Study Guide

4th edition

Basic Financial Management

David F. Scott, Jr.
University of Central Florida

John D. Martin
University of Texas at Austin

J. William Petty
Abilene Christian University

Arthur J. Keown
Virginia Polytechnic Institute and State University

Prentice Hall, Englewood Cliffs, New Jersey 07632

Editorial/production supervision and
   interior design: John A. Nestor
Cover design: Janet Schmid
Manufacturing buyer: Ed O'Dougherty

Printed in the United States of America

10 9 8 7 6 5 4 3 2

ISBN 0-13-060757-6 01

Prentice-Hall International (UK) Limited, *London*
Prentice-Hall of Australia Pty. Limited, *Sydney*
Prentice-Hall Canada Inc., *Toronto*
Prentice-Hall Hispanoamericana, S.A., *Mexico*
Prentice-Hall of India Private Limited, *New Delhi*
Prentice-Hall of Japan, Inc., *Tokyo*
Simon & Schuster Asia Pte. Ltd., *Singapore*
Editora Prentice-Hall do Brasil, Ltda., *Rio de Janeiro*

CONTENTS

PREFACE

The objective of this Study Guide is to provide a student-oriented supplement to Basic Financial Management. There are two basic ways in which we have attempted to accomplish that end. The first involves providing a condensation of each chapter in the form of a detailed sentence outline. This overview of the key points of the chapter can serve both as a preview and quick survey of the chapter content and as a review. A second way in which we have attempted to accomplish our overall objective is through providing problems (with detailed solutions) and self-tests which can be used to aid in the preparation of outside assignments and in studying for examinations. The problems were keyed to the end-of-chapter problems in the text in order to provide a direct and meaningful student aid. Both multiple-choice and true-false questions are used to provide a self-test over the descriptive chapter material. The outline, problems and solutions, and self-tests combined provide what we believe is a valuable learning tool for the student of financial management.

1

The Role of Financial Management

Orientation: The role of the financial manager has undergone dramatic changes during this century. Currently the financial manager has a major voice in all aspects of both the raising and allocation of financial capital. This chapter focuses on the development of financial thought, the goal of the firm, the financial decision-making process and a brief preview of the book.

I. Development of financial thought

   A. To a large extent, the economic and business activity of the time determined what was of primary importance in the field of finance.

      1. During the early 1900's financial and economic news emphasized consolidations, mergers, and public regulation. Thus, these topics received the majority of attention in the field of finance.

      2. As the economy began to expand in the 1920's emphasis in finance shifted to methods and procedures for acquiring funds.

      3. The business failures of the 1930's caused an increased emphasis to be placed on bankruptcy, liquidity management, and avoidance of financial problems.

      4. During the 1940's and early 1950's an increased emphasis was given to liquidity management and cash budgeting.

1

B. While the economic environment continued to affect financial thought, many factors together helped to bring about dramatic changes in the mid-1950's. During this time the field of finance evolved to one dealing with all aspects of acquiring and efficiently utilizing those funds.

C. The field of finance continues to develop, being reshaped by economic activity, primarily increased inflationary worries, and new theoretical developments.

II. Goal of the firm

A. In this book we will designate maximization of share-holder wealth, by which we mean maximization of the total market value of the firm's common stock, to be the goal of the firm. To understand this goal and its inclusive nature it is first necessary to understand the difficulties involved with the frequently suggested goal of profit maximization.

B. While the goal of profit maximization stresses the efficient use of capital resources, it assumes away many of the complexities of the real world and for this reason is unacceptable.

1. One of the major criticisms of profit maximization is that it assumes away uncertainty of returns. That is, projects are compared by examining their expected values or weighted average profit.

2. Profit maximization is also criticized because it assumes away timing differences of returns.

C. Profit maximization is unacceptable and a more realistic goal is needed.

III. Maximization of shareholder wealth

A. We have chosen the goal of shareholder wealth maximization because the effects of all financial decisions are included in this goal.

B. In order to employ this goal we need not consider every price change to be a market interpretation of the worth of our decisions. What we do focus on is the effect that our decision should have on the stock price if everything were held constant.

C. The _agency_ _problem_ is a result of the separation between the decision makers and the owners of the firm. As a result managers may make decisions that are not in line with the goal of maximization of shareholder wealth.

IV. Financial decisions and risk-return relationships

   A. Almost all financial decisions involve some sort of risk-return tradeoff.

   B. In general, the more risk the firm is willing to assume, the higher will be the expected return from the given course of action.

Self-Tests

TRUE-FALSE

F   1. Profit maximization is considered to be a more appropriate goal than shareholder wealth maximization because it considers the timing of the expected returns of the firm.

T   2. Shareholder wealth maximization considers the effects of the riskiness of a prospective earnings stream.

F   3. Originally, the role of the financial manager of a firm was very extensive (covering many areas of the firm); recently, however, the manager's responsibilities have been narrowed so that he or she might devote more time to raising funds.

T   4. Two major criticisms of the profit maximization goal are that it does not deal adequately with the uncertainty and the timing of returns.

T   5. Historically, economic activity and business activity have strongly affected the development of financial thought.

F   6. During the mid-1950's the point of view of finance shifted from that of an insider charged with the management and control of the firm's operations to that of an outsider assessing the condition and performance of a firm.

F   7. In general, the less risk a firm is willing to assume, the higher the expected return will be from a given course of action.

_____I_____ 8. Business failures of the 1930's caused an increased emphasis to be placed on bankruptcy, liquidity management, and avoidance of financial problems.

_____F_____ 9. The business expansion of the 1920's caused a shift in the emphasis in finance from mergers and regulation to methods and procedures for acquiring funds.

_____F_____ 10. In order to employ the goal of shareholder wealth maximization, every stock price change should be considered to be a market interpretation of the worth of our financial decisions.

_____T_____ 11. The agency problem is a result of a separation of management and the owners of the firm.

MULTIPLE CHOICE

1. The long-run goal of the firm is to

    a. Hold large quantities of cash.
    b. Increase sales regularly.
    c. Maximize earnings per share.
    d. Maximize shareholder wealth.

2. Maximizing shareholder wealth means maximizing the

    a. Value of the firm's assets.
    b. Value of the firm's cash.
    c. Value of the firm's investments.
    d. Value of the firm's profits.
    e. Market value of the firm's common stock.

3. The financial manager is concerned with which of the following

    a. Determining the proper amount of funds to employ in the firm.
    b. Seeing that the financial statements of the firm are properly presented.
    c. Raising funds for the firm on the most favorable terms possible.
    d. a and b.
    e. a and c.

4. Important functions of financial management are

    a. To provide for adequate financing.
    b. Long-range planning.
    c. To control costs.
    d. To identify desirable investment projects.
    e. All of the above.

4

5. Profit maximization is not the proper objective of a firm because

    a. It is not as inclusive a goal as the maximization of shareholder wealth.
    b. It does not consider the uncertainty of the return.
    c. It does not consider the timing of the returns.
    d. All of the above.
    e. None of the above.

6. The market price of a share of stock is determined by

    a. The New York Stock Exchange.
    b. The Federal Reserve.
    c. The company's management.
    d. Individuals buying and selling the stock.

7. The management of working capital deals with

    a. The management of long-term assets.
    b. The management of long-term liabilities.
    c. The management of current assets.
    d. All of the above.
    e. None of the above.

8. The agency problem is:

    a. Associated with insuring the firm.
    b. No longer important.
    c. Invalidates the goal of maximization of shareholder wealth.
    d. Is a result of the separation of the decision makers and the owners of the firm.
    f. All of the above.

2

Legal Forms
of Organization
and the
Tax Environment

Orientation: The objective of this chapter is to afford the student a familiarity with the legal setting in which the firm operates. In this regard, the basic forms of business organization are reviewed. Also, a highlight of the basic tax implications relating to financial decisions is given consideration.

I. Legal forms of business organization

    A. Sole proprietorship: A business owned by a single person and that has a minimum amount of legal structure.

        1. Advantages

            a. Easily established with few complications.
            b. Minimal organizational costs.
            c. Does not have to share profits or control with others.

        2. Disadvantages

            a. Unlimited liability for the owner.
            b. Owner must absorb all losses.
            c. Equity capital limited to the owner's personal investment.
            d. Business terminates immediately upon death of owner.

B. Partnership: An association of two or more individuals coming together as co-owners to operate a business for profit.

1. Two types of partnerships

    a. General partnership: Relationship between partners is dictated by the partnership agreement.

        (1) Advantages

            (a) Minimal organizational requirements.
            (b) Negligible government regulations.

        (2) Disadvantages

            (a) All partners have unlimited liability.
            (b) Difficult to raise large amounts of capital.
            (c) Partnership dissolved by the death or withdrawal of general partner.

    b. Limited partnership

        (1) Advantages

            (a) For the limited partners, liability is limited to the amount of capital invested in the company.
            (b) Withdrawal or death of a limited partner does not affect the continuity of the business.
            (c) Stronger inducement in raising capital.

        (2) Disadvantages

            (a) There must be at least one general partner who has unlimited liability in the partnership.
            (b) Names of limited partners may not appear in the name of the firm.
            (c) Limited partners may not participate in the management of the business.

(d) More expensive to organize than general partnership, as a written agreement is mandatory.

C. The corporation: An "impersonal" legal entity having the power to purchase, sell, and own assets and to incur liabilities while existing separately and apart from its owners.

   1. Ownership is evidenced by shares of stock.

   2. Advantages

      a. Limited liability of owners.
      b. Ease of transferability of ownership, i.e., by the sale of one's shares of stock.
      c. The death of an owner does not result in the discontinuity of the firm's life.
      d. Ability to raise large amounts of capital is increased.

   3. Disadvantages

      a. Most difficult and expensive form of business to establish.
      b. Control of corporation not guaranteed by partial ownership of stock.

II. Federal income taxation

   A. Objectives of federal income taxation

      1. Provide government revenues.
      2. Achieve socially desirable goals.
      3. Stabilize the economy

   B. Income taxes for sole proprietorship

      1. All income and expenses for the business are reported on the owner's personal income tax forms.
      2. Taxation of the business income is the same as for the owner's personal income.

   C. Income taxes for partnerships

      1. Partnership tax return reports every transaction that has a tax consequence and allocates the transactions as specified by the partnership agreement.

2. The individual partners report their portions of the partnership income within their personal tax returns.

D. Income taxes for corporations

1. A tax return must be filed and the resulting taxes paid by the corporation.
2. Taxable income is basically determined as income less allowable exclusions and tax deductible expenses.
3. Eighty percent of any dividends received from another corporation are tax exempt.
4. Dividends paid by the corporation to its stockholders are not tax deductible.
5. Corporate rate structure:

15%	$0 - 50,000
25%	$50,001 - 75,000
34%	$75,001 - 100,000
39%	$100,001 - 335,000 _5% surtax_
34%	$335,001 and over

6. Depreciation

   a. For assets acquired prior to 1981, two depreciation methods, among others, may be used for tax purposes.

      (1) Straight-line.
      (2) Double-declining balance.

   b. For assets acquired in 1981 or later, the Accelerated Cost Recovery Systems, ACRS, should be used.

      (1) Allows for a more rapid depreciation schedule.
      (2) Assigns property to a 3, 5, 10, or 15-year property class.
      (3) Allows for the alternative use of straight-line depreciation.

   c. Effective January 1, 1987 the Accelerated Cost Recovery System, ACRS, was modified to include:

      (1) The Asset Depreciation Range
      (2) The method of depreciation
      (3) The averaging convention

d. There are two averaging conventions based upon the type of asset being depreciated:

(1) Half-year convention
(2) Mid-month convention

7. Net operating loss: If a corporation has an operating loss in any year, the loss may be applied against the profits in the 3 prior years. If the loss has not been completely absorbed by the profits in these 3 years, the loss may be carried forward to each of the 15 following years.

8. If after deducting all capital gains and capital losses the company has a net capital loss, such losses may be carried back for 3 years and forward for 5 years to offset any capital gains occurring during those periods.

9. Accumulated earnings tax is a penalty surtax assessed on the corporation on any accumulation of earnings by a corporation for the purpose of avoiding taxes by its shareholders.

10. Subchapter S corporation

a. Subchapter S of the Internal Revenue Code permits the owners of a small corporation with 35 or fewer stockholders to use the corporation organizational form but be taxed as though the firm were a partnership.
b. This treatment eliminates the double taxation normally associated with the corporate entity, yet provides limited personal liability and other favorable features of the corporate structure.
c. This provision became even more important in 1987 when individual tax rates fell below corporate tax rates.

D. Implications of taxes in financial decision making

1. Taxes and capital investment decisions

a. When a plant or equipment acquisition is being considered, the returns from the investment should be measured on an after-tax basis using the marginal not average tax rate in the computations.

10

b. The depreciation method will have an impact on the timing of taxes.

c. The estimated salvage value also may have a tax impact; the greater the anticipated salvage value, the less the amount of annual depreciation charges.

2. Taxes and the firm's capital structure: The tax deductibility of interest payments gives debt financing a definite cost advantage over preferred and common stock financing.

3. Taxes and corporate dividend policies: The differential tax treatment for the firm's common stockholders might influence the firm's preference between stock price appreciation, i.e., capital gains for the investor, and dividends, i.e., ordinary income for the investor.

Study Problems

1. A corporation had $145,000 in taxable earnings. What is the tax liability?

SOLUTION

Income		Marginal Tax Rate	Tax Liability
$ 50,000	X	15%	$ 7,500
25,000	X	25%	6,250
25,000	X	34%	8,500
45,000	X	39%	17,550
$145,000		Total tax liability =	$39,800

2. A corporation has earnings before interest and taxes of $86,000, dividend income of $8,000, and interest expenses of $9,000. Also, a contribution to a university was made in the amount of $1,000. What is the corporation's (a) taxable income and (b) tax liability?

SOLUTION

(a)	Operating income		$86,000
	Dividend income	$8,000	
	Dividend exclusion		
	80% X $8,000	(6,400)	
	Taxable dividend income		1,600
	Interest expense		(9,000)
	Contribution		(1,000)
	Taxable income		$77,600

(b)
$$15\% \times \$50,000 = \$7,500$$
$$25\% \times 25,000 = 6,250$$
$$34\% \times \underline{2,600} = \underline{884}$$
$$\underline{\$77,600} \qquad \underline{\$14,634} = \text{Tax liability}$$

3. The taxable income of Broghm Corporation is as follows (losses are shown in parentheses):

1982	$(125,000)
1983	150,000
1984	300,000
1985	(150,000)
1986	(20,000)
1987	350,000
1988	400,000

What is Broghm's tax payment or tax refund in each year?

SOLUTION

Year	Taxable Income Before Carry-Back or Carry-Forward	Tax Payment	Carry-Back	Carry-Forward	Tax Refunds
1982	$(125,000)	$ 0			
1983	150,000	3,750	$ 25,000 from 1985	$125,000 from 1982	
1984	300,000	100,250	$125,000 from 1985 $ 20,000 from 1986		
1985	(150,000)	0			$55,250[a]
1986	(20,000)	0			7,800[b]
1987	350,000	119,000			
1988	400,000	136,000			

[a]1985 refund = $3,750 (1980 taxes) + $51,500 (correction of 1984 taxes from $300,000 to $175,000).

[b]1986 refund = $7,800 (correction of 1984 taxes from $175,000 to $155,000).

Self-Tests

TRUE-FALSE

F 1. Many businesses are formed as corporations because of the ease of establishment.

12

_T_   2. In a limited partnership there must be at least one general partner with unlimited liability.

_T_   3. The income from a partnership is reported by the partners on their personal tax returns.

_F_   4. If an asset is depreciated by ACRS and sold at midyear, the owner may use 50% of the allowable depreciation for that year.

_F_   5. Assets purchased prior to 1981 may also use ACRS, by following certain provisions.

_F_   6. Interest and dividend payments made by a corporation are both tax deductible by the paying corporation.

_F_   7. When an acquisition of a plant or equipment is being considered, the returns from the investment should be measured on a before-tax basis.

_T_   8. A business that is formed as a Subchapter S corporation avoids the double taxation of income.

_F_   9. If the double-declining balance form of depreciation is used, the asset is never fully depreciated.

_T_   10 Using the Accelerated Cost Recovery System an asset is assigned to either a 3, 5, 10, or 15 year property class, regardless of its economic life.

MULTIPLE CHOICE

1. Advantages of the corporation include:

     a. Transferability of ownership.
     b. Unlimited liability.
     c. Ability of the corporation to raise capital.
     d. Double taxation of dividend income.
     e. a and c.
     f. a and b.

2. Disadvantages of the partnership are:

     a. Expense of formation.
     b. Lack of permanence.
     c. Double taxation on income.
     d. Unlimited liability.
     e. b and d.
     f. a and d.

3. A corporation owning stock in another corporation is taxed on what percentage of the dividends received from the owned corporation?

    a. 20%.
    b. 80%.
    c. 48%.
    d. 50%.

4. Which of the following is an advantage of the partnership?

    a. Limited liability.
    b. A voice in the management of the partnership.
    c. Limited life.
    d. a and b.
    e. a and c.

5. Which of the following forms of business organization is the largest in number?

    a. Corporation.
    b. Partnership.
    c. Sole proprietorship.

6. If a corporation sustains a net operating loss, this loss may be:

    a. Deducted against long-term capital gains.
    b. Carried back 3 years and forward 15 years to offset taxable income.
    c. Carried back 5 years and forward 7 years to offset taxable income.

7. Advantages of the sole proprietorship are:

    a. Unlimited liability.
    b. Ease of formation.
    c. Double taxation.
    d. Nominal organizational costs.
    e. b and d.

8. The pair containing one advantage and one disadvantage of the corporation is:
    a. Costly to form and lack of secrecy.
    b. Unlimited liability and ease of transferability of ownership.
    c. Limited liability and more complex to form.
    d. Limited liability and perpetual life.
    e. a and c.
    f. b and c.

14

3

Financial Analysis

Orientation: Financial analysis can be defined as the process of assessing the financial condition of a firm. The principal analytical tool of financial analysis is the financial ratio. In Chapter 3 we provide an overview of a firm's basic financial statements followed by a survey of a set of key financial ratios and a discussion of their effective use.

I. Basic financial statements

   A. The <u>balance sheet</u> represents a statement of the financial position of the firm on a given date, its asset holdings, liabilities, and owner supplied equity. This statement is considered to be the most important financial statement for judging the economic well-being of the firm. The balance sheet consists of two basic components: (1) assets and (2) liabilities plus owner's equity.

      1. On the asset side of the balance sheet we usually find two categories.

         a. <u>Current assets</u> are those assets that are expected to be realized in cash, sold, or consumed either in 1 year or within the operating cycle of the firm, whichever is longer.

b. Fixed or noncurrent assets contain all those resources which are not expected to be converted into cash within the operating cycle of the firm. Security investments, plant and equipment, and land are the most common fixed assets.

2. Liabilities represent the outstanding claims held against a firm's assets and are reported at their stated or face value. There are two basic categories of liabilities.

   a. Current liabilities represent obligations that are reasonably expected to be liquidated within 1 year.
   b. Long-term or noncurrent liabilities include permanent obligations of the firm that are not reasonably expected to be liquidated within the normal operating cycle of the firm but are payable at some later date. Noncurrent liabilities are often referred to as long-term liabilities.

3. Owner's equity represents the book value of the owner's interest in the assets of the firm. Owner's equity is comprised of capital stock (par value of common stock plus paid in capital) and retained earnings (undistributed earnings).

B. The income statement represents an attempt to measure the net results of a firm's operations over a specified time interval. Some of the more important components of the income statement are discussed below:

1. Sales represent the total sales of products or services net of returns and allowances attributable to the period. Under the accrual method of accounting, no distinction is made between cash and credit sales. In addition, only those sales directly attributable to normal operations are included under this sales category.

2. Cost of goods sold is simply the cost of the product sold or service provided. There are two widely used methods for computing cost of goods sold. The FIFO, or first-in, first-out method assigns to cost of goods sold the prices the firm paid on the oldest item in inventory. The LIFO, or last-in, first-out method, assigns cost to items sold based on the cost of the most recently purchased inventory item. The

16

method selected can have an important effect on net earnings for a period in which prices have risen or fallen significantly. During a period of rising prices LIFO results in lower taxes being paid and higher cash flow and the converse is true for FIFO.

3. Gross profit represents the amount by which sales exceed cost of goods sold.

4. Selling expense includes all those expenses incurred in the process of making the period's sales.

5. General and administrative expenses include all those operating expenses not directly attributed to the cost of merchandise sold or selling expenses. These expenses usually include administrative salaries, utilities, non-income related taxes, insurance, and depreciation. Depreciation is not a cash expense; it represents an attempt to allocate the cost of the firm's plant and equipment against the periods in which those assets are being used. The Accelerated Cost Recovery System, which was described in Chapter 2, provides an accelerated cost write-off because it provides for a more rapid rate of expensing the capitalized cost of the asset than does the straight-line method.

6. Net operating income reflects the net results of a firm's operations before considering financing costs and income taxes.

7. Net income after taxes represents net earnings for the period after income taxes.

8. Retained earnings for the period represent any earnings that remain after all dividends have been paid to stockholders. This amount is then added to the existing retained earnings figure on the balance sheet.

C. The statement of changes in financial position, often referred to as a sources and uses statement, provides a description of the sources of cash for a specific period of time and the uses to which they were put. The information contained in this statement makes it a very useful tool of financial analysis. Two forms of source and use statements are currently acceptable although the second is most frequently used in financial analyses (and is the only one discussed in Chapter 3 of the text).

1. The <u>statement of sources and uses of working capital</u> is designed to "explain" the change in the net working capital position of a firm for some stated period of time. Sources and uses of net working capital can be summarized in terms of the following grid:

	Sources	Uses
Fixed assets	−	+
Long-term debt	+	−
Common stock	+	−
Net income	+	−

    where the minus sign (−) indicates a decrease and the plus sign (+) an increase in the asset, liability, or owner's equity account. Thus, a decrease in fixed assets would be a source of net working capital whereas an increase in common stock would involve a use. The source and use of working capital statement does not detail the changes in current assets and current liabilities. To obtain this information, it is necessary to either add on a section to the working capital statement or prepare the more detailed <u>source and use of funds (cash) statement</u>.

2. The <u>sources and uses of funds statement</u> on a cash basis explains the change in cash for the period rather than net working capital. In this statement we analyze changes in current assets and liabilities individually as well as long-term assets and liabilities. In preparing this statement the analyst must consider the changes in the items in the above grid plus the following:

	Sources	Uses
Current asset account	−	+
Current liability account	+	−

    The basic form of the source and use of funds statement is quite simple; for example

Cash (Beginning Balance)	$100
Plus: Sources of cash for the period	300
Less: Uses of cash for the period	(250)
Cash (Ending Balance)	$150

II. Overview of financial ratios

A. Financial ratios provide the analyst with a means for making meaningful comparison of a firm's financial data over time and with other firms. Thus, financial ratios represent an attempt to standardize financial information in order to facilitate meaningful comparisons.

B. Financial ratios can be divided into four basic categories. These categories consist of liquidity ratios, efficiency ratios, leverage ratios, and profitability ratios.

III. Types of ratios

A. Liquidity ratios are used to measure the ability of a firm to meet its short-term financial obligations. The principal measures of liquidity follow:

1. The current ratio is defined as

$$\frac{current\ assets}{current\ liabilities}$$

Higher the better

with a higher ratio indicating increased liquidity.

2. The acid-test ratio is computed as

$$\frac{current\ assets\ -\ inventories}{current\ liabilities}$$

Inventories are omitted because they are generally the least liquid of a firm's current assets.

B. Efficiency ratios provide the basis for assessing how effectively the firm is using its resources to generate sales. Some of the more common efficiency ratios are found below:

1. The average collection period, defined as

$$\frac{accounts\ receivable}{annual\ credit\ sales/360}$$

the lower the better

shows how rapidly a firm's accounts are being collected. Frequently net sales are used in the place of credit sales where the analyst does not know the proportion of the firm's sales which are credit sales.

19

2. The <u>inventory-turnover ratio</u> reflects the number of times that inventories are turned over (replaced) during the year. This ratio is defined as

$$\frac{\text{cost of goods sold}}{\text{inventories}}$$

3. The <u>fixed asset turnover</u> ratio is used to measure the efficiency with which the firm utilizes its investment in fixed assets. This ratio is calculated as

$$\frac{\text{sales}}{\text{net fixed assets}}$$

4. The <u>total asset turnover</u> ratio indicates how many dollars in sales the firm generates for each dollar it has invested in assets. This ratio is computed as

$$\frac{\text{sales}}{\text{total assets}}$$

C. <u>Leverage ratios</u> are used to measure the extent to which non-owner supplied funds have been used to finance a firm's assets. Leverage ratios can be categorized as being either balance-sheet ratios or coverage ratios.

1. <u>Balance-sheet leverage ratios</u> measure the proportion of the firm's assets financed with non-owner funds.

a. The <u>debt ratio</u> is equal to

$$\frac{\text{total liabilities}}{\text{total assets}}$$

b. The <u>long-term debt to total capitalization ratio</u> measures the relative importance or long-term debt in the firm's capitalization.

2. <u>Coverage ratios</u> are used to measure a firm's ability to cover the finance changes associated with its use of financial leverage.

a. The <u>times interest earned ratio</u> is defined as

20

$$\frac{\text{net operating income}}{\text{annual interest expense}}$$

and represents the most popular coverage ratio.

b. The cash flow overall coverage ratio is computed as

$$\frac{\text{net operating income + lease expense + depreciation}}{\text{interest + lease expense + } \dfrac{\text{preferred dividends}}{(1 - T)} + \dfrac{\text{principal payments}}{(1 - T)}}$$

and reflects the total amount of earnings that are available to meet interest and other finance related charges. It also improves on the times interest earned ratio in that it considers lease payments, principal payments, and preferred dividends, in addition to interest or finance charges that must be covered.

C. Profitability ratios serve as overall measures of the effectiveness of the firm's management. These ratios can be divided into those that measure profitability in relation to sales and those that measure profitability in relation to investment.

1. Profitability in relation to sales ratios reflects the ability of the firm's management to control the various expenses involved in generating sales.

a. The gross profit margin is defined as

$$\frac{\text{gross profit}}{\text{net sales}}$$

and indicates both the efficiency of the firm's operations and the pricing policies of the firm.

b. The operating profit margin serves as an overall measure of operating effectiveness and is computed as

$$\frac{\text{net operating income}}{\text{sales}}$$

c. The net profit margin is equal to

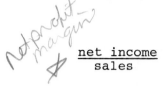

net income
———————
sales

Net income in this ratio is after taxes.

2. <u>Profitability in relation to investment ratios</u> measures the firm's profitability in relation to invested funds used to generate those profits

   a. <u>Operating income return on investment</u> is defined as

   operating income
   ————————————
   total assets

   and represents the before-tax and interest expense return on invested capital. This ratio is particularly useful since it reflects the total earnings produced by the total assets of the firm. In fact, when we decompose this ratio into the product of the <u>operating profit margin</u> and <u>total asset turnover</u> ratio it forms the basis for <u>earning power analysis</u>, that is, this ratio also equals

   operating income   sales
   ——————————— x ——————————
        sales   total assets

   Using this form of the operating income return on investment ratio the analyst can analyze, individually, the determinants of firm profitability.

   b. The rate of return earned on total invested capital after interest and taxes is indicated by the <u>return on total assets</u> ratio which is computed as follows:

    net income
   ———————————
   total assets

   c. The <u>return on total assets ratio</u> is often broken down into the following components:

   net income   sales
   —————————— x ——————————
      sales   total assets

   By breaking this ratio into two parts--net profit margin and sales to total invested capital--the analyst can easily determine

22

the underlying reason for a particular return on assets produced by a firm.

d. The return on common equity ratio is defined as

$$\frac{\text{net income available to common}}{\text{common equity}}$$

and measures the net return on investment of the common shareholders.

Still another useful relationship can be defined between the return on total asset ratio and return on common equity ratio. This relationship is

$$\frac{\text{return on total assets}}{1 - \text{debt ratio}}$$

which simply recognizes the fact that the return on common equity depends on the after tax profitability of the firm on its total investment (the return on total assets) and how much of the firm's investment was financed by its creditors (the debt ratio).

IV. Using financial ratios

A. To fully understand a firm's strengths and weaknesses, the analyst should use one of the two following standards against which ratios can be compared:

1. Similar ratios can be computed for the same firm from its previous financial statements. This is commonly referred to as trend analysis and requires that the analyst look at each ratio over several statement periods.

2. A second type of standard for comparison comes from ratios generated from firms that have characteristics similar to the subject firm. These are referred to as industry average ratios and the two most common sources for such ratios are Dun and Bradstreet's Key Business Ratios and Statement Studies published by Robert Morris Associates.

Study Problems

1. Prepare a balance sheet for the A. R. Peterson MFG. Co. from the scrambled list of items below. The owner's equity balance is not given but it can be determined as a balancing figure.

Building	$49,100	Office equipment	4,100
Accounts receivable	21,600	Land	22,000
Machinery	2,950	Notes payable	14,000
Cash	9,200	Owner's equity	
Accounts payable	16,500		

SOLUTION

A. R. Peterson Mfg. Co.
Balance Sheet

Cash	$ 9,200	Accounts payable	16,500
Accounts receivable	21,600	Notes payable	14,000
Land	22,000	Owner's equity	78,450
Building	49,100		
Machinery	2,950		
Office equipment	4,100	Total liabilities	
Total assets	$108,950	& owner's equity	$108,950

2. By studying the successive balance sheets for AMP, Inc. found below, determine what transactions have occurred. Prepare a list of the transactions and the corresponding balance-sheet dates. For example, on March 31, 1988, the firm's owners invested $200,000 in AMP, Inc. and started the business.

(a)
AMP, Inc.
Balance Sheet
March 31, 1988

Assets		Owner's Equity	
Cash	$200,000	Owner's equity	$200,000

(b)
AMP, Inc.
Balance Sheet
April 2, 1988

Assets		Owner's Equity	
Cash	$100,000	Owner's equity	$200,000
Land	100,000		
	$200,000		$200,000

24

(c)
AMP, Inc.
Balance Sheet
April 15, 1988

Assets		Owner's Equity	
Cash	$ 50,000	Owner's equity	$200,000
Building	50,000		
Land	100,000		
	$200,000		$200,000

(d)
AMP, Inc.
Balance Sheet
March 2, 1988

Assets		Liabilities & Owner's Equity	
Cash	$ 50,000	Accounts payable	$ 25,000
Inventories	25,000	Owner's equity	200,000
Building	50,000		
Land	100,000		
	$225,000		$225,000

(e)
AMP, Inc.
Balance Sheet
March 15, 1988

Assets		Liabilities & Owner's Equity	
Cash	$ 60,000	Accounts payable	$ 25,000
Inventories	25,000	Notes payable	25,000
Equipment	15,000	Owner's equity	200,000
Building	50,000		
Land	100,000		
	$250,000		$250,000

SOLUTION

(a) On March 31, 1988, the firm's owners invested
$200,000 in AMP, Inc. and started the business.

(b) On April 2, 1988, $100,000 of the original invest-
ment by the owners was used to acquire land.

(c) On April 15, 1988, $50,000 of the original cash was
used to acquire a building.

(d) On May 2, 1988, $25,000 of inventory was purchased on account (credit).

(e) On May 15, 1988, a $25,000 loan was obtained of which $15,000 of the proceeds were used to purchase equipment.

3. Balance sheets for Marion Mfg. Co. and the Sterlington Corp. are found below. Both firms are involved in the manufacture of electrical components used in small electronic calculators and digital wristwatches. Since both firms are less than 3 years old, their book values are reasonably close to actual market value.

Marion Mfg. Co.
Balance Sheet
November 30, 1988

Assets			
Cash	$ 50,000	Notes payable	$ 520,000
Accounts receivable	90,000	(due in 30 days)	
Building	225,000	Accounts payable	420,000
Machinery	350,000	Owner's equity	150,000
Land	375,000		
	$1,090,000		$1,090,000

Sterlington Co.
Balance Sheet
November 30, 1988

Assets			
Cash	$ 50,000	Notes payable	$120,000
Accounts receivable	200,000	(due in 30 days)	
Land	10,000	Accounts payable	150,000
Machinery	350,000	Owner's equity	640,000
Building	300,000		
	$910,000		$910,000

(a) Assume the role of a commercial banker who has been approached by both of the above firms with a request for a 90-day loan for $200,000. For which of the firms are you most likely to approve the loan? Why?

(b) If you were considering the purchase of one of these firms and assume the liabilities of each, which one would you be willing to pay the higher price for? (Obviously, you would want more information in order to make a

26

complete analysis, but make your evaluation based on the balance sheets above.)

SOLUTION

(a) Sterlington Corp. In reviewing requests for short-term loans, the commercial loan officer is most inter-ested in the liquidity of the subject firm. The current ratio of Marion Mfg. Co. is a very weak 0.15 while Sterlington Corp.'s current ratio is .93. In addition, a quick glance at the balance sheet of Marion Mfg. shows that a very substantial note of $520,000 comes due in 30 days which the company may have difficulty paying.

(b) Sterlington Corp. If it is assumed that book values are reasonably close to actual market values, the differ-ence between Sterlington's total assets and assumed debt is $640,000 as opposed to Marion's net difference of $150,000.

4. Burruss Inc. had the following condensed balance sheet at the end of operation for 1988:

Burruss, Inc.
Balance Sheet
December 31, 1988

Cash	$ 24,000	Current liabilities	$ 30,000
Other current assets	51,000	Long-term notes	33,000
	$ 75,000	payable	
Investments	40,000	Bonds payable	40,000
Fixed assets (net)	125,000	Capital stock	150,000
Land	62,000	Retained earnings	$ 49,000
	$302,000		$302,000

During 1989 the following occurred:

(a) Burruss, Inc. sold some of its investments for $20,600 which resulted in a gain of $600.

(b) Additional land for a plant expansion was purchased for $12,000.

(c) Bonds payable were paid in the amount of $10,000.

(d) An additional $20,000 in capital stock was issued.

(e) Dividends of $15,000 were paid to stockholders.

(f) Net income for 1989 was $42,000 after allowing for $18,000 in depreciation.

(g) A second parcel of land was purchased through the issuance of $12,000 in bonds, $6,000 in long-term notes payable, and internally generated funds.

Required:

(a) Prepare a statement of changes in financial position for 1989.

(b) Prepare a condensed balance sheet for Burruss, Inc. at December 1989.

Assume that current liabilities remain at $30,000 and other current assets did not change during the year.

SOLUTION

Burruss, Inc.
Statement of Changes in Financial Position
For the Year Ended December 31, 1989

Cash (12/31/88)	$ 24,000

Sources:

Increase (decrease) in working capital from operations:

Net income	$ 42,000
Depreciation	18,000
Gain on sales of investments	(600)
	$59,400
Sale of investments	20,600
Issuance of capital stock	20,000
Increase in bonds payable	12,000
Increase in long-term notes payable	6,000
Total sources of funds	$118,000

Uses:

Purchase of land	$ 30,000
Payment of bond payable	10,000
Payment of dividends to stockholders	15,000
Total use of funds	$ 55,000
Cash (12/31/89)	$ 87,000

```
                    Burruss, Inc.
                    Balance Sheet
                  December 31, 1989
```

Cash	$ 87,000	Current liabilities	$ 30,000
Other current assets	51,000	Long-term notes	39,000
Total Current Assets	$138,000	payable	
Investments	20,000	Bonds payable	42,000
Fixed assets (net)	107,000	Capital stock	170,000
Land	92,000	Retained earnings	76,000
	$357,000		$357,000

5. The financial manager of Sudhop, Inc. has hired you as a recent finance graduate. Now he wishes to test your familiarity with financial ratios and your overall ability to work with financial statements. He gives you the following incomplete year-end balance sheet:

```
                    Sudhop, Inc.
                    Balance Sheet
                  December 31, 1989
```

Cash	$	Accounts payable	$
Accounts receivable		Long-term debt	
Inventory		Total Debt	$
Total Current Assets	$	Common stock	125,000
Fixed assets	400,000	Retained earnings	275,000
	$		$

He then gives you the following additional information and asks you to complete the above balance sheet.

Average collection period (360-day year)	30 days
Interest paid on long-term debt (10% rate)	$5,000
Debt-to-equity ratio	75%
Sales to operating (current) assets	2.0 times
Quick ratio	1.1
Current ratio	1.2

SOLUTION

```
                    Sudhop, Inc.
                    Balance Sheet
                  December 31, 1989
```

Cash	$225,000	Accounts payable	$250,000
Accounts receivable	50,000	Long-term debt	50,000
Inventory	25,000	Total Debt	$300,000
	$300,000	Common stock	125,000
Fixed assets	400,000	Retained earnings	275,000
	$ 70,000		$700,000

6. The balance sheet and income statement for Miller Company are given for the year 1988 in addition to various financial ratios for the industry in which Miller operates.

Miller Company
Balance Sheet
December 31, 1988
(000's)

Cash	$ 230	Notes payable	$ 1,015
Accounts receivable	9,380	Accounts payable	3,545
Inventories	7,515	Accrued taxes	225
Current assets	17,125	Current liabilities	4,785
Fixed assets (net)	34,125	Long-term debt	18,035
Total Assets	$51,250	Deferred income taxes	2,840
		Total Debt	$20,875
		Common stock-par	575
		Capital in excess of par	7,945
		Retained earnings	17,070
		Common equity	25,590
		Total liabilities & net worth	$51,250

Miller Company
Income Statement
Year Ended December 31, 1988

Net sales (credit)	$46,235
Cost of sales	33,167
Gross profit	13,068
General and administrative expense	9,590
Operating income	3,478
Interest changes	1,120
Net income before taxes	2,358
Income taxes	1,130
Net income	$ 1,228

	Industry
Current	4.02
Acid test	3.00
Inventory turnover	7.50
Average collection period	63.1%
Operating income margin	6.0%
Gross profit margin	26.0%
Operating income margin	6.0%
Net profit margin	5.0%
Return on total assets	2.5%
Debt ratio	38.0%
Times interest earned	3.90

Required:

(a) Compute the various ratios indicated for Miller Company.

(b) Discuss the liquidity and leverage portion and profitability of Miller in relation to the industry norms.

SOLUTION

(a)

	Industry	Miller
Current ratio	4.02	3.58
Acid-test ratio	3.00	2.01
Inventory turnover	7.50	4.41
Average collection period	63.1	73.04
Gross profit	26.0%	28.3%
Operating income margin	6.0%	7.5%
Net profit margin	5.0%	2.7%
Return on total assets	2.5%	2.4%
Debt ratio	38.0%	50.1%
Times interest earned	3.90	3.11

(b) Miller's liquidity and efficiency ratios are well below the industry averages. The most serious problem is with inventory turnover which is almost one-half the industry norm.

Miller's leverage position, based upon its debt ratio, is also very unfavorable. It appears that any additional debt financing would be difficult to acquire at this point.

The _gross profit_ and _operating profit_ margins compare
favorably with the industry average which could indicate that
the operational and administrative operations of the firm are
relatively efficient. However, the net profit margin is well
below the industry average and appears to result from relatively high interest expense. This is also indicated by
comparing the times interest earned ratio with the industry
norm. This high degree of interest expense is undoubtedly
directly related to the leverage position of Miller discussed
above.

Self-Tests

TRUE-FALSE

_F_ 1. The balance sheet is a statement of the firm's
financial position over a specified time interval.

_T_ 2. Noncurrent assets are those which are not expected
to be converted into cash within the firm's operating cycle.

_F_ 3. The income statement represents an attempt to
measure the net results of the firm's operations on
a given date.

_T_ 4. The owner's equity represents the book value of the
owner's investment in the assets of the firm.

_T_ 5. A firm attempts to match revenues from the period's
operations with the expenses incurred in generating
those revenues by compiling the income statement on
an accrual basis.

_F_ 6. Reported revenues and expenses must represent actual
cash flows for the period when the income statement
is prepared on an accrual basis.

_T_ 7. The LIFO method of inventory valuation assigns cost
of the items sold based on the cost of the most
recently purchased inventory items.

_F_ 8. During a period of rising prices the FIFO method
results in lower taxes being paid than would be the
case if the LIFO method were used.

_T_ 9. Accelerated methods of depreciation offer the
advantage of deferring the payment of taxes which
increases the present worth of the firm's operating
cash flows.

_____**T**_____10. The statement of changes in financial position is sometimes referred to as a sources and uses of funds statement.

MULTIPLE CHOICE

1. Which of the following is generally considered to be the most important financial statement for judging the economic well-being of a firm?

   a. Income statement.
   b. Balance sheet.
   c. Statement of sources and uses of funds.
   d. All of the above.
   e. None of the above.

2. One of the limitations of the balance sheet is the fact that:

   a. Historical cost is used as the basis for valuation of assets and liabilities.
   b. Items which have financial value are omitted because of problems of objective valuation.
   c. Appreciation in asset values is ignored.
   d. Estimates must be used in the valuation of several accounts.
   e. All of the above.

3. The _____ method of inventory valuation assigns to cost of goods sold the prices paid on the oldest items of inventory.

   a. FIFO.
   b. LIFO.
   c. Average cost.
   d. Insufficient information.
   e. None of the above.

4. Use of the FIFO method in a period of rising prices will have the effect of _underr_ the true cost of goods sold and _over_ the firm's gross profits.

   a. Overstating; overstating.
   b. Overstating; understating.
   c. Understating; understating.
   d. Understating; overstating.
   e. Cannot be determined.

5. Under conditions of rising inventory prices, the use of LIFO will _overstate_ cost of goods sold and _understa_ gross profit.

a. Overstate; overstate.
b. Overstate; understate.
c. Understate; understate.
d. Understate; overstate.
e. Cannot be determined.

6. The firm's cash flow from operations is largest when the method for determining cost of goods sold _____ the true cost and _____ the firm's earnings for the period.

a. Overstates; overstates.
b. Overstates; understates.
c. Understates; understates.
d. Understates; overstates.
e. Cannot be determined.

7. A source of funds would be _____ in fixed assets or _____ in long-term debt.

a. An increase; an increase.
b. An increase; a decrease.
c. A decrease; a decrease.
d. A decrease; an increase.
e. Cannot be determined.

8. A use of funds would be _____ in common stock or _____ in fixed assets.

a. An increase; an increase.
b. An increase; a decrease.
c. A decrease; a decrease.
d. A decrease; an increase.
e. Cannot be determined.

9. The debt ratio is considered to be in the category of _____ ratios.

a. Liquidity.
b. Profitability.
c. Leverage.
d. Efficiency.
e. None of the above.

10. The average collection period is considered to be in the category of _____ ratios.

a. Leverage.
b. Efficiency.
c. Liquidity.
d. Leverage.
e. None of the above.

4

Financial Forecasting, Planning, and Budgeting

Orientation: This chapter is divided into two sections. The first section includes an overview of the role played by forecasting in the firm's planning process. The second section focuses on the construction of detailed financial plans. This involves the preparation of budgets and pro forma financial statements for future periods of the firm's operations. A budget is a forecast of future events and provides the basis for taking corrective action in the event that budgeted figures do not reasonably match actual results. Budgets can also be used for performance evaluation of individuals responsible for implementing budgeted plans. The cash budget and pro forma financial statements provide the necessary information to determine estimates of future financing requirements of the firm. These estimates are the key element in our discussion of financial planning and budgeting.

I.   Financial forecasting and planning

   A.   The need for forecasting in financial management arises whenever the future financing needs of the firm are being estimated. There are three basic steps involved in predicting financing requirements.

       1.   Project the firm's sales revenues and expenses over the planning period.

       2.   Estimate the levels of investment in current and fixed assets which are necessary to support the projected sales level.

3. Determine the financing needs of the firm throughout the planning period.

B. The key ingredient in the firm's planning process is the sales forecast. This forecast should reflect (1) any past trend in sales that is expected to continue and (2) the effects of any events which are expected to have a material effect on the firm's sales during the forecast period.

C. The traditional problem faced in financial forecasting begins with the sales forecast and involves making forecasts of the impact of predicted sales on the firm's various expenses, assets, and liabilities. There are a number of techniques that can be used to make these forecasts:

1. The percent of sales method involves projecting the financial variable as a percent of projected sales.

2. A slightly more refined technique involves the use of a scatter diagram in which the financial variable is plotted against corresponding levels of sales (or another predictor variable). A line is then visually fitted to the scatter plot and is used to predict the financial variable.

3. Regression analysis represents a method for mathematically "fitting" a line to a scatter plot. The resulting equation can then be used to predict the level of the subject financial variable. The regression method can be used whenever there is a single "predictor" variable (referred to as the independent variable, e.g., firm sales) and a single "predicted" variable (referred to as the dependent variable, e.g., firm inventories). Furthermore, a multiple regression analysis can be used whenever more than one predictor (independent) variable is used to predict a single financial variable.

II. Financial planning and budgeting

A. In general, a business will use four types of budgets: physical, cost, profit, and cash.

1. Physical budgets include budgets for unit sales, personnel or manpower, unit production, inventories, and actual physical facilities. They are also used as a basis for generating cost and profit budgets.

36

2. <u>Cost budgets</u> are prepared for every major expense category of the firm, such as manufacturing or production cost, selling cost, and administrative cost.

3. The <u>profit budget</u> is prepared based upon information generated from the sales budget and cost budget.

4. The <u>cash budget</u> is generated by converting all budget information previously discussed into a cash basis.

B. The cash budget represents a detailed plan of future cash flows and can be broken down into four components: cash receipts, cash disbursements, net change in cash for the period, and new financing needed. Cash budgets can also be either fixed or variable.

1. In a <u>fixed cash budget</u>, cash flow estimates are made for a single set of sales estimates.

2. The <u>variable cash budget</u> involves the preparation of several budgets with each budget corresponding to a different set of sales estimates. This budget fulfills the two following basic needs:

a. The variable budget gives management more information on the range of possible financing needs of the firm.

b. Management is provided with a standard against which it can measure the performance of subordinates responsible for various cost and revenue items contained in the budget.

C. Although no strict rules exist, as a general rule, the budget period shall be long enough to show the effect of management policies, yet short enough so that estimates can be made with reasonable accuracy. For instance, the capital expenditure budget may be properly developed for a 10-year period while a cash budget may only cover 12 months.

D. The development of pro forma financial statements represents the final stage of the budgeting process.

1. A <u>pro forma income statement</u> represents a statement of planned profit or loss for the future period and is based primarily on information generated in the cash budget.

2. The <u>pro forma balance sheet</u> for a future date is developed by adjusting present balance-sheet figures for projected information found primarily within the cash budget and pro forma income statement.

Study Problems

1. TAM Manufacturing Company is attempting to estimate its needs for funds during each of the months covering the third quarter of 1988. Pertinent information is given in the table.

   (1) Past and estimated future sales:

April	$100,000	July	$100,000
May	80,000	August	110,000
June	90,000	September	120,000
		October	100,000

   (2) Rent expense is $4,000 per month.

   (3) A quarterly interest payment on $100,000 in 5% notes payable is paid during September, 1988.

   (4) Wages and salaries are estimated as follows:

July	$10,000
August	11,000
September	12,000

   Payments are made within the month in which the wages are earned.

   (5) Fifty percent of sales are for cash, with the remaining 50% collected in the month following the sale. (Bad debts are negligible.)

   (6) TAM pays 80% of the sales price for merchandise and makes payment in the same month in which the sales occur, although purchases are made in the month prior to the anticipated sales.

   (7) TAM plans to pay $10,000 in cash for a new forklift truck in July, 1988.

   (8) Short-term loans can be obtained at 12% annual interest with interest paid during each month for which the loan is outstanding.

   (9) TAM's ending cash balance for June 30, 1988 is $55,000: the minimum balance the firm wishes to have in any month is $45,000.

38

(a) Set up, in a logical and easy-to-follow format, a cash budget for TAM for the quarter ended September 30, 1988.

SOLUTION

Worksheet

	June	July	August	September
Sales	$90,000	$100,000	$110,000	$120,000
Cash sales		50,000	55,000	60,000
Collections (50% 1 month later)		45,000	50,000	55,000
Total cash collections		$ 95,000	$105,000	$115,000

Cash Budget

	July	August	September
Cash receipts			
From sales	$ 95,000	$105,000	$115,000
Cash disbursements			
Payments on purchases	(80,000)	(88,000)	(96,000)
Rent	(4,000)	(4,000)	(4,000)
Wages and salaries	(10,000)	(11,000)	(12,000)
Interest (0.05 X 100,000 X 1/4)			(1,250)
Purchase of forklift truck	(10,000)		
Short-term-borrowing interest (0.12)			
Total cash disbursement	(104,000)	(103,000)	(113,250)
Net	(9,000)	2,000	1,750
Beginning cash balance	55,000	46,000	48,000
Borrowing (repayment)	0	0	0
Ending balance	$ 46,000	$ 48,000	$ 49,750

(b) Prepare a pro forma income statement for TAM covering the quarter ended September 30, 1988. You may assume that TAM's marginal tax rate is 17%. Also, TAM has $110,000 in fixed assets with an average expected useful life of 10 years. (TAM uses straight-line depreciation.)

SOLUTION

TAM Mfg. Co.
Pro Forma Income Statement
for the Quarter Ended
September 30, 1988

Sales	$330,000
Cost of goods sold	(264,000)
Gross profit	66,000
Operating expenses:	
Wages and salaries	(33,000)
Rent	(12,000)
Depreciation	(2,750)
Total operating expenses	(47,750)
Earnings before interest and taxes	18,250
Interest	(1,250)
Earnings before taxes	17,000
Taxes (17%)	(2,890)
Net profit after taxes	$ 14,110

(c) Given the following balance sheet for TAM (dated June 30, 1988) and the results of parts (a) and (b), construct a pro forma balance sheet as of September 30, 1988.

TAM Mfg. Co.
Balance Sheet
June 30, 1988

Cash	$ 55,000	Accounts payable	$ 0
Accounts receivable	45,000	Accrued taxes	0
Inventories	100,000	Notes payable	100,000
Fixed assets, net	100,000	Common equity	200,000
	$300,000		$300,000

SOLUTION

TAM Mfg. Co.
Pro Forma Balance Sheet
September 30, 1988

Cash	$ 49,750	Accounts payable	$ 0[d]
Accounts receivable	60,000[a]	Accrued taxes	2,890
Inventory	100,000[b]	Notes payable	100,000
Fixed assets, net	107,250[c]	Common equity	214,110[e]
	$317,000		$317,000

40

[a]Accounts receivable (beginning balance) $ 45,000
  +credit sales   165,000
  -collections   (150,000)
  Ending balance $ 60,000

[b]Inventories (beginning balance) $100,000
  +purchases   264,000
  -cost of goods sold   (264,000)
  Ending balance $100,000

[c]Fixed assets (beginning balance) $100,000
  +purchases   10,000
  -depreciation   (2,750)
  Ending balance $107,250

[d]Accounts payable $ 0
  +purchases   264,000
  -payments   (264,000)
  Ending balance $ 0

[e]Common equity (beginning balance) $200,000
  +net income   14,110
  -cash dividends   0
  Ending balance $214,110

2. The Horn Corporation's projected sales for the first 8 months of 1988 are as follows:

January	$300,000	May	$1,200,000
February	450,000	June	1,000,000
March	540,000	July	900,000
April	960,000	August	700,000

   Twenty percent of Horn's sales are for cash, another 40% is collected in the month following sale, and 40% is collected in the second month following sale. November and December sales for 1987 were $800,000 and $650,000, respectively.

   Horn purchases raw materials equal to 60% of sales and it makes its purchases 2 months in advance of sales. The supplier is paid 1 month after the purchase. For example, purchases for April sales are made in February and are paid for in March.

   Furthermore, Horn pays $42,000 per month for rent and $90,000 per month for other expenditures. Finally, tax deposits of $85,000 are made each quarter, beginning in March.

The company's cash balance at December 31, 1987, was $80,000 and a minimum balance of $50,000 must be maintained at all times. Assume that any short-term financing needed to maintain the minimum cash balance would be paid off in the month following the month of financing with interest paid at a 12% annual rate.

Prepare a cash budget for Horn covering the first 6 months of 1988.

SOLUTION

	January	February	March	April	May	June	July
Sales	$300,000	$450,000	$540,000	$960,000	$1,200,000	$1,000,000	$ 900,000
Cash sales	60,000	90,000	108,000	192,000	240,000	200,000	180,000
Collections 1 month later	260,000	120,000	180,000	216,000	384,000	480,000	400,000
Collections 2 months later	320,000	260,000	120,000	180,000	216,000	384,000	480,000
Total collections from sales	640,000	470,000	408,000	588,000	840,000	1,064,000	1,060,000
Purchases	324,000	576,000	720,000	600,000	540,000	420,000	
Payments on purchases	270,000	324,000	576,000	720,000	600,000	540,000	420,000

Cash receipts:

	January	February	March	April	May	June	July
Collections from sales	640,000	470,000	408,000	588,000	840,000	1,064,000	1,060,000

Cash disbursements:

	January	February	March	April	May	June	July
Payments on purchases	270,000	324,000	576,000	720,000	600,000	540,000	420,000
Other expenditures	90,000	90,000	90,000	90,000	90,000	90,000	90,000
Rent	42,000	42,000	42,000	42,000	42,000	42,000	42,000
Tax deposits			85,000			85,000	
Total disbursements	402,000	456,000	793,000	852,000	732,000	757,000	552,000
Net change for the month	238,000	14,000	(385,000)	(264,000)	108,000	307,000	
Beginning cash balance	80,000	318,000	332,000	50,000	50,000	50,000	
Plus: net change	238,000	14,000	(385,000)	(264,000)	108,000	307,000	
Borrowing	—	—	103,000	265,030	104,320	(263,710)	
Interest for prior month's borrowing	—	—	—	1,030*	3,680	2,637	
Ending cash balance	$318,000	$332,000	$ 50,000	$ 50,000	$ 50,000	$ 90,653	
Cumulative borrowing	—	—	—	$368,030	$ 263,710	—	

*0.12 X 103,000 X 1/12 = $1,030

Self-Tests

TRUE-FALSE

_____ T   1. Budgets perform the basic functions of (1) providing the basis for taking corrective action and (2) providing the basis for performance evaluation.

_____ T   2. Physical budgets are used as the basis for generating cost and profit budgets.

_____ F   3. Depreciation expense is an essential element in the cash budget.

_____ T   4. Performance evaluation is a principal function that can be performed through the use of budgets.

_____ F   5. A budget of expected research and development costs for the coming year is an example of a physical budget.

_____ T   6. A fixed cash budget differs from a variable cash budget in that a fixed budget reflects cash flow estimates for only one set of sales estimates whereas a variable budget reflects cash flow estimates for several possible sales levels.

_____ F   7. As a general rule, all budgets of the firm should project no longer than 1 year in the future so that estimates can be made with reasonable accuracy.

_____ F   8. A pro forma income statement can be developed wholly from information found in the cash budget prepared for the same period.

_____ T   9. The cash budget is only as useful as the accuracy of the forecasts that are used in its preparation.

_____ F   10. Future net fixed assets are estimated for the pro forma balance sheet by adding planned expenditures to existing net fixed assets and adding to this sun depreciation for the period.

MULTIPLE CHOICE

1. The most important element in determining the accuracy of most cash budgets is the:

   a. Forecast of cash disbursements.
   b. Forecast of collection schedule.
   c. Forecast of sales.
   d. Cannot be determined.
   e. None of the above.

2. Pro forma statements embody:

   a. Forecasts of prospective future cash positions of the firm.
   b. Forecasts of all assets and liabilities.
   c. Forecasts of the firm's long-range goals and objectives.
   d. All of the above.
   e. a and b only.

3. Which of the following items would be included in the cash budget?

   a. Depreciation charges.
   b. Goodwill.
   c. Patent amortization.
   d. All of the above.
   e. None of the above.

4. The cash budget provides the following information:

   a. The exact amount of borrowing needed for the budget interval.
   b. The type of loan which should be obtained to meet the cash needs for the time interval.
   c. A point estimate of the borrowing needs for the budget interval.
   d. An estimate of the cash needed for depreciation expense.
   e. None of the above.

5. In general, a firm will use the following type(s) of budgets:

   a. Profit budgets.
   b. Cash budgets.
   c. Cost budgets.
   d. Physical budgets.
   e. All of the above.

6. Which of the following would not fall under the physical budget classification?

   a. Unit sales budget.
   b. Physical facilities budget.
   c. Production cost budget.
   d. Unit production budget.
   e. None of the above.

45

5

Introduction to Working Capital Management

Orientation: In this chapter we introduce working-capital management in terms of managing the firm's liquidity. Specifically, working capital is defined as the difference in current assets and current liabilities. The hedging principle is offered as one approach to addressing the firm's liquidity problems.

I. Managing current assets

   A. The firm's investment in current assets (like fixed assets) is determined by the marginal benefits derived from investing in them compared with their acquisition cost.

   B. However, the current-fixed asset mix of the firm's investment in assets is an important determinant of the firm's liquidity. That is, the greater the firm's investment in current assets, other things remaining the same, the greater the firm's liquidity. This is generally true since current assets are usually more easily converted into cash.

   C. The firm can invest in marketable securities to increase its liquidity. However, such a policy involves committing the firm's funds to a relatively low-yielding (in comparison to fixed assets) investment.

II. Managing the firm's use of current liabilities

A. The greater the firm's use of current liabilities, other things being the same, the less will be the firm's liquidity.

B. There are a number of advantages associated with the use of current liabilities for financing the firm's asset investments.

   1. Flexibility. Current liabilities can be used to match the timing of a firm's short-term financing needs exactly.

   2. Interest cost. Historically, the interest cost on short-term debt has been lower than that on long-term debt.

C. Following are the disadvantages commonly associated with the use of short-term debt:

   1. Short-term debt exposes the firm to an increased risk of illiquidity because short-term debt matures sooner and in greater frequency, by definition, than does long-term debt.

   2. Since short-term debt agreements must be renegotiated from year to year, the interest cost of each year's financing is uncertain.

III. Determining the appropriate level of working capital

A. Pragmatically, it is impossible to derive the "optimal" level of working capital for the firm. Such a derivation would require estimation of the potential costs of illiquidity which, to date, have eluded precise measurement.

B. However, the "hedging principle" provides the basis for the firm's working-capital decisions.

   1. The hedging principle or rule of self-liquidating debt involves the following: Those asset needs of the firm not financed by spontaneous sources (i.e., payables and accruals) should be financed in accordance with the following rule: Permanent asset investments are financed with permanent sources and temporary investments are financed with temporary sources of financing.

2. A _permanent investment in an asset_ is one which the firm expects to hold for a period longer than 1 year. Such an investment may involve current or fixed assets.

3. Temporary asset investments comprise the firm's investment in current assets what will be liquidated and _not_ replaced during the year.

4. _Spontaneous sources of financing_ include all those sources which are available upon demand (e.g., trade credit--Accounts Payable) or which arise naturally as a part of doing business (e.g., wages payable, interest payable, taxes payable, etc.).

5. _Temporary sources of financing_ include all forms of current or short-term financing not categorized as spontaneous. Examples include bank loans, commercial paper, and finance company loans.

6. _Permanent sources of financing_ include all long-term sources such as debt having a maturity longer than 1 year, preferred stock, and common stock.

C. Although the hedging principle provides a useful guide to the firm's working-capital decisions, no firm will follow its tenets strictly. At times a firm may find itself overly reliant on temporary financing but at other times it may have excess cash as a result of excessive use of permanent financing.

Study Problem

1. The Harrison Mfg. Co. has projected its needs for both current and fixed assets over the next 5 years. At present Harrison has financed its assets using $75 million in common equity, $9 million in long-term debt, and the balance in payables. Payables generally equal 50% of current assets.

	Current Assets	Fixed Assets
1/01/88 (now)	$18,000,000	$75,000,000
6/30/88	26,000,000	77,000,000
1/01/89	20,000,000	80,000,000
6/30/89	30,000,000	80,000,000
1/01/90	22,000,000	81,000,000
6/30/90	32,000,000	83,000,000
1/01/91	34,000,000	86,000,000
6/30/91	34,000,000	88,000,000
1/01/92	26,000,000	90,000,000
6/30/92	36,000,000	93,000,000

Devise a financing plan for Harrison that is consistent with the hedging principle.

SOLUTION

Date	Fixed Assets	Current Assets	Total Assets	Temporary Assets	Permanent Assets
1/01/88	$75M	$18M	$ 93M	$ 0	$ 93M
6/30/88	77M	26M	103M	3M	100M
1/01/89	80M	20M	100M	0	100M
6/30/89	80M	30M	110M	7M	103M
1/01/90	81M	22M	103M	0	103M
6/30/90	83M	32M	115M	0	115M
1/01/91	86M	34M	120M	4M	116M
6/30/91	88M	34M	122M	6M	116M
1/01/92	90M	26M	116M	0	116M
6/30/92	93M	36M	129M	13M	116M

Date	Permanent Financing[a]	Spontaneous Financing[b]	Short-term Debt[c]
1/01/88	$84M	$ 9M	$ 0
6/30/88	87M	13M	3M
1/01/89	88M	10M	2M
6/30/89	88M	15M	7M
1/01/90	92M	111	0
6/30/90	99M	16M	0
1/01/91	99M	12M	9M
6/30/91	99M	17M	6M
1/01/92	99M	13M	4M
6/30/92	99M	18M	12M

[a]Permanent financing includes both common equity and long-term debt; ordinarily these sources of financing are issued for prolonged periods of time and thus do not fluctuate downward in the short run.

[b]Spontaneous financing (including payables) is estimated to be 50% of current assets.

[c]Short-term debt equals the difference in total financing needs and that provided by permanent plus spontaneous sources.

COMMENTS:

(1) Note that since we are dealing with 6-month intervals and since assets are growing throughout the planning horizon, temporary financing or short-term debt does not periodically go to zero. This does not mean that short-term notes are not repaid. However, if Harrison is to avoid having to issue and then repay permanent funds or if the firm does not want excess cash due to over financing through permanent sources, then it appears that some short-term debt will be needed throughout most of the planning period.

(2) Note that we have not distinguished between debt and equity sources of permanent financing. This decision relates to the firm's choosing a financing mix and is discussed in Chapter 15.

Self-Tests

TRUE-FALSE

<u>F</u> 1. Working capital has traditionally been defined as the firm's investment in assets.

<u>F</u> 2. Generally interest rates on short-term debt are higher than they are on long-term debt for a given borrower.

<u>T</u> 3. The guiding principle for the firm's working capital policies is referred to as the "principle of self-liquidating debt" or the "hedging principle."

F <u>T</u> 4. The use of short-term sources of financing enhances the firm's liquidity and reduces the firm's rate of return on assets.

<u>T</u> 5. There are two basic problems encountered in attempting to manage the firm's use of short-term financing: determining how much short-term debt to use and determining what sources to select.

<u>T</u> 6. Investment decisions are undertaken in the expectation of receiving future benefits.

_F_ 7. In order to reduce the risk of illiquidity, a firm should decrease its investment in cash and marketable securities.

_T_ 8. Current liabilities provide a flexible source of financing.

_F_ 9. The "hedging principle" is founded in valuation theory.

_T_ 10. Spontaneous financing consists of trade credit and other accounts payable which arise "automatically" in the firm's day-to-day operations.

MULTIPLE CHOICE

1. Which of the following is an advantage associated with the use of current liabilities?

    a. The use of current liabilities subjects the firm to greater risk of illiquidity.
    b. The firm's interest costs can vary from year to year.
    c. All of the above.
    d. None of the above.

2. Spontaneous financing consists of:

    a. Accounts payable.
    b. Trade credit.
    c. Short-term notes payable.
    d. Common stock.
    e. All of the above.
    f. a and b only.

3. Which of the following accounts would <u>not</u> be a prime consideration in working-capital management?

C

    a. Cash.
    b. Accounts payable.
    c. Bonds payable.
    d. Marketable securities.
    e. Accounts receivable.

4. The greatest margin of safety for a firm would be provided by:

    a. More current assets and less current liabilities.
    b. More current assets and more current liabilities.
    c. Less current assets and more current liabilities.
    d. Less current assets and less current liabilities.

51

5. Which asset-liability combination would result in the firm having the greatest risk of technical insolvency?

    a. More current assets and less current liabilities.
    b. More current assets and more current liabilities.
    c. Less current assets and more current liabilities.
    d. Less current assets and less current liabilities.

6. Which of the following illustrates the use of the hedging approach?

    a. Temporary assets financed with long-term liabilities.
    b. Permanent assets financed with long-term liabilities.
    c. Temporary assets financed with short-term liabilities.
    d. All of the above.
    e. b and c.

6

Cash and Marketable Securities Management

Orientation: This chapter initiates our study of cash management. Here, we focus on the cash flow process and the reasons why a firm holds cash balances. The objectives of a sound cash management system are identified. The concept of float is defined. Several techniques that firms can use to favorably affect their cash receipts and disbursements patterns are examined. Finally, the composition of the firm's marketable securities portfolio is discussed.

I.   Why a company holds cash

    A.   The firm's cash balance is constantly affected by a variety of influences. Sound cash management techniques are based on a thorough understanding of the cash flow process.

        1.   On an irregular basis cash holdings are increased from several external sources, such as from the sale of securities.

        2.   In a similar fashion, irregular cash outflows reduce the firm's cash balance. Typical examples include cash dividend payments and the interest requirements on debt agreements.

        3.   Other major sources of cash arising from internal operations occur on a rather regular basis. Accounts receivable collections are an example.

B.   Three motives for holding cash balances have been identified by Keynes.[1]

    1.   The _transactions motive_ is the need for cash to meet payments that arise in the ordinary course of doing business. Holding cash to meet a payroll or to acquire raw materials characterizes this motive.

    2.   The _precautionary motive_ describes the investment in liquid assets that are used to satisfy possible but as yet indefinite needs for cash. Precautionary balances are a buffer against all kinds of things that might happen to drain the firm's cash resources.

    3.   The _speculative motive_ describes holding cash to take advantage of hoped-for, profit-making situations.

II. Variations in liquid asset holdings

A.   Considerable variation is present in the liquid asset holdings of major industry groups and individual firms.

    1.   This is because (1) not all of the factors noted above affect every firm and (2) the executives in different firms who are ultimately responsible for cash management tasks have different risk-bearing preferences.

    2.   Some industries invest very heavily in liquid assets. For example, the total liquid assets to total assets ratio of the contract construction industry greatly exceeds that of the utility industry.

B.   Because assets are acquired, wasted, and sold every day, the management of liquid assets must be viewed as a dynamic process. The cash flow process is complex. In order to cut through this complexity, it is necessary that the firm's cash management system operate within clearly defined objectives.

---

[1] John Maynard Keynes, _The General Theory of Employment Interest and Money_ (New York: Harcourt Brace Jovanovich, Inc., 1936).

III. Cash management objectives and decisions

   A. A properly designed cash management program forces the financial manager to come to grips with a risk-return trade off.

      1. He or she must strike an acceptable balance between holding too much cash and holding too little cash.

      2. A large cash investment minimizes the chances of insolvency, but it penalizes company profitability.

      3. A small cash investment frees excess (cash) balances for investment in longer-lived and more profitable assets, which increases the firm's profitability.

   B. The firm's cash management system should strive to achieve two prime objectives:

      1. Enough cash must be on hand to dispense effectively with the disbursal needs that arise in the course of doing business.

      2. The firm's investment in idle cash balances must be reduced to a minimum.

   C. In the attempt to meet the two objectives noted above, certain decisions dominate the cash management process. These decision areas can be reduced to the three following questions:

      1. What can be done to speed up cash collections and slow down or better control cash outflows?

      2. What should be the composition of the marketable securities portfolio?

      3. How should the investment in liquid assets be split between actual cash holdings and marketable securities? This is covered in the Appendix to this chapter.

IV. Collection and disbursement procedures

   A. Cash acceleration and deceleration techniques revolve around the concept of _float_. Float can be broken down into four elements:

1. <u>Mail float</u> refers to funds that are tied up as a result of the time that elapses from the moment a customer mails his or her remittance check until the firm begins to process the check.

2. <u>Processing float</u> refers to funds that are tied up as a result of the firm's recording and processing remittance checks prior to their deposit in the bank.

3. <u>Transit float</u> refers to funds that are tied up as a result of the time needed for a deposited check to clear through the commercial banking system and become "usable" funds to the firm.

4. <u>Disbursing float</u> refers to funds that are technically usable to the firm until its <u>payment</u> check has cleared through the banking system and has been charged against its deposit account.

B. Float reduction can result in considerable benefits in terms of (1) usable funds that are released for company use and (2) in the returns produced on these freed-up balances. A study problem at the end of this chapter illustrates the calculation of such savings.

C. Several techniques are available to improve the management of the firm's cash inflows. These techniques may also provide for a reduction in float.

1. The <u>lock-box</u> arrangement is a widely used commercial banking service for expediting cash gathering.

    a. The objective is to reduce <u>both</u> mail and processing float.

    b. The procedure behind a lock-box system is very simple. The firm rents a local post office box and authorizes a local bank in which a deposit account is maintained to pick up remittances from the box.

        (1) Customers are instructed to mail their payments to the numbered post office box.

56

(2) A deposit form is prepared by the bank for each batch of processed checks.

(3) The bank may notify the firm daily as to the amount of funds deposited on the firm's behalf.

(4) The firm that receives checks from all over the country establishes several lock boxes.

c. A lock-box arrangement provides for (1) increased working cash, (2) elimination of clerical functions, and (3) early knowlledge of dishonored checks.

d. The firm must carefully evaluate whether this or any cash management service is worth the added costs. Usually, the bank levies a charge for each check processed through the system. The marginal income generated from released funds must exceed the added costs of the system to make it economically beneficial. A study problem at the end of this chapter illustrates this kind of calculation.

2. Pre-authorized checks (PAC's) are another method for speeding up the conversion of receipts into working cash.

a. The objective of the PAC is to reduce mail and processing float.

b. A PAC (1) is created with the individual's legal authorization, (2) resembles an ordinary check, and (3) does not contain the signature of the person on whose account it is being drawn.

c. PAC systems are most useful to firms that (1) regularly receive a large volume of payments of a fixed amount (2) from the same customers. Insurance companies and savings and loan associations are prominent examples.

d. The principle behind the PAC system is straight-forward. The firm simply obtains an authorization from its customers to draw checks (at specified times and for

specified amounts) on their (the customers') demand deposit accounts.

e.   Figure 6.1 shows the operation of a PAC
system.

f.   The benefits derived from a PAC system
include (1) highly predictable cash flows,
(2) reduced billing, postage, and clerical
expenses, (3) customer preference, and (4)
increased working cash stemming from
reduced mail and processing float.

3.   <u>Depository transfer checks</u> are used in conjunction with <u>concentration banking</u>. A concentration bank is one in which the firm maintains a
major disbursing account.

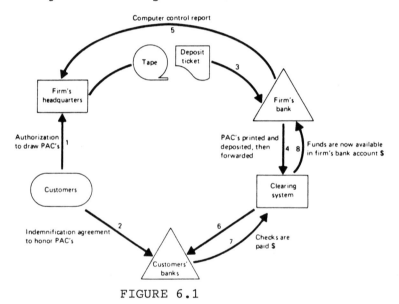

FIGURE 6.1

Pre-Authorized Check Systems (PAC)

a.   The major objective of using depository
transfer checks (DTC's) is to eliminate
excess cash balances held by the firm in
its several regional banks. A secondary
objective, which is achieved through use
of the <u>automated depository transfer check</u>
(ADTC) is to reduce float incurred by
mailing (ordinary) DTC's from a regional
bank to a concentration bank.

58

b. The DTC provides a means for moving
    (transferring) funds from a local bank to
    a concentration bank.

    (1) The DTC is an unsigned, non-negotia-
        ble instrument.

    (2) The DTC is payable only to the bank
        of ultimate deposit.

    (3) DTC's can operate through the use of
        the U.S. mail system or an automated
        system (ADTC).

c. With the conventional DTC, a company
    employee deposits the day's cash receipts
    in a local bank, fills out a DTC for the
    amount of the deposit, and mails the DTC
    to the concentration bank. When the DTC
    is received at the concentration bank, the
    transferred funds are credited to the
    firm's demand deposit account.

d. The ADTC eliminates the time required for
    the conventional DTC to travel through the
    mails and physically reach the concentra-
    tion bank. The deposit information is
    transmitted electronically at the concen-
    tration bank, which results in the saved
    time. This system is shown in Figure 6.2.

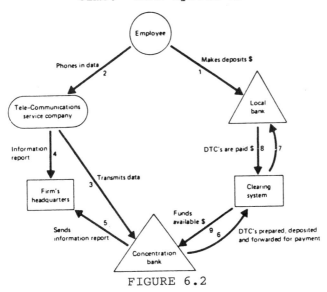

FIGURE 6.2

Automated Depository Transfer Check System (DTC)

59

4. <u>Wire transfers</u> offer the fastest method for moving funds between commercial banks. Usable ("good") funds are transferred and thereby immediately become usable funds at the receiving bank. There is no <u>transit</u> float with wire transfers. Two major communication facilities are used to accommodate wire transfers: (1) bank wire, which is privately operated by about 250 major commercial banks in the United States, and (2) Federal Reserve wire system, which is accessible to members of the Federal Reserve system. The movement of small dollar amounts does not usually justify use of this system.

D. Techniques used by firms that hope to improve the management of their cash outflows include: (1) zero balance accounts, (2) payable-through drafts, and (3) remote disbursing.

1. <u>Zero balance accounts</u> (ZBA's) permit centralized control (i.e., at the head office) over cash disbursements, but at the same time they allow the firm to maintain disbursing authority at the local or divisional level.

   a. The major objective of a ZBA system is to achieve better control over cash payments. A secondary benefit of this technique <u>might</u> be an increase in disbursement float.

   b. Under a ZBA system, each profit center (division) has a disbursing account located in the <u>same</u> concentration bank.

      (1) The firm's authorized employees write payment checks in the usual manner.

      (2) These checks then clear through the banking system and are presented to the firm's concentration bank for payment.

      (3) The checks are paid by the bank and negative balances build up in the appropriate disbursing accounts.

      (4) Daily, the negative balances are restored to a zero level by means of credits to the various ZBA's and a corresponding reduction in the firm's

master demand deposit account in the concentration bank.

c. For the firm that has several operating units, the benefits from using a ZBA system include:

    (1) Centralized control over disbursements.

    (2) Reduction of time spent on superficial cash management activities.

    (3) Reduction of excess cash balances held in outlying accounts.

    (4) An increase in disbursement float.

2. <u>Payable-through drafts</u> (PTD's) have the physical appearance of ordinary checks but they are drawn on and paid by the issuing firm instead of the bank. The bank serves as a collection point for the documents and passes the documents on to the firm for inspection and authorization for payment.

a. The objective of a payable-through draft system is to provide for effective control of field authorized payments. An example would be a claim settlement authorized by an insurance agent.

b. Stop payment orders can be initiated by the firm's headquarters on any drafts considered inappropriate.

c. Legal payment of <u>individual</u> drafts takes place <u>after</u> review and approval of the drafts by the company. Disbursing float, however, is usually <u>not</u> increased by the use of drafts. For purposes of measuring usable funds to the firm, drafts presented daily for payment are charged in <u>total</u> against the corporate master demand deposit account.

3. <u>Remote disbursing</u>, rather obviously, is intended to increase disbursing float.

a. To implement such a procedure, the firm only needs to open and use a deposit account located in a city distant from its customers' banks.

      b.   Since checks written on that account take longer to clear, the firm has use of its funds for a longer period of time.

      c.   The major constraint on this procedure is the possible alienation of important customers who must wait longer for their remittance checks to become usable funds.

4.   <u>Electronic funds transfer</u> methods are serving to reduce transit, mail, and processing float

      a.   If Firm A owes money to Firm B, this situation ought to be immediately reflected on both the books and bank accounts of these companies.

      b.   This ideal within the U.S. financial system has not been reached; the trend towards it is readily observable. Business firms, for example, are using systems like terminal-based wire transfers to move funds within their cash management systems.

      c.   The heart of electronic funds transfer (EFT) is the elimination of the check as a method of transferring funds. The process of EFT should provide for a more efficient economy, since funds (cash) will be released for more productive purposes.

• Evaluating the costs of cash management services

A.   Whether a particular cash management system will provide an economic benefit to the firm can be evaluated by use of this relationship:

added costs = added benefits

B.   Clearly, if the benefits exceed the costs of using the system, then the system is economically feasible.

C.   On a per unit basis, this relationship can be expressed as follows:

$P = (D)(S)(i)$

where P = increase in per-check processing cost, if the new system is adopted,
      D = days saved in the collection process, i.e., float reduction,
      S = average check size in dollars,

i = the daily, before-tax opportunity cost (rate of return) of carrying cash.

D. The sum of (D) (S) (i) must exceed P for the system to be beneficial to the firm. A study problem at the end of this chapter provides an example of this logic.

VI. Composition of the marketable securities portfolio

A. When selecting a proper marketable securities mix, five factors should be considered.

1. _Financial risk_ is the uncertainty of expected returns from a security due to unforeseeable changes in the financial capacity of the security issuer to make future payments to the security owner.

2. _Interest rate_ risk is the uncertainty in expected returns caused by possible changes in interest rates. This is particularly important for securities that have long, as opposed to short, terms of maturity. (See study problem 6 for an illustration of this point.)

3. _Liquidity_ is the ability to transform a security into cash. Consideration should be given to (1) the time needed to sell the security and (2) the likelihood that the security can be sold at or near its prevailing market price.

4. The _taxability_ of interest income and capital gains is seriously considered by some corporate treasurers.

   a. The interest income from _municipal obligations_ is tax-exempt.

   b. The following equation may be used to determine an equivalent before-tax yield on a taxable security.

      (1) Notation:

         r = equivalent before-tax yield.
         r* = after-tax yield on tax-exempt security.
         T = firm's marginal income tax rate.

(2) Computation

$$r = \frac{r*}{(1 - T)}$$

(3) Example: Suppose a firm has a choice between investing in a 1-year tax-free debt issue yielding 6% on a $1,000 outlay or a 1-year taxable issue that yields 10% on a $1,000 outlay. The firm pays federal taxes at the rate of 46%. Which security is more beneficial to the firm?

$$r = \frac{0.06}{(1 - 0.46)} = 11.11\%$$

(4) Clearly, this firm should choose the tax exempt security.

5. The <u>yield</u> criterion involves a weighing of the risks and benefits inherent in the four previously mentioned factors. The higher the risks associated with a particular security, the higher the expected yield (risk-return tradeoff).

B. Marketable security alternatives

1. A <u>Treasury bill</u> is a direct obligation of the U.S. government sold on a regular basis by the U.S. Treasury.

    a. These bills may be purchased in denominations of $10,000, $15,000, $50,000, $100,000, $500,000, and $1,000,000.

    b. The bills are currently offered with maturities of 91, 182, and 365 days. Nine-month bills are <u>not</u> presently sold.

    c. Since Treasury bills are sold on a discount basis, the investor does not receive an actual interest payment.

    d. The bills are marketed by the Treasury only in bearer form (without the name of the investor upon them) and are therefore easily transferable.

    e. Since Treasury bills are backed by the U.S. government they are considered risk-free and consequently sell at lower yields than those obtainable on other marketable securities.

f. The income from Treasury bills is only subject to federal income taxes and is always taxed as an ordinary gain.

2. Federal agency securities represent debt obligations of federal government agencies and were created to carry out leading programs of the U.S. government.

a. The Federal National Mortgage Association (FNMA) renders supplementary assistance to the secondary market for mortgages.

b. The Federal Home Loan Banks (FHLB) function as a credit reserve system for member banks.

c. The Federal Land Banks grant loans to members of Federal Land Bank Associations who are engaged in agriculture, provide agricultural services, or own rural homes

d. The Federal Intermediate Credit Banks grant loans to and purchase notes originating from loans made to farmers by other financial institutions.

e. The Banks for Cooperatives make loans to cooperative associations which are owned and controlled by individuals involved in general farm business.

f. Securities of these "big five" federally sponsored agencies are not directly backed by the U.S. government.

g. The maturities available range from 30 days to 15 years, with most (80%) maturing in 5 years or less.

h. The yields available always exceed those of Treasury bills of comparable maturity and are taxable at the federal, state, and local level.

3. Bankers' acceptances are largely concentrated in the financing of foreign transactions; this acceptance is a draft (order to pay) drawn on a

specific bank by an exporter in order to obtain payment for goods shipped to a customer who maintains an account with that bank.

   a. The maturities run mostly from 30 to 180 days, with the most common period being 90 days.

   b. Like Treasury bills, the acceptances are sold on a discount basis.

   c. Income generated from acceptances is fully taxable at all governmental levels.

   d. Acceptances provide investors with a higher yield than do Treasury bills and agency obligations of comparable maturity.

4. A negotiable certificate of deposit (CD), is a marketable receipt for funds that have been deposited in a bank for a fixed time period at a fixed interest rate.

   a. CD's are offered in denominations ranging from $25,000 to $10,000,000, with popular sizes of $100,000, $500,000 and $1,000,000.

   b. Original maturities on CD's range from 1 to 18 months.

   c. Yields on CD's are higher than yields on Treasury bills, and in recent years they have exceeded those available on acceptances.

   d. The income received from CD's is taxed at all governmental levels.

5. Commercial paper refers to short-term, unsecured promissory notes sold by large businesses in order to raise cash.

   a. Paper is usually sold in relatively large denominations, typically in excess of $25,000, and ranging up to $1,000,000.

   b. The notes are sold on a discount basis with maturities ranging from 3 to 270 days.

   c. It is the only investment instrument discussed here that has no active trading in a secondary market.

d. The return on commercial paper is fully taxable at all governmental levels.

6. <u>Repurchase agreements</u> are legal contracts that involve the actual sale of securities by a borrower to the lender, with a commitment on the part of the borrower to repurchase the securities at the contract price plus a stated interest charge.

   a. These agreements are usually executed in sizes of $500,000 or more.

   b. The maturity is either for a specified time period (tailored to the needs of the investor) or there is no fixed maturity date.

   c. The yields are generally less than those of Treasury bill rates of comparable maturities and are taxable at all governmental levels.

7. <u>Money market mutual funds</u> usually invest in a diversified portfolio of short-term, high-grade debt instruments like those described in this section.

   a. These funds sell their shares to a large number of small investors in order to raise cash.

   b. The funds offer the investing firm a high degree of liquidity and investment expertise.

   c. The returns earned from owning shares in a money market fund are taxable at all governmental levels.

   d. Table 6.1 summarizes the salient features of the major money market instruments important to businesses.

8. <u>Money market deposit accounts</u> became available to the public on December 14, 1982, on authorization of the Depository Institutions Deregulatory Committee.

   a. These accounts are offered by commercial banks and thrift institutions. The intent is to compete with money market mutual funds, but they <u>do</u> differ in significant

Features of Selected Money Market Instruments

Instrument	Denominations	Maturities	Basis	Form	Liquidity	Taxability
U.S. Treasury Bills: direct obligations of the U.S. government.	$ 10,000 15,000 50,000 100,000 500,000 1,000,000	91 days 182 days 365 days 9-month not presently issued	Discount	Bearer	Excellent secondary market	Exempt from state and local income; do not qualify for favorable capital gains rate
Federal Agency Securities: Obligations of corporations and agencies created to affect the federal government's lending programs.	Wide variation from $1,000 to $1,000,000	5 days* to more than ten years (*Farm Credit consolidated system-wide discount notes)	Discount or coupon; usually on coupon	Bearer or registered	Good for issues of "Big Five" agencies	Generally exempt at local level; FNMA issues are not
Bankers' Acceptances: Drafts accepted for future payment by commercial banks.	No set size; typically range from $25,000 to $1,000,000	Predominately from 30 to 180 days	Discount	Bearer	Good for acceptances of large "money market" banks	Taxed at all levels of government
Negotiable Certificates of Deposit: Marketable receipts for funds deposited in a bank for a fixed time period.	$15,000 to $10,000,000	1 to 18 months	Accrued interest	Bearer or registered bearer is preferable from liquidity standpoint	Fair to good	Taxed at all levels of government
Commercial Paper: Short-term, unsecured promissory notes.	$5,000 to $5,000,000; $1,000 and $5,000 multiples above the initial offering size are sometimes available	3 to 270 days	Discount	Bearer	Poor; no active, secondary market in usual sense	Taxed at all levels of government
Repurchase Agreements: Legal contracts between a borrower (security seller) and lender (security buyer). The borrower will repurchase at the contract price plus an interest charge	Typical sizes are $500,000 or more	According to terms of contract	Not applicable	Not applicable	Fixed by the agreement, i.e., borrower will repurchase	Taxed at all levels of borrower government
Money Market Mutual Funds: Hold a diversified portfolio of short-term, high-grade debt instruments.	Some require an initial investment as small as $1,000	Shares can be sold at any time	Net asset value	Registered	Good; provided by the fund itself	Taxed at all levels of government

68

ways from the funds. You should check these characteristics in the text of Chapter 6.

b. One characteristic of the money market deposit accounts (MMDAs) that makes them inappropriate for _most_ businesses is that the number of transactions per month on each account is limited. Firms generally do not want to be restricted on the number of times per month that they can tap their liquid asset reserves. That runs counter to the very logic of holding a buffer stock of liquidity.

c. Alternatively, the MMDAs have become very popular with _individual_ investors.

Study Problems

1. Buckeye equipment has $3,000,000 in excess cash that it might invest in marketable securities. In order to buy and sell the securities though, the company must pay a transactions fee of $67,500.

(a) Would you recommend purchasing the securities if they yield 13 percent annually and are held for:

1. one month?
2. two months?
3. three months?
4. six months?
5. one year?

(b) What minimum required yield would the securities have to return for the firm to hold them for three months?

SOLUTION

(a) It is necessary to calculate the dollar value of the estimated return for each holding period and compare it with the transactions fee. This will allow you to determine if a gain can be made by investing in the securities. The calculations and recommendations are shown below:

			Recommendation
1. $3,000,000(.13)(1/12)	=	$32,500<$67,500	NO
2. $3,000,000(.13)(2/12)	=	$65,000<$67,500	NO
3. $3,000,000(.13)(3/12)	=	$97,500>$67,500	YES
4. $3,000,000(.13)(6/12)	=	$195,000>$67,500	YES
5. $3,000,000(.13)(12/12)	=	$390,000>$67,500	YES

69

(b)   Now we find the breakeven yield for a three-month
      holding period. Let (%) be the required yield.
      With $3,000,000 to invest for three months we have:

$$\$3,000,000 \ (\%) \ (3/12) = \$ \ 67,500$$
$$\$3,000,000 \ (\%) \qquad\ \ = \$270,000$$
$$\qquad\qquad (\%) \qquad\qquad\ = \$270,000/\$3,000,000 = \underline{9\%}$$

2.   Portland Energy Products is evaluating whether or not to
      use an additional lock box. If the lock box is used,
      check processing costs will rise by $.20 a check. The
      average check size that will be mailed to the lock-box
      location is $1,000. Funds that are freed by using the
      lock box will be invested in marketable securities to
      yield an <u>annual</u> before-tax return of 7%. The firm uses a
      365 day year in its analysis procedures. What reduction
      in check-collection time is required to justify use of
      the lock box?

SOLUTION

Solve the following relationship for D:

$$P = (D)(S)(i)$$

$$\$.20 = (D)(\$1,000)\left(\frac{0.07}{365}\right)$$

$$\$.20 = (D)(\$.192)$$

$$\frac{\$.20}{\$.192} = D = \underline{1.0417 \ days}$$

Thus, the lock box is justified if it can speed up
collections by <u>more</u> than 1.0417 days.

3.   Annual sales for Austin Drilling Supply will total
      $250,000,000 next year. What would be the annual value
      of 1-day's float reduction to this firm if it could
      invest the freed-up balances at 8% per year?

SOLUTION

Compute Austin's sales per day:

$$\frac{annual \ revenues}{days \ in \ year} = \frac{250,000,000}{365} = \$684,932$$

Compute the annual value of the 1-day float reduction:

$$(\$684,932)(0.08) = \underline{\$54,795}$$

4. The corporate treasurer of Buckeye Bottling is considering purchasing a municipal obligation with a 7% coupon and a $1,000 par value. Mr. Inside Info has telephoned the treasurer about another $1,000 par value offering which provides a 12% yield. This latter offering is, however, fully taxable. Buckeye is taxed at a 48% rate.

   (a) Should the treasurer take Mr. Info's advice and purchase the 12% security?

   (b) What is the equivalent before-tax yield on the municipal assuming Buckeye is in a 48% tax bracket?

   SOLUTION

   (a) The after-tax yield to Buckeye on the 12% offering is $(0.12)(1-0.48) = 6.24\%$. Since the yield on the municipal is already stated on an after-tax basis the treasurer should ignore Mr Info's advice and purchase the municipal offering.

   (b) The equivalent before-tax yield is:

   $$r = \frac{0.07}{(1-0.48)} = \underline{13.46\%}$$

   Thus, the taxable issue would have to yield in excess of 13.46% to be more attractive than the municipal to Buckeye.

5. Tech Electronics, manufacturers of fine calculators, has recently purchased 10-year bonds at their par value of $1,000 per security. Texas Parts, a close competitor, has just purchased 5-year bonds at their $1,000 par value. Both securities have a coupon rate set at 8%, are compounded annually, and have a maturity value of $1,000. Suppose the prevailing interest rate 1 year from now rises to 10%. What would the decline in market price be for each bond in 1 year?

   SOLUTION

   One year from now the 5-year issue has 4 years remaining to maturity. The market price in 1 year can be found by computing P according to the following:

   $$P = \sum_{T=1}^{4} \frac{\$80}{(1+0.10)^T} + \frac{\$1,000}{(1+0.10)^4} = \$936.60$$

   where $\$80 = (0.08)(\$1,000)$. Similarly, for the 10-year issue which now has 9 years to maturity,

$$P = \sum_{T=1}^{9} \frac{\$80}{(1+0.10)^T} + \frac{\$1,000}{(1+0.10)^9} = \$884.82$$

Thus the 10-year security declines in price $115.18 ($1,000 - $884.82), while the 5-year security declines in price by only $63.40 ($1,000-$936.60). This illustrates the concept of <u>interest rate risk</u>, discussed in the text in Chapter 6.

6. Gavin International expects to generate sales of $74,000,000 in the coming year. All sales are done on a credit basis, net 30 days. Gavin has estimated that it takes an average of 4 days for payments to reach their central office and an additional day to process the payments. What is the opportunity cost of the funds tied up in the mail and processing? Gavin uses a 360 day year in all calculations and can invest free funds at 7%.

SOLUTION

Daily collections = 74,000,000/360 = $ 205,555.56

Opportunity Cost = (205,555.56)(5)(.07) = <u>$71,944</u>

7. The corporate treasurer of Chester Motors is considering the purchase of either an offering carrying a 7.6% coupon or a municipal obligation with a 5% coupon. Both bonds have a $1000 par value. The company is currently in the 34% marginal tax bracket. Which security should the treasurer recommend.

SOLUTION

The after-tax yield to Chester Motors on the 7.6% offering is (1-.34)(.076) = 5%. The municipal's after-tax rate is the stated 5%. There is no difference in yield. If the risk is considered equal for each security then the treasurer would be indifferent between the two.

<u>Self-Tests</u>

TRUE-FALSE

_____ 1. Accounts receivable are usually referred to as "near-cash assets."

_____ 2. Holding cash to pay for next week's labor bill (payroll) is an example of the precautionary motive for holding cash.

_____ 3. Ready borrowing power enables the firm to reduce the cash balances actually held for precautionary purposes.

_____ 4. Technical insolvency means that the firm is able to meet its short-term obligations on time but that its long-term obligations are in jeopardy.

_____ 5. Cash flow forecasting is the initial step in any effective cash management program.

_____ 6. Wire transfers provide the fastest and least costly method of transferring funds among depository institutions.

_____ 7. A possible benefit stemming from the use of pre-authorized checks is that cash flows can be more predictable.

_____ 8. The major objective of using payable-through drafts is to extend disbursing float.

_____ 9. The major reason for using lock boxes is to enjoy a reduction in transit float.

_____ 10. Zero balance accounts are used to accelerate cash receipts.

_____ 11. Although they have a lower yield, agency securities are more readily marketable by the purchasing corporation than are Treasury bills.

_____ 12. Bankers' acceptances generally mature from 9 to 12 months after "sight."

_____ 13. Commercial paper is backed by specific assets of the firm.

_____ 14. The most common denomination for the negotiable CD is $10,000.

_____ 15. The longer the term of maturity, the less sensitive the price of a security to changes in interest rates.

_____ 16. Long-term bonds may serve as a useful (comfortable) hedge against interest rate risk.

_____ 17. Because of their higher financial risk, agency securities always yield more than Treasury securities of a comparable maturity do.

73

_____ 18. The higher the marginal tax bracket the lower the after-tax rate of return on a taxable security.

_____ 19. Bankers' acceptances provide for a steady flow of interest payments to the investor in the form of coupon payments.

_____ 20. With respect to interest risk, Treasury securities are risk-free.

_____ 21. Money market deposit accounts (MMDAs) are more suited to individual investors than business firms as a tool of liquid asset management.

_____ 22. The lock-box system is the most widely used commercial banking service for expediting cash gathering.

_____ 23. A concentration bank is one where the firm generally maintains several minor disbursing accounts.

_____ 24. There is an inverse relationship between a financial instrument's chance of default and financial risk.

_____ 25. The contract price of the securities that make up the repurchase agreement is fixed for the duration of the transaction.

_____ 26. According to Keynes the demand for cash can be divided into three categories: transactions, precautionary, and speculative.

_____ 27. A PAC or Preauthorized Check does not ordinarily bear the name of the person on whose account the check was drawn.

_____ 28. To calculate the annual savings due to float reduction you would multiply the sales per day by the days of float reduction.

_____ 29. Payable-Through Drafts provide control over field payments.

_____ 30. A liquid asset is an asset that can be sold regardless of the time it takes to make the sale and the price concession suffered to make the sale.

_____ 31. Commercial paper is sometimes described as short-term, corporate IOU's.

MULTIPLE CHOICE

1. Indicate the item that is not an advantage of the lock-box system.

    a. The cost is minimal.
    b. Speeds up the flow of cash to the firm.
    c. Remittances are collected sooner.
    d. All of the above are advantages.

2. Which of the following is not a cash acceleration technique?

    a. Lock boxes.
    b. Automated depository transfer checks.
    c. Pre-authorized checks.
    d. Payable-through drafts.
    e. All of the above are cash acceleration techniques.

3. Depository transfer checks mainly:

    a. Reduce mail and processing float.
    b. Extend disbursing float.
    c. Provide a method of moving funds from local banks to concentration banks.
    d. Centralize disbursing authority.

4. Zero balance accounts:

    a. Permit centralized control over disbursements.
    b. Provide for effective control over field payments.
    c. Are an integral part of the lock-box system.
    d. Are the same thing as pre-authorized checks.

5. A pre-authorized check system:

    a. Reduces mail float.
    b. Reduces processing float.
    c. Extends disbursing float.
    d. a and b.
    e. b and c.

6. Generally, the least important component of a firm's preference for liquidity is:

    a. the transaction motive.
    b. the precautionary motive.
    c. the speculative motive.
    d. all motives are of equal importance.

75

7. Which of the following is <u>not</u> an objective of the lock-box system?

    a. reduce mail float.
    b. reduce processing float.
    c. reduce transit float.
    d. reduce disbursing float.

8. The advantages of a preauthorized check system include:

    a. reduced expenses.
    b. highly predictable cash flows.
    c. increased working cash.
    d. customer preference.
    e. all of the above are benefits of a PAC.

9. The uncertainty of expected returns from a security attributable to possible changes in the financial capacity of the security issuer to make future payments to the security owner refers to:

    a. interest rate risk.
    b. liquidity.
    c. financial risk.
    d. taxability.
    e. yield.

10. Which short-term investment has, for all practical purposes, <u>no</u> active trading in a secondary market?

    a. treasury bills.
    b. federal agency securities.
    c. negotiable certificates of deposit.
    d. commercial paper.
    e. banker's acceptances.

11. Which of the following is a benefit of centralizing the firm's pool of cash:

    a. Lower levels of excess cash.
    b. Stricter control over available cash.
    c. More efficient investments in near-cash assets.
    d. a and b.
    e. All of the above.

12. The fact that funds are available in the company's bank account until its payment check has cleared through the banking system refers to:

    a. Mail float.
    b. Processing float.
    c. Transit float.
    d. Disbursing float.

13. Which is <u>not</u> an objective of zero balance accounts:

    a. Achieve better control over cash payments.
    b. Reduce excess cash balances held in regional banks for disbursing purposes.
    c. Decrease disbursing float.

14. Firms use remote disbursements to:

    a. Decrease mail float.
    b. Increase disbursing float.
    c. Decrease disbursing float.
    d. Increase processing float.

77

Appendix 6A

CASH MANAGEMENT MODELS:
THE SPLIT BETWEEN CASH AND NEAR CASH

I. Dividing liquid assets between cash and marketable securities.

    A. When the need for cash is certain, the financial manager may utilize the economic order quantity formula (inventory model).

        1. Objective: The purpose of this analysis is to balance the lost income that the firm suffers from holding cash rather than marketable securities against the transactions costs involved in converting securities into cash.

        2. Strategy: The inventory model minimized the total cost of maintaining the cash balance whenever the costs include:

            a. The carrying cost of holding cash.

            b. The fixed cost of converting marketable securities into cash.

        3. Assumptions:

            a. Cash payments over the planning period are:

                (1) A regular or constant amount

                (2) Continuous

                (3) Certain

            b. No unanticipated cash receipts will be received during the planning period.

            c. The interest rate on investments remains constant over the analysis period.

            d. Transfers between cash and the securities portfolio may take place at any time at a cost that is fixed, regardless of the amount to be transferred.

        4. Computation

a. Notation:

C = the amount per order of marketable securities to be converted into cash.

i = the interest rate per period available on investments in marketable securities.

b = the fixed cost per order of converting marketable securities into cash.

T = the total cash requirements over the planning period.

TC = the total costs associated with maintenance of a particular average cash balance.

b. Computation of costs:

T/C = the number of transfers during the period.

C/2 = the average cash balance.

Thus the total costs (TC) of having cash on hand can be expressed as:

$$TC = i\left(\frac{C}{2}\right) + b\left(\frac{T}{C}\right)$$

total   total
interest   ordering
income   costs
forgone

c. Minimization of total costs: The optimal cash conversion size, C*, can be found by using the following equation:

$$C^* = \sqrt{\frac{2bT}{i}}$$

5. Example: Management estimates the total cash needs for the next 2 months to be \$15,000. The cost of transferring marketable securities into cash is \$30 for each trade, and the annual yield on securities is 12% (2% for 2 months). Find the optimal cash order size.

$$C^* = \sqrt{\frac{2bT}{i}} = \sqrt{\frac{2(30)(15,000)}{0.2}} = \$6,708.2$$

Further, the optimal average cash balance is \$3,354.10 (\$6,708.20/2).

6. Implications of the inventory model for cash management:

   a. Notice that the optimal case order size, C*, varies directly with the square root of the ordering costs, bT, and inversely with the yield, i, obtained on marketable securities.

   b. Also notice that as T increases, C* does not rise proportionately. This implies the existence of economies of scale in cash management.

   c. When the total cost of ordering and holding cash is minimized, the cash conversion cost and the interest income forgone are exactly equal.

   d. The strict assumptions of the inventory model for cash management will not be completely satisfied in actual business practice.

B. When cash balances fluctuate randomly, the financial manager may use a stochastic (probabilistic) control-limit model to facilitate the decision process.

   1. Objective: The control-limit model seeks to minimize the total costs of managing the firm's cash balance.

   2. Strategy: Through the use of control theory, the model determines upper and lower limits beyond (out of) which the cash balance is not permitted to reach (or wander).

      a. When the cash balance reaches the upper control limit (UL), a conversion of cash into marketable securities takes place. The amount converted is equal to UL-RP dollars, where RP is some calculated cash return point.

      b. When the cash balance reaches the lower control limit (LL), a conversion of marketable securities into cash is initiated by the financial officer. The amount converted is equal to RP-LL dollars.

   3. Assumptions:

      a. The firm's cash balance changes in an irregular, unpredictable manner over time.

b. The probability (chance) of a cash balance change being either positive or negative is 0.5 (i.e., equally likely).

4. Computation of UL and RP:

   a. Notation:

      b = the fixed cost per order of converting marketable securities into cash.

      i = the daily interest rate available on investments in marketable securities.

      σ^2 = the variance of daily changes in the firm's expected cash balances.

   b. The optimal cash return point, RP, can be determined by using the following equation:

$$RP = \sqrt[3]{\frac{3b\sigma^2}{4i}} + LL$$

   c. The upper control limit (UL) can be calculated:

      $UL = 3RP - 2\ LL$

   d. The lower control limit (LL) is determined by management.

5. Example: Assume that the annual yield available on marketable securities is 11%. During a 365-day year, it becomes 0.11/365 = 0.0003 per day. Also assume that the fixed cost of transacting a marketable securities trade (b) is $40. In addition, the firm has observed a variance of $490,000 in past daily cash balance changes. Management has decided that $2,000 is an appropriate lower control limit.

   a. The optimal cash return point becomes

$$RP = \sqrt[3]{\frac{3(40)(490,000)}{4(0.0003)}} = \$3,659 + \$2,000$$

      $= \$5,659$

   b. The upper cash balance limit is

      $UL = 3(\$5,659) - 2(\$2,000) = \$12,977$

c. Once the cash balance reaches the upper limit of $12,977, the financial manager would buy $7,318 (UL-RP) of marketable securities. Should the cash balance drop to the lower limit of $2,000, the financial manager would sell $3,659 (RP-LL) of marketable securities.

6. Implications of the control-limit model for cash management:

   a. The optimal cash return level, RP, will vary, directly with the cube root of both the transfer cost, b, and the volatility of daily cash balance changes, σ^2.

   b. The larger the transfer cost or cash balance volatility, the greater the absolute dollar spread between the upper control limit and the cash return point.

   c. The optimal cash return point varies inversely with the cube root of the lost interest rate.

   d. Like the inventory model, the control-limit model implies the existence of economies of scale in cash management.

• Compensating balances.

1. The bank requires that the firm maintain deposits of a given minimum amount in its demand deposit account.

2. These balances are normally required of corporate customers in three situations:

   a. Whenever the firm has a loan commitment at the bank which is not entirely used, a compensating balance is required.

   b. If the firm has a loan outstanding at the bank, a compensating balance is required.

   c. Instead of paying directly for certain banking services (e.g., check clearing), a firm will be asked to maintain such a balance. The current trend, however, is toward unit pricing for these services.

3. Compensating balance policies vary among commercial banks and are influenced by general economic and financial market conditions. Several guidelines may, however, be offered.

a. For the case of the unused portion of a loan commitment, the bank might require that the compensating balance range from 5% to 10% of the commitment.

b. If a loan is outstanding with the bank, the requirement may be 10% to 20% of the unpaid balance.

c. In order to compensate for various bank services, the firm may be asked to maintain a balance based on either an absolute amount or an average amount.

4. When determining the optimal split between cash and marketable securities the financial officer must explicitly consider the compensating balance requirement.

   a. One approach is to ignore the requirement when performing the necessary calculations and then select the maximum of that suggested by the model or the bank's compensating balance requirement.

   b. A second approach is to include the compensating balance requirement in the requisite calculations.

      (1) The requirement could be treated as a safety stock in the inventory model.

      (2) The requirement could be considered the lower control limit in the control-limit model.

Study Problems

1. Using the inventory model, determine: (a) the optimal cash conversion size; (b) the optimal level of cash the firm should hold; and (c) the total cost of having the optimal amount of cash on hand during the next 6 months. The financial officer has developed the following information:

   (1) The firm needs $5,000 in cash for transactions purposes during the next 6 months.

   (2) The cost of transferring marketable securities into cash is $60 per order.

   (3) The interest rate on marketable securities is 10% for the next year (5% for 6 months).

83

SOLUTION

(a) $C* = \sqrt{\dfrac{2(60)(5,000)}{0.05}} = \underline{\$3,464}$

(b) Optimal level of cash is

$$\frac{C*}{2} = \frac{\$3,464}{2} = \underline{\$1,732}$$

(c) $TC = 0.05(\$1,732) + \$60\left(\dfrac{\$5,000}{\$3,464}\right) = \underline{\$173.20}$

2. Using the inventory model, determine the optimal level of cash the firm should hold if:

   (a) The available annual yield on marketable securities is 6%.

   (b) The cost of converting from cash to marketable securities is $50 per transaction.

   (c) The firm's transaction needs will total $1,000 over the next year.

SOLUTION

$$\text{transaction balance} = C* = \sqrt{\dfrac{2(50)(1,000)}{0.06}} = \underline{\$1,291}$$

$$\begin{matrix}\text{optimal level}\\ \text{of cash}\end{matrix} = \text{transaction balance} \div 2 = \frac{C*}{2} = \frac{\$1,291}{2}$$

$$= \$645.50$$

3. Wolfpack Industries is considering taking out a loan at the Piedmont National Bank. The firm is evaluating the option of a 10%, 1-year loan for $1,000, with interest and principal due at the end of the year. The alternative is a 9%, 1-year loan for $1,000 with the same repayment terms as the other loan, but a 13% compensating balance is required. Which loan do you recommend that Wolfpack take?

SOLUTION

The cost of the 10% loan is actually 10%. The cost of the 9% loan is

$$\frac{\$\text{interest}}{\text{funds available}} = \frac{\$90}{\$1,000 - \$130} = \frac{\$90}{\$870} = 10.34\%$$

Wolfpack should take the straight 10% loan option.

4. The cash balances of South Tampa Cigars fluctuate randomly, with a standard deviation of daily cash flows of $500. The current annual rate of interest on securities is 9%, with fixed conversion costs of $150. Also, management desires to have at least $3,000 in cash on hand at any point in time. The firm uses a 365-day year in its analysis procedures.

(a) Find the upper and lower control limits.

(b) In what lot sizes will marketable securities be purchased and sold?

SOLUTION

(a) The lower control limit (LL) is simply $3,000.

$$RP = \sqrt[3]{\frac{3(150)(500)^2}{4(0.000247)}} = \$4,847 + \$3,000 = \$7,847$$

where $i = \frac{0.09}{365} = 0.000247$ and the optimal upper limit (UL) is

$$UL = 3RP - 2LL = \$23,541 - \$6,000 = \underline{\$17,541}.$$

(b) Marketable securities will be purchased in lot sizes equal to

$$UL - RP = \$17,541 - \$7,847 = \underline{\$9,694}.$$

Securities will be sold in lot sizes equal to

$$RP - LL = \$7,847 - \$3,000 = \underline{\$4,847}.$$

7

Accounts Receivable
and Inventory
Management

<u>Orientation</u>: The investment of funds in accounts receivable
inventory involves a trade-off between profitability and risk.
For accounts receivable this trade-off occurs as less credit-
worthy customers with a higher probability of bad debts are
taken on to increase sales. With respect to inventory management, a larger investment in inventory leads to more efficient
production and speedier delivery, hence, increased sales.
However, additional financing to support the increase in
inventory and increased handling and carrying costs is
required.

I.   Accounts receivable

    A.   Typically, accounts receivable accounts for just
         over 25% of a firm's assets.

    B.   The size of the investment in accounts receivable
         varies from industry to industry and is affected by
         several factors including the percentage of credit
         sales to total sales, the level of sales, and the
         credit and collection policies, more specifically
         the terms of sale, the quality of customer, and
         collection efforts.

    C.   Although all these factors affect the size of the
         investment, only the credit and collection policies
         are decision variables under the control of the
         financial manager.

D. The terms of sale are generally stated in the form a/b net c, indicating that the customer can deduct a% if the account is paid within b days; otherwise, the account must be paid within c days.

E. If the customer decides to forego the discount and not pay until the final payment date, the annualized opportunity cost of passing up this a% discount and withholding payment until the cth day is determined as follows:

annualized opportunity

$$\text{cost of foregoing the discount} = \frac{a}{1-a} \times \frac{360}{c-b}$$

Example: Given the trade credit terms of 3/20 net 60, what is the annualized opportunity cost of passing up the 3% discount and withholding payment until the 60th day?

Solution: Substituting in the values from the example, we get:

$$27.8\% = \frac{0.03}{1-0.03} \times \frac{360}{60-20}$$

F. A second decision variable in determining the size of the investment in accounts receivable in addition to the trade credit terms is the type of customer.

   1. The costs associated with extending credit to lower-quality customers include:

       a. Increased costs of credit investigation.
       b. Increased probability of customer default.
       c. Increased collection costs.

G. Analyzing the credit application is a major part of accounts receivable management.

   1. Several avenues are open to the firm in considering the credit rating of an applicant. Among these are financial statements, independent credit ratings and reports, bank checking, information from other companies, and past experiences.

   2. One commonly used method for credit evaluation is called credit scoring and involves the numerical evaluation of each applicant in which an applicant receives a score based upon the

answers to a simple set of questions. The score is then evaluated relative to a predetermined standard, its level relative to that standard determining whether or not credit scoring should be extended to the applicant. The major advantage of credit scoring is that it is inexpensive and easy to perform.

3. Once the decision to extend credit has been made and if the decision is yes, a maximum credit line is established as a ceiling on the amount of credit to be extended.

H. The third and final decision variable in determining the size of the investment in accounts receivable is the firm's collection policies.

1. Collection policy is a combination of letter sending, telephone calls, personal visits, and legal actions.

2. The greater the amount spent on collecting, the lower the volume of bad debts.

a. The relationship is not linear, however, and beyond a point is not helpful.

b. If sales are independent of collection efforts, then methods of collection should be evaluated with respect to the reduction in bad debts against the cost of lowering those bad debts.

I. Credit should be extended to the point that marginal profitability on additional sales equals the required rate of return on the additional investment in receivables necessary to generate those sales.

I. Inventory

A. Typically, inventory accounts for about 5.88% of a firm's assets.

B. The purpose of carrying inventories is to uncouple the operations of the firm, that is, to make each function of the business independent of each other function.

C. As such, the decision with respect to the size of the investment in inventory involves a basic trade-off between risk and return.

D. The risk comes from the possibility of running out of inventory if too little inventory is held, while the return aspect of this tradeoff results because increased inventory investment costs money.

E. There are several general types of inventory including:

1. Raw materials inventory consists of the basic materials that have been purchased from other firms to be used in the firm's productions operations. This type of inventory uncouples the production function from the purchasing function.

2. Work in process inventory consists of partially finished goods that require additional work before they become finished goods. This type of inventory uncouples the various production operations.

3. Finished goods inventory consists of goods on which the production has been completed but the goods are not yet sold. This type of inventory uncouples the production and sales function.

4. Stock of cash inventory, already discussed in some detail in previous chapters, serves to make the payment of bills independent of the collection of accounts due.

F. In order to effectively manage the investment in inventory, two problems must be dealt with: the order quantity problem and the order point problem.

G. The order quantity problem involves the determination of the optimal order size for an inventory item given its expected usage, carrying, and ordering costs.

H. The economic order quantity (EOQ) model attempts to determine the order size that will minimize total inventory costs. The EOQ is given as:

$$Q* = \sqrt{\frac{250}{C}}$$

where C = carrying costs per unit,
O = ordering costs per order,
S = total demand in units over the planning period,
Q* = the optimal order quantity in units.

89

I. The order point problem attempts to answer the following question: How low should inventory be depleted before it is reordered?

J. In answering this question two factors become important:

   1. What is the usual procurement or delivery time and how much stock is needed to accommodate this time period?

   2. How much safety stock does the management desire?

K. Modification for safety stocks is necessary since the usage rate of inventory is seldom stable over a given timetable.

L. This safety stock is used to safeguard the firm against changes in order time and receipt of shipped goods.

M. The greater the uncertainty associated with fore-casted demand or order time, the larger the safety stock.

   1. The costs associated with running out of inventory will also determine the safety stock levels.

   2. A point is reached where it is too costly to carry a larger safety stock given the associated risk.

N. Inflation can also have an impact on the level of inventory carried.

   1. Goods may be purchased in large quantities in anticipation of price rises.

   2. The cost of carrying goods may increase causing a decline in Q*, the optional order quantity.

O. The just-in-time inventory control system is more than just an inventory control system, it is a production and management system.

   1. Under this system inventory is cut down to a minimum and the time and physical distance between the various production operations is also minimized.

2. Actually the just-in-time inventory control system is just a new approach to the EOQ model which tries to produce the lowest average level of inventory possible.

3. Average inventory is reduced by locating inventory supplies in convenient locations and setting up restocking strategies that cut time and thereby reducing the needed level of safety stock.

Study Problems

1. The Swank Furniture Company is trying to determine the optimal order quantity for sofas. Annual sales for sofas are 800 and the retail price is $300 per sofa. The cost of carrying sofas is $50 per sofa per year. It costs $35 to prepare and receive an order. The inventory planning period is one year.

   a. Determine the EOQ (assuming a one-year planning period).

   b. If the annual sales are 1200, what is the EOQ? If the annual sales are 300, what is the EOQ?

   SOLUTION

   a. $$EOQ = \sqrt{\frac{2(800)(35)}{50}} = \sqrt{1120} = 33.47 = 33 \text{ sofas}$$

   b. $$EOQ = \sqrt{\frac{2(1200)(35)}{50}} = \sqrt{1680} = 40.99 = 41 \text{ sofas}$$

   $$\sqrt{\frac{2(300)(35)}{50}} = \sqrt{420} = 20.49 = 20 \text{ sofas}$$

2. (From Appendix A - Marginal or Incremental Analysis) The Celeccorp makers of Sum'a'dis is considering relaxing its current credit policy. Currently the firm has annual sales (all credit) of $15 million and an average collection period of 50 days. The firm's required rate of return on new investment in receivables and inventory is 20 percent, and of the current sales 5 percent result in bad debt losses. Variable costs account for 70 percent of the selling price on their product, Sum'a'dis. Given the following information should Celeccorp adopt the proposed policy (assume a 360 day year)?

	Present Policy	Proposed Policy
Annual Sales (all credit)	15,000,000	18,000,000
Average Collection Period		
Original Sales	50 days	70 days
New Sales		70 days
Average Inventory	1,200,000	1,300,000
Bad Debt Losses in Percent		
Original Sales	4%	4%
New Sales		7%

SOLUTION

Step 1: Estimate the incremental profit contribution (ΔP) resulting from the proposed change in credit policy.

Discussion: This is equal to the portion of incremental (new) sales that goes towards profits ($\Delta S(1-V)$) less the increased loss to bad debts (ΔB).

Formula: ΔP = (New Sales)(Contribution Margin) - (Increased Bad Debts)

$$= (\Delta S)(1-V) - \Delta B$$

$$= \$3,000,000(1-.70) - \$210,000$$

$$= \$690,000$$

Step 2: Determine the opportunity loss associated with the delay in collection of accounts receivable caused by original customers changing their payment patterns.

Discussion: This involved multiplying the required rate of return on investment in receivables (R) times the incremental increase in collectible receivables due to original customers taking longer to pay (ΔACP)(Sorig-Borig)(360).

Formula:

$$OL = \begin{pmatrix} \text{Required} \\ \text{Return} \end{pmatrix} \begin{pmatrix} \text{Change in the} \\ \text{average collection} \\ \text{period on original} \\ \text{collectible sales} \end{pmatrix} \begin{pmatrix} \text{Daily level of} \\ \text{collectible sales} \\ \text{from original} \\ \text{customers} \end{pmatrix}$$

$$= (R)(\Delta ACP)(\text{Sorig-Borig}/360)$$
$$= (.20)(20)(\$15,000,000 - \$600,000)/360$$
$$= \$160,000$$

Step 3: Determine the dollar level required return on the marginal increase in investment in receivables and inventory due to new sales.

Discussion: The marginal increase in investment in collectable receivables due to new sales $[(\Delta S - \Delta B)/360] \cdot (ACP)(V)$ is added to the increased investment in inventory (ΔI) and multiplied times the required return on investment in inventory and receivables (R).

Formula:

$$DRR = \begin{array}{l}\text{Average} \\ \text{collection} \\ \text{period on} \\ \text{Collectable} \\ \text{New Receiv-} \\ \text{ables (non} \\ \text{bad debt} \\ \text{receivables)}\end{array} \begin{array}{l}\text{Daily} \\ \text{level of} \\ \text{new} \\ \text{collect-} \\ \text{able} \\ \text{sales}\end{array} \begin{array}{l}\text{Vari-} \\ \text{able} \\ \text{Costs}\end{array} + \begin{array}{l}\text{New} \\ \text{Invest-} \\ \text{ment in} \\ \text{Inven-} \\ \text{tory}\end{array} \begin{array}{l}\text{Required} \\ \text{Return}\end{array}$$

$$= \{(ACP_{new})\,[(\Delta S - \Delta B)/360]\,(V) + \Delta I\} \cdot R$$

$$= (70)(\$3,000,000 - \$210,000/360)(.70) + \$100,000(.20)$$

$$= \$95,950$$

Step 4: Compare the incremental revenues with the incremental costs.

Formula:

$$\begin{pmatrix}\text{Profit} \\ \text{contribution} \\ \text{from} \\ \text{Step 1}\end{pmatrix} - \begin{pmatrix}\text{Opportunity} \\ \text{loss associated} \\ \text{with original} \\ \text{sales - from} \\ \text{Step 2}\end{pmatrix} - \begin{pmatrix}\text{Required return} \\ \text{associated with} \\ \text{the investment} \\ \text{in receivables} \\ \text{from new sales -} \\ \text{from Step 3}\end{pmatrix}$$

$$= (\Delta P) - (OL) - (DRR)$$
$$= \$690,000 - \$160,000 - \$95,950$$
$$= \$434,050$$

Thus since the incremental revenues outweigh the incremental costs the project should be accepted.

3. What is the effective annualized cost of foregoing a trade discount with terms 4/40 net 60?

SOLUTION

The annualized opportunity cost of foregoing the trade discount $= \dfrac{a}{1-a} \times \dfrac{360}{c-b}$

where the terms of sale are stated in the form a/b net c, indicating that they can deduct a% if the account is paid within b days; otherwise, the account must be paid within c days.

Thus,

annualized opportunity cost of foregoing the trade discount

$$= \frac{a}{1-a} \times \frac{360}{c-b}$$

$$= \frac{.04}{1 - .04} \times \frac{360}{60 - 40}$$

$$= 0.75$$

$$= 75\%$$

Self-Tests

TRUE-FALSE

_____ 1. The objective in credit policy management is to minimize losses.

_____ 2. An increase in the time period over which credit must be repaid will increase demand.

_____ 3. Receivables arise from credit sales.

_____ 4. To speed up the turnover of receivables, a firm may either shorten the discount term or increase the discount offered.

_____ 5. The expression "5/10, net 30" means that the customers receive a 10% discount if they pay within 5 days; otherwise, they must pay within 30 days.

_____ 6. There is no one level of inventory that is efficient for all firms.

_____ 7. In determining the level of safety stock it is important to evaluate the tradeoff between the cost of carrying the additional inventory with the risk of running out of inventory.

_____ 8. Lead time in determining the reorder point refers to the time between the receipt of a customer's order and the shipment of that order.

_____ 9. Large safety stocks tend to reduce the possibility of stockouts.

_____ 10. The EOQ provides for an optimal safety stock determination.

MULTIPLE CHOICE

1. The major objective of a credit policy is to:

   a. Maximize sales.
   b. Minimize losses.
   c. Maximize profits.
   d. None of the above.

2. Which of the following is not part of the firm's credit
   and collection policy decisions?

   a. The credit period.
   b. The cash discount given.
   c. The dividend decision.
   d. The level of collection expenditures.
   e. The quality of account accepted.

3. Which of the following would be a source of credit information?

   a. Firm's financial statement.
   b. Credit ratings from Dun & Bradstreet.
   c. A credit check through a bank.
   d. The company's past experience.
   e. All of the above.

4. Which of the following is a cost associated with relaxed
   credit standards?

   a. Enlarged credit department.
   b. Increased probability of bad debt.
   c. Additional investment in receivables.
   d. All of the above.
   e. None of the above.

5. All of the following are relationships that exist for
   safety stock except:

   a. The greater the risk of running out of stock, the
      larger the safety stock.
   b. The larger the opportunity cost of the funds
      invested in inventory, the smaller the safety stock.
   c. The greater the uncertainty associated with future
      forecasts of use, the larger the safety stock.
   d. The higher the profit margin per unit, the lower the
      safety stock necessary.

95

6. In the basic model the optimal inventory level is the point at which

    a. total depreciation is minimized.
    b. total cost is minimized.
    c. total revenue is maximized.
    d. carrying costs are minimized.
    e. ordinary costs are minimized.

7. Determine the effective annualized cost of forgoing the trade discount on terms 2/10 net 45 (round to nearest .01%).

    a. 21.0%
    b. 16.3%
    c. 16.0%
    d. 20.6%

8. The Janjigian Company uses approximately 4,000 oxygen tanks in its manufacturing process each year. The carrying cost of the oxygen tanks inventory is $.60 per tank and the ordering cost per order is $20. What is Janjigian's economic ordering quantity of tanks (round to the nearest unit)?

    a. 15
    b. 365
    c. 417
    d. 516

8

Short-term Financing

Orientation: This chapter is one of the four chapters dealing with the sources of financing. Specifically, it deals with the sources of short-term financing that must be repaid within 1 year.

I. Determining the appropriate level of short-term financing

    A. In Chapter 5 the hedging concept was presented as one basis for determining the firm's use of short-term debt.

    B. Hedging involves attempting to match temporary needs for funds with short-term sources of financing and permanent needs with long-term sources.

II. Selecting a source of short-term financing

    A. In general, there are three basic factors that should be considered in selecting a source of short-term financing;

        1. The effective cost of the credit source.

        2. The availability of credit.

        3. The effect of the use of a particular source of credit on the cost and availability of other sources.

    B. The basic procedure used in estimating the cost of short-term credit utilizes the basic interest equation, i.e., interest = principal X rate X time.

C. The problem faced in assessing the cost of a source of short-term financing involves estimating the annual effective rate (RATE) where the interest amount, the principal sum, and the time for which financing will be needed is known. Thus, the basic interest equation is "rearranged" as follows:

$$RATE = \frac{interest}{principal} \times \frac{1}{time}$$

D. Compound interest was not considered in the simple RATE calculation. To consider compounding, the following relation is used:

$$APR = \left(1 + \frac{R}{M}\right)^M - 1$$

where APR is the <u>annual percentage rate</u>, R is the nominal rate of interest per year and M is the number of compounding periods within 1 year. The effect of compounding is thus to raise the effective cost of short-term credit.

III. Sources of short-term credit

A. The two basic sources of short-term credit are unsecured and secured credit.

   1. Unsecured credit consists of all those sources which have as their security only the lender's faith in the ability of the borrower to repay the funds when due.

   2. Secured funds include additional security in the form of assets that are pledged as collateral in the event the borrower defaults in payment of principal or interest.

B. There are three major sources of unsecured short-term credit: trade credit, unsecured bank loans, and commercial paper.

   1. Trade credit provides one of the most flexible sources of financing available to the firm. To arrange for credit, the firm need only place an order with one of its suppliers. The supplier then checks the firm's credit and if the credit is good, the supplier sends the merchandise.

   2. Commercial banks provide unsecured short-term credit in two basic forms: lines of credit and transaction loans (notes payable). Maturities

of both types of loans are usually 1 year or less with rates of interest depending on the credit worthiness of the borrower and the level of interest rates in the economy as a whole.

3. A line of credit is generally an informal agreement or understanding between the borrower and the bank as to the maximum amount of credit that the bank will provide the borrower at any one time. There is no "legal" commitment on the part of the bank to provide the stated credit. There is another variant of this form of financing referred to as a <u>revolving credit agreement</u> whereby such a legal obligation is involved. The line of credit generally covers a period of 1 year corresponding to the borrower's "fiscal" year.

4. Transaction loans are another form of unsecured short-term bank credit; the transaction loan, in contrast to a line of credit, is made for a specific purpose.

5. Only the largest and most credit worthy companies are able to use commercial paper which consists of unsecured promissory notes in the money market.

   a. The maturities of commercial paper are generally 6 months or less with the interest rate slightly lower than the prime rate on commercial bank loans. The new issues of commercial paper are either directly placed or dealer placed.

   b. There are a number of advantages that accrue to the user of commercial paper: Interest rates are generally lower than rates on bank loans and comparable sources of short-term financing. No minimum balance requirements are associated with commercial paper. Commercial paper offers the firm with very large credit needs a single source for all its short-term financing needs. Since it is widely recognized that only the most credit worthy borrowers have access to the commercial paper market, its use signifies a firm's credit status.

   c. However, a very important "risk" is involved in using this source of short-term financing; the commercial paper market is highly impersonal and denies even the most credit worthy borrower any flexibility in terms of repayment.

B. Secured sources of short-term credit have certain assets of the firm, such as accounts receivable or inventories pledged as collateral to secure a loan. Upon default of the loan agreement, the lender has first claim to the pledged assets.

    1. Generally, a firm's receivables are among its most liquid assets. Two secured loan arrangements are generally made with accounts receivable as collateral: (a) Under the arrangement of <u>pledged accounts receivable</u>, the amount of the loan is stated as a percent of the face value of the receivables pledged. (b) <u>Factoring accounts receivable</u> involves the outright sale of a firm's accounts receivables to a factor.

    2. Four secured loan arrangements are generally made with inventory as collateral: (a) Under the <u>floating lien agreement</u>, the borrower gives the lender a lien against all his or her inventories. (b) The <u>chattel mortgage agreement</u> involves having specific items of inventory identified in the security agreement. (c) The <u>field warehouse financing agreements</u> means that the inventories used as collateral are physically separated from the firm's other inventories and are placed under the control of a third-party field warehousing firm. (d) <u>Terminal warehouse agreements</u> involve transporting the inventories pledged as collateral to a public warehouse which is physically removed from the borrower's premises.

Study Problems

1. In order to meet a temporary need for working capital during an upcoming seasonal peak in sales, Gregory Sales Co. will require $500,000. Gregory's bank has agreed to lend the funds for the necessary 3-month interval at a rate of 12% with a 20% compensating balance. Gregory Sales Co. normally maintains a demand deposit amount of $20,000. Estimate the annual (effective) cost of the loan to Gregory.

SOLUTION

To obtain the needed $500,000 and meet the compensating balance requirement, Gregory must borrow X dollars, where X is found as follows:

$$X - [0.20X - 20,000] = 500,000$$

$$0.80X = 480,000$$

$$X = \$600,000$$

Thus, Gregory borrows $600,000 for which it must maintain a compensating balance of 0.20 X 600,000 = $120,000, of which $20,000 will come from its normal demand deposit and $100,000 must be borrowed, which will leave the firm the use of $500,000. The interest cost of the loan is computed as follows:

interest = 0.12 x 600,000 ÷ 4 = $18,000

Divide by 4 since the loan is for only 3 months or one-fourth of a year. The effective annual cost of the loan is:

$$\text{annual rate} = \frac{\$ \text{ loan cost}}{\$\text{funds available}} - \begin{array}{l}\text{loan maturity as a} \\ \text{fraction of 1 year}\end{array}$$

$$= \frac{18,000}{500,000} \div \frac{3}{12}$$

$$= \underline{0.144} \text{ or } \underline{14.4\%}$$

2. A factor has agreed to buy Thomas Brothers Company's receivables ($250,000 per month) which have an average collection period of 90 days. The factor will advance up to 80% of the face value of the receivables for an annual charge of 10% of the funds advanced. The factor also charges a handling fee of 5% of the face value of all accounts purchased. What is the effective annual cost of the factoring arrangement to Thomas Brothers if the maximum advance is taken every month?

SOLUTION

With an average collection period of 90 days and monthly credit sales, Thomas Brothers could build up a loan advance over 3 months of 0.80 X 750,000 = $600,000. This loan would be constantly rolling over as accounts were being collected and as new credit sales were being made. The 90-day interest cost of the loan would be computed:

interest = $600,000 X 0.10 ÷ 4 = $15,000

The factor's fee would be as follows:

fee = 0.05 x $750,000 = $37,500

Thus, the effective annual cost of the 90-day loan would be:

$$\text{annual rate} = \frac{\$15,000 + \$37,500}{\$600,000} \div \frac{3}{12}$$

$$= \underline{0.35} \text{ or } \underline{35\%}$$

3. For the past 7 years Warden Company has been factoring its accounts receivables. The factor's fee is 3% and the factor will lend up to 90% of the volume of receivables purchased for an additional 1% per month. The firm typically has sales of $200,000 per month; 75% are on credit. Warden Company will save credit department costs of $3,500, since it will no longer need to operate a credit department. In addition, there will no longer be bad-debt losses which previously were 1-1/4% per month.

The firm's bank has recently offered to lend the firm up to 90% of the face value of the receivables shown on the schedule of accounts. The bank would charge 9% per annum interest plus a 2% processing charge per dollar of receivables pledged. The firm extends terms of net 30, and all customers who plan to pay will do so by the thirtieth of the month. Should the firm discontinue its factoring arrangement in favor of the bank's offer if the firm borrows, on the average, $100,000 per month on its receivables?

SOLUTION

The cost of factoring is:

Fee (0.03 x $200,000 x 75)	$4,500
Interest cost (0.01 x $100,000)	1,000
	$5,500

The cost of the bank loan is:

Fee (0.02 x $100,000/.90)	$2,222
Interest (0.09 x $200,000 x 1/12)	1,500
	$3,722

Plus:

Credit department cost per month	$3,722
Bad-debt losses ($200,000 x .75 x 0.0125)	1,875
Total cost	$5,597

No, in this case factoring is slightly cheaper.

TRUE/FALSE

_____ 1. The amount of trade credit available to the firm varies inversely with the size of the cash discount.

_____ 2. Compensating balances are never required when a firm has a line of credit with a bank.

_____ 3. A transaction loan is made for a specific purpose or use for the funds involved.

_____ 4. An advantage of commercial paper to a credit worthy borrower is that repayment can be postponed if necessary.

_____ 5. Pledging involves selling accounts receivable to a factor.

_____ 6. The primary sources of collateral for secured short-term credit are accounts receivable and inventories.

_____ 7. Field warehouse financing agreements involve physically moving the pledged inventories to a public warehouse.

_____ 8. Commercial paper and trade credit are both forms of secured credit.

_____ 9. An advantage of trade credit is that the amount of credit extended expands and contracts with the needs of the firm.

_____ 10. The "prime rate of interest" represents the rate a bank charges its most credit worthy borrowers.

MULTIPLE CHOICE

1. Which of the following is not a form of secured short-term credit.

   a. General lien.
   b. Chattel mortgages.
   c. Commercial paper.
   d. Terminal warehouse receipt.
   e. Factoring.

2. Under which of the following agreements does the borrower retain physical possession of the inventory used as collateral for a loan?

   a. Field warehouse financing.
   b. Chattel mortgage.
   c. Terminal warehouse.
   d. All of the above.
   e. None of the above.

3. An informal agreement between a bank and its customer with respect to the maximum amount of unsecured credit the bank will permit the firm to owe at any one time is a:

   a. Line of credit
   b. Revolving credit agreement.
   c. Transaction loan.
   d. None of the above.

4. When a firm needs short-term funds for only one purpose, it usually obtains a _____.

   a. Line of credit
   b. Revolving credit agreement.
   c. Transaction loan.
   d. Compensating balance.
   e. None of the above.

5. If a firm borrows $1 million at 8% and is required to maintain $100,000 in a compensating balance, the effective annual interest cost is:

   a. 8%
   b. 8.88%.
   c. 7.27%.
   d. 9.5%.
   e. None of the above.

6. Inventory is in the possession of a third party under which of the following arrangements?

   a. Floating lien agreement.
   b. Terminal warehouse receipt loan.
   c. Chattel mortgage.
   d. Line of credit.
   e. None of the above.

9

Mathematics of Finance

Orientation: In this chapter the concept of a time value of money is introduced, that is, a dollar today is worth more than a dollar received a year from now. Thus if we are to logically compare projects and financial strategies, we must either move all dollar flows back to the present or out to some common future date.

I. Compound interest results when the interest paid on the investment during the first period is added to the principal and during the second period the interest is earned on the original principal plus the interest earned during the first period.

    A. Mathematically, the future value of an investment if compounded annually at a rate of i for n years will be:

$$FV_n = P(1 + i)^n$$

        where n = the number of years during which the compounding occurs,

            i = the annual compound interest rate,

           P = the principal or original amount invested at the beginning of the first period,

        FV_n = the future value of the investment at the end of n years.

1. The future value of an investment can be increased by either increasing the number of years we let it compound or by compounding it at a higher rate.

2. If the compounded period is less than 1 year, the future value of an investment can be determined as follows:

$$FV_n = P \left(1 + \frac{i}{m}\right)^{mn}$$

where m = the number of times compounding occurs during the year.

B. In the case of continuous compounding, the value of M in the above equation is allowed to approach infinity. As this happens, the value of

$$\left(1 + \frac{i}{m}\right)^{mn}$$

approaches e^{in}, with e being defined as follows and having a value of approximately 2.71828,

$$e = \lim_{m \to \infty} \left(1 + \frac{1}{m}\right)^{m}$$

where ∞ indicates infinity.

1. Thus, the future value of an investment compounded continuously for n years can be determined as follows:

$$FV_n = P \cdot e^{in}$$

where e = 2.71828,

n = the number of years during which compounding occurs,

i = the annual compounded interest rate,

P = the principal or original amount invested at the beginning of the first period,

FV_n = the future value of the investment at the end of n years.

106

II. Determining the present value, that is the value in today's dollars, of a sum of money to be received in the future involves nothing other than inverse compounding. The differences in these techniques come about merely from the investor's point of view.

A. Mathematically, the present value of a sum of money to be received in the future can be determined with the following equation:

$$P = FV_n \left(\frac{1}{(1 + i)^n} \right)$$

where n = the number of years until payment will be received,

i = the opportunity rate or discount rate,

P = the present value of the future sum of money,

FV_n = the future value of the investment at the end of n years

1. The present value of a future sum of money is inversely related to both the number of years until the payment will be received and the opportunity rate.

III. An annuity is a series of equal dollar payments for a specified number of years. Because annuities occur frequently in finance, for example, bond interest payments, we treat them specially.

A. A compound annuity involves depositing or investing an equal sum of money at the end of each year for a certain number of years and allowing it to grow.

1. This can be done by using our compounding equation and compounding each one of the individual deposits to the future or by using the following compound annuity equation:

$$FV_n = A \sum_{t=0}^{n-1} (1 + i)^t$$

where A = the annuity value deposited at the end of each year,

i = the annual compound interest rate,

107

n = the number of years for which the annuity will last,

FV_n = the future value of the annuity at the end of the nth year.

B. Pension funds, insurance obligation, and interest received from bonds all involve annuities. To compare these financial instruments we would like to know the present value of each of these annuities.

   1. This can be done by using our present value equation and discounting each one of the individual cash flows back to the present or by using the following present value of an annuity equation:

   $$P = \left[A \sum_{t=1}^{n} \frac{1}{(1 + i)^t} \right]$$

   where A = the annuity withdrawn at the end of each year,

   i = the annual interest or discount rate,

   P = the present value of the future annuity,

   n = the number of years for which the annuity will last.

C. This procedure of solving for A, the annuity value when i, n, and P are known is also the procedure used to determine what payments are associated with paying off a loan in equal installments. Loans paid off in this way, in periodic payments, are called amortized loans.

   1. Here again we know three of the four values in the annuity equation and are solving for a value of A, the annual annuity.

   2. For example: Suppose a firm borrows $5,000 to be repaid in five equal payments at the end of each of the next five years to purchase some machinery and the interest rate that is paid to the lender is 15 percent on the outstanding portion of the loan. Using the annuity equation to solve we get

$$\$5{,}000 = \left[A \sum_{Z=1}^{5} \frac{1}{(1 + .15)^t} \right]$$

$$\$5{,}000 = A(3.352)$$

$$A = \$1{,}491.65$$

IV. A perpetuity is an annuity that continues forever, that is every year from now on this investment pays the same dollar amount.

    A. An example of a perpetuity is preferred stock which yields a constant dollar dividend infinitely.

    B. The following equation can be used to determine the present value of a perpetuity:

$$P = \frac{pp}{i}$$

    where P = the present value of the perpetuity,

           pp = the constant dollar amount provided by the perpetuity,

           i = the annual interest or discount rate.

V. Bond valuation illustrates a combination of several discounting techniques and procedures including an annuity, a single cash flow and semiannual periods. When a bond is purchased the owner receives two things: interest payments which are generally made semiannually and at maturity repayment of the full principal, regardless of how much the bond was purchased for.

    A. The present value of a bond can be illustrated as follows:

$$\text{Bond value} = \begin{pmatrix} \text{Present} \\ \text{Value of} \\ \text{Interest} \\ \text{Payments} \end{pmatrix} + \begin{pmatrix} \text{Present Value} \\ \text{of Return of} \\ \text{Principal} \end{pmatrix}$$

$$= A \left[\sum_{t=1}^{n.m} \frac{1}{(1 + \frac{i}{m})^t} \right] + FV_{n.m} \left[\frac{1}{(1 + \frac{i}{m})^{n.m}} \right]$$

VI. To aid in the calculations of present and future values, tables are provided at the back of <u>Basic Financial Management</u> (<u>BFM</u>).

A. To aid in determining the value of FV_n in the compounding formula

$$FV_n = P(1 + i)^n$$

tables have been compiled for values of $(1 + i)^n$ in Appendix A, "Compound Sum of $1," in *BFM*.

B. Thus to determine the value of:

$$FV_{10} = \$1,000(1 + 0.08)^{10}$$

we need merely to look up the value of $(1 + 0.08)^{10}$ in Appendix A and substitute it in. The table value given in the $n = 10$ row and 8% column of Appendix A is 2.159. Substituting this in the equation, we get

$$FV_{10} = \$1,000(2.159)$$

$$FV_{10} = \$2,159$$

C. To aid in the computation of present values

$$P = FV_n \frac{1}{(1 + i)^n}$$

tables have been compiled for values of

$$\frac{1}{(1 + i)^n}$$

and appear in Appendix B in the back of *BFM*.

D. Because of the time-consuming nature of compounding an annuity,

$$FV_n = A \sum_{t=0}^{n-1} (1 + i)^t$$

tables are provided in Appendix C of *BFM* for

$$\sum_{t=0}^{n-1} (1 + i)^t$$

for various combinations of n and i.

E. To simplify the process of determining the present value of an annuity

$$P = A \left(\sum_{t=1}^{n} \frac{1}{(1 + i)^t} \right)$$

tables are provided in Appendix D of <u>BFM</u> for various combinations of n and i for the value

$$\sum_{t=1}^{n} \frac{1}{(1 + i)^t}$$

Study Problems

1. What will $1,000 invested for 10 years at 10% compounded annually accumulate to?

   SOLUTION

   Substituting into the compound value formula, we get:

   $$FV_n = P(1 + i)^n$$

   $$FV_{10} = \$1,000(1 + 0.10)^{10}$$

   $$FV_{10} = \$1,000(2.594)$$

   $$FV_{10} = \$2,594$$

2. How many years will it take $500 to grow to $1,586 if it is invested at 8% compounded annually?

   SOLUTION

   From the compound value formula we know:

   $$FV_n = P(1 + i)^n$$

   Substituting in the values that we know, we get:

   $$\$1,586 = \$500(1 + 0.08)^n$$

   or using table values, we get:

   $$\$1,586 = \$500 \begin{bmatrix} \text{Table Value} \\ \text{Appendix A} \\ \text{n years} \\ 8\% \end{bmatrix}$$

Dividing both sides by $500, we get:

$$3.172 = \begin{bmatrix} \text{Table Value} \\ \text{Appendix A} \\ \text{n years} \\ 8\% \end{bmatrix}$$

Looking in the 8% column, we find a value of 3.172 in the 15-year row. Thus, it will take 15 years.

3. At what annual rate would $1,000 have to be invested in order to grow to $4,046 in 10 years?

SOLUTION

From the compound value formula we know:

$$FV_n = P(1 + i)^n$$

Substituting the table value given in Appendix A of BFM for $(1 + i)^n$, we get:

$$FV_n = P \begin{bmatrix} \text{Table Value} \\ \text{Appendix A} \\ \text{n years} \\ i\% \end{bmatrix}$$

Substituting in the given values, we get:

$$\$4,046 = \$1,000 \begin{bmatrix} \text{Table Value} \\ \text{Appendix A} \\ 10 \text{ years} \\ i\% \end{bmatrix}$$

$$4.046 = \begin{bmatrix} \text{Table Value} \\ \text{Appendix A} \\ 10 \text{ years} \\ i\% \end{bmatrix}$$

Thus, we are looking for a table value of 4.046 in the 10-year row of Appendix A. This appears in the 15% column; thus, 15% is the annual rate we are looking for.

4. What is the present value of $1,000 to be received 8 years from now discounted back to present at 10%?

SOLUTION

Substituting in the present value formula we get:

$$P = FV_n \left[\frac{1}{(1 + i)^n} \right]$$

$$P = \$1,000 \left[\frac{1}{(1 + 0.10)^8} \right]$$

$$P = \$1,000[0.467]$$

$$P = \$467$$

5. What is the accumulated sum of the following streams of payments, $1,000 per year for 5 years compounded annually at 5%?

SOLUTION

Substituting into the compound annuity formula, we get:

$$FV_n = A \sum_{t=0}^{n-1} (1 + i)^t$$

$$FV_5 = \$1,000 \sum_{t=0}^{5-1} (1 + 0.05)^t$$

$$FV_5 = \$1,000(5.526)$$

$$FV_5 = \$5,526$$

6. What is the present value of $100 a year for 15 years discounted back to the present at 15%?

SOLUTION

Substituting into the present value of an annuity formula:

$$P = A \left[\sum_{t=1}^{n} \frac{1}{(1 + i)^t} \right]$$

$$P = \$100 \left[\sum_{t=1}^{15} \frac{1}{(1 + 0.15)^t} \right]$$

$$P = \$100(5.847)$$

$$P = \$584.70$$

7. If you receive a 9 percent $100,000 loan that has annual payments of $14,695.08, how many loan payments must you make in order to pay off the loan?

SOLUTION

Substituting into the present value of an annuity formula:

$$P = A \left[\sum_{t=1}^{n} \frac{1}{(1 + i)^t} \right]$$

$$\$100,000 = \$14,695.08 \begin{bmatrix} \text{TABLE VALUE} \\ \text{APPENDIX D} \\ \text{? YEARS} \\ \text{9 PERCENT} \end{bmatrix}$$

$$6.805 = \begin{bmatrix} \text{TABLE VALUE} \\ \text{APPENDIX D} \\ \text{? YEARS} \\ \text{9 PERCENT} \end{bmatrix}$$

Looking down the 9% column of Appendix D we find a value of 6.805 in the 11 year row. Thus, in 11 years the loan will be paid off.

Self-Tests

TRUE/FALSE

_____ 1. The fact that there is an opportunity cost to money brings on the concept of the time value of money.

_____ 2. The higher the rate used to compound a given sum, the larger it will be at some future date.

_____ 3. The future value of an investment can be increased by reducing the number of years we let it compound.

_____ 4. There is an inverse relationship between the effective annual interest rate and the length of the compounding period.

_____ 5. Continuous compounding takes on importance because it allows interest to be earned on interest more frequently than any other compounding period.

_____ 6. Determining present value is merely the inverse of compounding.

_____ 7. A compound annuity involves depositing or investing an equal sum of money at the end of each year for a certain number of years and allowing it to grow.

_____ 8. A perpetuity is an annuity that continues for 30 years or more.

114

_____ 9. The present value of an annuity increases as the discount rate decreases.

_____ 10. An example of perpetuity is the interest received on long-term bonds.

MULTIPLE CHOICE

1. To determine the present value of a future sum we need only multiply it by:

   a. $\dfrac{1}{(1 + i)^n}$.

   b. $\dfrac{1}{(1 + n)^1}$.

   c. $(1 + n)^i$.

   d. $(1 + i)^n$.

2. The present value of a $100 perpetuity discounted back to present at 6% is:

   a. $6,000.00.
   b. $6,666.66.
   c. $1,666.67.
   d. $1,200.00.

3. If we place $100 in a savings account that yields 6% compounded semiannually, what will our investment grow to at the end of 5 years?

   a. $133.80.
   b. $130.00.
   c. $125.00.
   d. $134.40.

4. The future value of an investment compounded continuously for n years can be determined from the following formula (e = 2.71828):

   a. $FV_n = e \cdot P^{in}$.

   b. $FV_n = P \cdot e^{in}$.

   c. $FV_n = P \dfrac{1}{e}in$.

   d. $FV_n = P \cdot e \cdot i^n$.

5. The future value of an investment compounded continuously is calculated by the formula:

   a. $FV_n = P/e^{in}$

   b. $FV_n = Pe^{-in}$

   c. $FV_n = Pe^{in}$

   d. $FV_n = Pe(1 + i)n$

6. A bond maturing in 10 years pays $80 each year and $1,000 upon maturity. Assuming 10 percent to be the appropriate discount rate, the present value of the bond is:

   a. $1,010.84
   b. $925.74
   c   877.60
   d. $1,000.00

7. The Fuller Company has received a $50,000 loan. The annual payments are $6,202.70. If the Fuller Company is paying 9 percent interest per year, how many loan payments must the company make?

   a. 15
   b. 13
   c. 12
   d. 19

10

Capital Budgeting

Orientation: Capital budgeting involves the decision-making process with respect to investment in fixed assets; specifically, it involves measuring the incremental cash flows associated with investment proposals and evaluating the attractiveness of these cash flows relative to the project's costs. This chapter focuses on the estimation of those cash flows based on various decision criteria.

I. What criteria should we use in the evaluation of alternative investment proposals?

   A. Use cash flows rather than accounting profits because cash flows allow us to correctly analyze the time element of the flows.

   B. Examine cash flows on an after-tax basis because they are the flows available to shareholders.

   C. Only include the incremental cash flows resulting from the investment decision. Ignore all other flows.

II. Measure cash flows: We are interested in measuring the incremental after-tax cash flows resulting from the investment proposal. In general, there will be three major sources of cash flows: initial outlays, differential cash flows over the project's life, and terminal cash flows.

   A. Initial outlays include whatever cash flows are necessary to get the project in running order: for example:

117

1. The installed cost of the asset.

2. In the case of a replacement proposal, the selling price of the old machine plus (or minus) any tax gain (or loss) offsetting the initial outlay.

3. Any expense items (for example, training) necessary for the operation of the proposal.

4. Any other non-expense cash outlays required, such as increased working-capital needs.

B. Differential cash flows over the project's life include the incremental after-tax flows over the life of the project: for example:

1. Added revenue (less added selling expenses) for the proposal.

2. Any labor and/or material savings incurred.

3. Increases in overhead incurred.

4. These values are measured on an after-tax basis, thus allowing for the tax savings (or loss) from incremental increase (or decrease) in depreciation to be included.

5. A word of warning not to include financing charges (such as interest or preferred stock dividends), for they are implicitly taken care of in the discounting process.

C. Terminal cash flows include any incremental cash flows that result at the termination of the project; for example:

1. The project's salvage value plus (or minus) any taxable gains or losses associated with the project.

2. Any terminal cash flow needed, perhaps disposal of obsolete equipment.

3. Recovery of any non-expense cash outlays associated with the project, such as recovery of increased working-capital needs associated with the proposal.

III. Methods for evaluating projects

A. Average rate of return is

$$\text{average rate of return} = \sum_{t=1}^{n} \left[\frac{\dfrac{\text{annual profits after tax}_t}{n}}{\dfrac{\text{investment + expected salvage value}}{2}} \right]$$

   1. This formula assumes straight-line depreciation; thus, the average investment in the project is equal to the sum of the investment plus the expected salvage value divided by 2.

   2. Although this measure has the advantages of being easy to calculate and of having familiar terms it uses profits rather than cash flows in its calculations and does not consider the time value of money.

B. The payback method

   1. The payback period of an investment tells the number of years required to recover the initial investment. The payback period is calculated by adding the cash flows up until they are equal to the initial fixed investment.

   2. Although this measure does, in fact, deal with cash flows and is easy to calculate and understand, it ignores any cash flows that occur after the payback period and does not consider the time value of money within the payback period.

C. Present-value methods

   1. The net present value of an investment project is the present value of the cash inflows less the present value of the cash outflows. By assigning negative values to cash outflows, it becomes:

$$\text{NPV} = \sum_{t=1}^{n} \frac{\text{ACF}_t}{(1 + k)^t} - \text{IO}$$

      where ACF_t = the annual after-tax cash flow in time period t (this can take on either positive or negative values),

119

$$k = \text{the \underline{required} rate of \underline{return} or appropriate discount rate or cost of capital}^{1},$$

$$\text{IO} = \text{the initial cash outlay,}$$

$$n = \text{the project's expected life.}$$

a. The acceptance criteria are:

accept if NPV > 0
reject if NPV < 0

b. The advantage of this approach is that it takes the time value of money into consideration in addition to dealing with cash flows.

2. The profitability index is the ratio of the present value of the expected future net cash flows to the initial cash outlay, or

$$\text{profitability index} = \frac{\sum_{t=1}^{n} \frac{ACF_t}{(1 + k)^t}}{IO}$$

a. The acceptance criteria are:

accept if PI > 1.0
reject if PI < 1.0

b. The advantages of this method are the same as those for the net present value.

c. Either of these present-value methods will give the same accept-reject decisions to a project.

D. The internal rate of return is the discount rate that equates the present value of the project's future net cash flows with the project's initial outlay. Thus the internal rate of return is represented by IRR in the equation below:

$$IO = \sum_{t=1}^{n} \frac{ACF_t}{(1 + IRR)^t}$$

[1]The cost of capital is discussed in Chapter 13.

1. The acceptance-rejection criteria are:

    accept if IRR > required rate of return
    reject if IRR < required rate of return

    The required rate of return is often taken to be the firm's cost of capital, which will be discussed in Chapter 13.

2. The advantages of this method are that it deals with cash flows and recognizes the time value of money; however, the procedure is rather complicated and time-consuming.

IV. Mutually exclusive projects: Although the IRR and the present-value methods will, in general, give consistent accept-reject decisions, they may not rank projects identically. This becomes important in the case of mutually exclusive projects.

A. A project is mutually exclusive if acceptance of it precludes the acceptance of one or more projects. In this case, the project's relative ranking becomes important.

B. Ranking conflicts come as a result of the different assumptions on the reinvestment rate on funds released from the proposals.

C. Thus, when conflicting ranking of mutually exclusive projects results from the different reinvestment assumptions, the decision boils down to which assumption is best.

D. In general, the net present value method is considered to be theoretically superior.

V. Capital rationing is the situation in which a budget ceiling or constraint is placed upon the amount of funds that can be invested during a time period.

A. Theoretically, a firm should never reject a project that yields more than the required rate of return. Although there are circumstances that may create complicated situations in general, an investment policy limited by capital rationing is less than optimal.

Study Problems

1. The cost of new machinery for a given investment project will be $100,000. Incremental cash flows after taxes will be $40,000 in years 1 and 2 and will be $60,000 in year 3. What is the payback period for this project, and if acceptable projects must recover the initial investment in 2.5 years, should this project be accepted or rejected?

   SOLUTION

   After 2 years they will have recovered $80,000 of the $100,000 outlay and they expect to recover an additional $60,000 in the third year. Thus, the payback period becomes

   $$2 \text{ years} + \frac{\$20,000}{\$60,000} = 2.33 \text{ years}$$

   2.33 years 2.5 years

   Therefore, accept the project.

2. A given investment project will cost $50,000. Incremental annual cash flows after taxes are expected to be $10,000 per year for the life of the investment, which is 5 years. There will be no salvage value at the end of the 5 years. The required rate of return is 14%. On the basis of the profitability index method, should the investment be accepted?

   SOLUTION

   PV of cash flow = $10,000(3.433) = $34,330

   PV of cash outlay = $50,000

   $$PI = \frac{\$34,330}{\$50,000} = 0.6866 < 1$$

   Therefore, the project should be rejected.

3. The G. Wolfe Corporation is considering replacing one of its bottling machines with a new, more efficient one. The old machine presently has a book value of $75,000 and could be sold for $60,000 The old machine is being depreciated using a simplified straight line method down to zero over the next five years generating depreciation of $15,000 per year. The replacement machine would cost $250,000, and have an expected life of five years after

which it could be sold for $20,000. Because of reductions in defects and materials savings, the new machine would produce cash benefits of $100,000 per year before depreciation and taxes. Assume simplified straight line depreciation, a 40 percent marginal tax rate, and a required rate of return of 18 percent, find:

a. The payback period.
b. The net present value.
c. The profitability index.

SOLUTION

Initial Outlay

Outflows:	
Purchase Price	$250,000
Inflows:	
Tax Savings from sale of old machine below book value ($75,000-60,000) .40	- 6,000
Salvage Value on Old Machine	- 60,000
Net Initial Outlay	$184,000

Differential Annual Cash Flows (Years 1-4)

	Book Profit	Cash Flow
Savings:		
Cash Savings	$100,000	$100,000
Costs:		
Increased depreciation ($50,000 - $15,000)*	- 35,000	
Net Savings Before Taxes	$ 65,000	$100,000
Taxes (40%)	- 26,000	- 26,000
		$ 74,000

*Note: Annual depreciation on the new machine was calculated by taking the purchase price ($250,000) and dividing by the expected life (5 years).

Terminal Cash Flow (Year 5)

Inflows:	
Differential Cash Flow Year 5	$ 74,000
Salvage Value	20,000
Outflows:	
Taxes due on sale of new machine ($20,000-0)(.40)	- 8,000
	$ 86,000

a. Payback Period = $\dfrac{\$184,000}{\$74,000}$ = _____ years

b. Net Present Value =

$$\sum_{t=1}^{4} \frac{\$74,000}{(1+.18)^t} + \frac{\$86,000}{(1+.18)^5} - \$184,000$$

= \$74,000(2.690) + \$86,000(.437) - \$184,000

= \$201,750 + \$37,582 - \$184,000 = \$55,332

c. The Profitability Index = 1.3

Self-Tests

TRUE/FALSE

_____ 1. Cash flow, not income, is what is important in capital budgeting.

_____ 2. The net present value of a project decreases as the required rate of return increases.

_____ 3. The higher the discount rate, the more valued is the proposal with the early cash flows.

_____ 4. The net-present-value approach is preferred over the profitability index for mutually exclusive projects because it measures worth in absolute terms and the profitability index measures worth in relative terms.

_____ 5. Capital rationing occurs when profitable projects must be rejected because of shortage of capital.

_____ 6. The net present value of a project will equal zero whenever the average rate of return equals the required rate of return.

_____ 7. The net present value of a project will equal zero whenever the payback period of a project equals the required payback period.

_____ 8. The average rate of return will always equal the internal rate of return.

_____ 9. One difference in the net-present-value approach and the internal-rate-of-return method is the reinvestment-rate assumption.

_____ 10. Capital rationing is not an optimal capital budgeting strategy.

_____ 11. The probability index provides the same decision result as the net present value method.

_____ 12. Implied in the accounting rate of return is the double-declining balance method of depreciation.

_____ 13. Both the internal rate of return rule and the accounting rate of return rule take into consideration the time value of money.

MULTIPLE CHOICE

1. Which of the following considers the time value of money?

   a. Payback method.
   b. Average rate of return.
   c. Profitability index.
   d. None of the above.

2. Which of the following is important to capital budgeting decisions?

   a. Depreciation method.
   b. Salvage value.
   c. Timing of cash flows.
   d. Taxes.
   e. All of the above.

3. Which of the following is an estimate approach?

   a. Average rate of return.
   b. Profitability index.
   c. Internal rate of return.
   d. Net present value.

4. The net-present-value approach and the internal-rate-of-return method may lead to discrepancies when:

   a. Projects are dependent.
   b. The discount rate equals zero.
   c. Projects are mutually exclusive.
   d. All of the above.

125

5. The average-rate-of-return method will always lead to the same accept or reject decision as will the:

    e

    a. Profitability index.
    b. Net-present-value method.
    c. Payback method.
    d. Internal-rate-of-return method.
    e. None of the above.

6. If the internal rate of return is greater than the required rate of return

    C

    a. the present value of all the cash flows will be less than the initial outlay.
    b. the payback will be less than the life of the investment.
    c. the project should be accepted.
    d. a and c.

7. If the federal income tax rate were increased, the result would be to

    d

    a. decrease the net present value.
    b. increase the net present value.
    c. increase the payback period.
    d. a and c.

8. If the cash flow pattern for a project has two sign reversals, then there can be as many as _____ positive IRR's.

    b

    a. 1
    b. 2
    c. 3
    d. 4

11

Capital Budgeting Under Uncertainty

<u>Orientation</u>: The focus of this chapter will be on how to measure and adjust for the riskiness of a given project or combination of projects and on understanding how risk affects the value of a firm.

I.   Risk and the investment decision

A.   Up to this point we have treated the expected cash flows resulting from an investment proposal as being known with perfect certainty. We will now introduce risk.

B.   The riskiness of an investment project is defined as the variability of its cash flows from the expected cash flow.

II.   Quantitative risk measures

A.   Probability distributions illustrate the complete set of probabilities for all possible outcomes for one particular event.

1.   A discrete probability distribution is one in which a probability is assigned to each possible outcome in the set of all possible outcomes.

2.   In a continuous probability distribution there are an infinite number of possible outcomes, in which the probability of an event is related to a range of possible outcomes.

127

Average 3. The expected value of a distribution is the arithmetic mean or average of all possible outcomes: those outcomes are weighted by the probability that each outcome will occur.

B. Risk, that is the dispersion of the distribution, can be measured in either relative or absolute terms.

   1. The standard deviation provides a measure of the absolute spread of the probability distribution. Quantitatively, it is defined as:

$$\alpha = \sqrt{\sum_{i=1}^{n} (X_i - \bar{X})^2 P(X_i)}$$

   where n = the number of possible outcomes,

   X_i = the value of the ith possible outcome,

   $\bar{X}$ = the expected value,

   $P(X_i)$ = the probability that the ith outcome will occur.

EXAMPLE 1

State	Prob-ability	Proposal A	Weighted Average	Proposal B	Weighted Average
Deep re-cession	0.2	$20,000	$ 4,000	$10,000	$ 2,000
Normal	0.6	25,000	15,000	25,000	15,000
Major boom	0.2	30,000	6,000	40,000	8,000
		Expected value=	$25,000		$25,000

$$A = \sqrt{(\$20{,}000 - \$25{,}000)^2 (0.2) + (\$25{,}000 - \$25{,}000)^2 (0.6) + (\$30{,}000 - \$25{,}000)^2 (0.2)}$$

$$= \sqrt{\$5{,}000{,}000 + \$5{,}000{,}000} = \underline{\$3{,}162.28}$$

$$B = \sqrt{(\$10{,}000 - \$25{,}000)^2 (0.2) + (\$25{,}000 - \$25{,}000)^2 (0.6) + (\$40{,}000 - \$25{,}000)^2 (0.2)}$$

$$= \sqrt{\$45{,}000{,}000 + \$45{,}000{,}000} = \underline{\$9{,}486{,}833}$$

   a. The standard deviation simply measures the tightness of a probability distribution.

128

　　　　b.　The lower the standard deviation of the
　　　　　　cash flow, the lower the perceived risk.

　　2.　The coefficient of variation is <u>the measure of
　　　　<u>relative dispersion or risk in a project.</u></u>

　　　　a.　Whereas the standard deviation gives us a
　　　　　　measure of absolute risk, the coefficient
　　　　　　of variation gives us a measure of rela-
　　　　　　tive risk (i.e., risk per unit of return).

II. Methods for incorporating risk into capital budgeting

　　A.　The certainty equivalent approach involves a direct
　　　　attempt to allow the decision maker to incorporate
　　　　his or her utility function into the analysis.

　　　　1.　In effect, a riskless set of cash flows is
　　　　　　substituted for the original set of cash flows
　　　　　　between both of which the financial manager is
　　　　　　indifferent.

　　　　2.　To simplify calculations certainty equivalent
　　　　　　coefficients (α_t's) are defined as the ratio of
　　　　　　the certain outcome to the risky outcome
　　　　　　between which the financial manager is
　　　　　　indifferent.

　　　　3.　Mathematically, certainty equivalent coeffi-
　　　　　　cients can be defined as follows:

$$\alpha_t = \frac{\text{certain cash flow}_t}{\text{risky cash flow}_t}$$

　　　　4.　The appropriate certainty equivalent coeffi-
　　　　　　cient is multiplied by the original cash flow
　　　　　　(which is the risky cash flow) with this
　　　　　　product being equal to the equivalent certain
　　　　　　cash flow.

　　　　5.　Once risk is taken out of the cash flows, those
　　　　　　cash flows are discounted back to present at
　　　　　　the risk-free rate of interest and the pro-
　　　　　　ject's net present value or profitability index
　　　　　　is determined.

　　　　6.　If the internal rate of return is calculated,
　　　　　　it is then compared to the risk-free rate of
　　　　　　interest rather than to the firm's required
　　　　　　rate of return

　　　　7.　Mathematically, the certainty equivalent can be
　　　　　　summarized as follows:

$$NPV = \sum_{t=1}^{n} \frac{\alpha_t ACF_t}{(1+i_F)^t} - IO$$

where α_t =   the certainty equivalent coefficient for time period t,

      ACF_t =   the annual after-tax expected cash flow in time period t,

      IO =   the initial cash outlay,

      n =   the project's expected life,

      i_F =   the risk-free interest rate.

B.   The use of the risk-adjusted discount rate is based on the concept that investors demand higher returns for more risky projects.

    1.   If the risk associated with the investment is greater than the risk involved in a typical endeavor, then the discount rate is adjusted upward to compensate for this risk.

    2.   The expected cash flows are then discounted back to present at the risk-adjusted discount rate. Then the normal capital budgeting criteria are applied, except in the case of the internal rate of return, in which case the hurdle rate to which the project's internal rate of return is compared now becomes the risk-adjusted discount rate.

    3.   Expressed mathematically the net present value using the risk-adjusted discount rate becomes

$$NPV = \sum_{t=1}^{n} \frac{ACF_t}{(1+i^*)^t} - IO$$

where ACF_t =   the annual after-tax cash flow in time period t,

      IO =   the initial outlay,

      i^* =   the risk-adjusted discount rate,

      n =   the project's expected life.

IV.   Additional approaches for dealing with risk in capital budgeting

A. A simulation imitates the performance of the project being evaluated by randomly selecting observations from each of the distributions that affect the outcome of the project, combining those observations to determine the final output of the final project, and continuing with this process until a representative record of the project's probable outcome is assembled.

   1. The firm's management then examines the resultant probability distribution, and if management considers enough of the distribution of possible net present values to be greater than zero, it will accept the project.

   2. The use of a simulation approach to analyze investment proposals offers two major advantages:

      a. The financial managers are able to examine and base their decisions on the whole range of possible outcomes rather than just point estimates.

      b. They can undertake subsequent sensitivity analysis of the project.

B. A probability tree is a graphical exposition of the sequence of possible outcomes; it presents the decision maker with a schematic representation of the problem in which all possible outcomes are graphically displayed.

V. Other sources and measures of risk

A. Many times, especially with the introduction of a new product the cash flows experienced in early years affect the size of the cash flows experienced in later years. This is called time dependence of cash flows, and it has the effect of increasing the riskiness of the project over time.

B. A distribution that is not symmetric is said to be skewed. When distributions are skewed, the expected value and standard deviation alone may not be enough to differentiate between two distributions.

C. The addition of some projects because of their particular cyclical patterns is able to lower the overall riskiness of the firm better than the addition of other projects. Risk in this context is called portfolio risk.

1. In order to measure the relationship between two projects, we use the concept of correlation.

2. If the correlation coefficient between two projects is close to -1.0, the projects move in linearly opposite directions. If the correlation coefficient is close to 1.0, the projects move together linearly.

3. Since firm diversification can reduce the chance of bankruptcy, there is value to diversification.

Study Problems

1. A firm with a 15% required rate of return is considering a project with an expected life of 5 years. The initial outlay associated with this project involves a certain cash outflow of $100,000. The expected cash inflows and certainty equivalent coefficients, α_t's, are as follows:

Year	Expected Cash Flow	Certainty Equivalent Coefficient, α_t
1	$20,000	0.90
2	30,000	0.80
3	40,000	0.75
4	50,000	0.60
5	60,000	0.50

The risk-free rate of interest is 6%. What is the project's net present value?

SOLUTION

To determine the net present value of this project by using the certainty equivalent we must first remove the risk from the future cash flows. We do so by multiplying each expected cash flow by the corresponding certainty equivalent coefficient:

Year	Expected Cash Flow	Certainty Equivalent Coefficient, α_t	$\alpha_t \times$ (Expected Cash Flow) = Equivalent Riskless Cash Flow
1	$20,000	0.90	$18,000
2	30,000	0.80	24,000
3	40,000	0.75	30,000
4	50,000	0.60	30,000
5	60,000	0.50	30,000

The equivalent riskless cash flows are then discounted back to the present at the riskless interest rate, not the firm's required rate of return:

Year	Equivalent Riskless Cash Flow	Present Value Factor at 6%	Present Value
1	$18,000	0.943	16,974
2	24,000	0.890	21,360
3	30,000	0.840	25,200
4	30,000	0.792	23,760
5	30,000	0.747	22,410

NPV = -$100,000+$16,974+$21,360+$25,200+$23,760+$22,410

$\quad$ = $9,704

Applying the normal capital budgeting decision criteria, we find that the project should be accepted because its net present value is greater than zero.

2. A firm is considering introducing a new product that has an expected life of 5 years. Since this product is much riskier than a typical project for this firm, the management feels that the normal required rate of return of 12% is not sufficient; instead, the minimally acceptable rate of return on this project should be 20%. The initial outlay would be $100,000 and the expected cash flows from this project are as given below:

Year	Expected Cash Flow
1	$40,000
2	40,000
3	40,000
4	40,000
5	40,000

Should this project be accepted?

SOLUTION

Discounting this annuity back to present at 20% yields a present value of the future cash flows of $119,640. Since the initial outlay on this project is $100,000, the net present value becomes $19,640. The project should be accepted.

3. Project A is expected to net a present value of $24,000. Project A's standard deviation is expected to be $12,000. Project B is expected to net a present value of $60,000 with a standard deviation of $20,000. What are the

133

coefficients of variation for these projects? Which project has the more relative risk?

SOLUTION

$$\gamma A = \frac{\$12,000}{\$24,000} = 0.5$$

$$\gamma B = \frac{\$20,000}{\$60,000} = 0.33$$

Project A has the largest coefficient of variation and therefore the most relative risk.

Self-Tests

TRUE/FALSE

_____ 1. The coefficient of variation is synonymous with the standard deviation.

_____ 2. Independent cash flows means that the outcome in period T is not dependent on the outcome of the T-1 cash flow.

_____ 3. If two projects are mutually exclusive, the one with the highest expected value should always be chosen, even if it is riskier.

_____ 4. The coefficient of variation serves as a relative measure of risk.

_____ 5. The certainty equivalent coefficient is the ratio of the risky outcome to the certain outcome between which the financial manager is indifferent.

_____ 6. Projects which are negatively correlated move together.

_____ 7. The correlation among projects is an essential element in measuring the risk of a portfolio.

_____ 8. Standard deviation is a measure of dispersion from an expected value.

_____ 9. A continuous distribution is one in which a probability is assigned to each possible outcome in the set of all possible outcomes.

_____ 10. The standard deviation loses meaning if the distribution is skewed.

_____ 11. The standard deviation indicates the relative dispersion of a distribution.

_____ 12. The use of risk-adjusted discount rates is based on the concept that investors require a higher rate of return for more risky projects.

_____ 13. Probability trees allow the financial manager to see possible future events, their probabilities and their outcomes.

_____ 14. A diversification effect occurs only when cash flows from two different projects have zero correlation.

_____ 15. A continuous probability indicates the probability that a specific outcome will occur.

MULTIPLE CHOICE

1. If two projects are completely independent, the measure of correlation between them is:

    a. +1.
    b. 0.
    c. -1.

2. To reduce risk most effectively, projects would ideally be chosen with the following correlation coefficient:

    a. +1.
    b. 0.
    c. -1.

3. Which of the following is not a method for adjusting for risk in capital budgeting?

    a. Certainty equivalent approach.
    b. Risk-adjusted discount rate.
    c. Skewed distributions.

4. The proposal with the greatest relative risk would have:

    a. The greatest standard deviation.
    b. The greatest coefficient of variation.
    c. The highest expected NPV.

135

• An investment project will be more desirable:

a. The smaller the standard deviation.
b. The less positive its correlations with existing average cash flows.
c. The larger the coefficient of variation of cash flow.
d. a and b.

• Probability tree analysis:

a. Illustrates the impact of diversification.
b. Fails to consider the probability distribution of cash flows.
c. Is good only for single period investments since discounting is not possible.
d. Graphically displays all possible outcomes of the investment.

12

Valuation
and Rates of Return

Orientation: This chapter introduces the concepts that underlie the valuation of securities. We are specifically concerned with common stock, preferred stock, and bonds. We also look at the concept of the investor's expected rate of return on an investment.

I.   The importance of valuation

   A.   Understanding valuation concepts helps the financial manager to implement the overall objective of the firm-maximization of common stock value.

   B.   Cost of capital used in capital budgeting decisions is derived from the required rates of return of the firm's investors.

II. Definitions of value

   A.   Book value is the value of an asset shown on a firm's balance sheet which is determined by its historical cost rather than its current worth.

   B.   Liquidation value is the amount that could be realized if an asset is sold individually and not as part of a going concern.

   C.   Market value is the observed value of an asset in the marketplace where buyers and sellers negotiate an acceptable price for the asset.

D.   Intrinsic value is the value based upon the expected cash flows from the investment, the riskiness of the asset, and the investor's required rate of return. It is the value in the eyes of the investor and is the same as the present value.

III. Basic determinants of intrinsic value

A.   Value is a function of three elements:

1.   The amount and timing of the asset's expected cash flow.

2.   The riskiness of these cash flows.

3.   The investors' required rate of return for undertaking the investment.

B. Expected cash flows

1.   Cash flows are the relevant variable to be measured in determining returns.

2.   An expected cash flow in an uncertain world can be measured by

$$\bar{X} = \sum_{i=1}^{N} X_i P(X_i)$$

where X_i = the ith possible outcome (cash flow).
$P(X_i)$ = the probability of the ith's event occurring.

C.   Riskiness of the cash flows

1.   Risk can be defined as the possible variation in cash flow about an expected cash flow.

2.   Statistically, risk may be measured by the standard deviation about the expected cash flow, σ, and may be computed as follows:

$$\sigma = \sqrt{\sum_{i=1}^{N} (X_i - \bar{X})^2 \, P(X_i)}$$

3.   Example: A firm has two mutually exclusive projects to choose from, which we will designate as projects A and B. Each project costs $100,000. During different states of the

138

economy, the following outcomes are assigned to each probability that the state of economy will occur. The risk level of each project is assessed as follows:

State of the Economy	Prob- ability	Project A Outcome	Project A Rate of Return	Project B Outcome	Project B Rate of Return
Recession	0.2	$10,000	10%	$ 5,000	5%
Normal	0.6	15,000	15%	15,000	15%
Boom	0.2	20,000	20%	25,000	25%

Expected Cash Flow: Project A

$$= 0.2(\$10,000) + 0.6(\$15,000) + 0.2(\$20,000)$$

$$= \underline{\$15,000}$$

Expected Cash Flow: Project B

$$= 0.2(\$5,000) + 0.6(\$15,000) + 0.2(\$25,000)$$

$$= \underline{\$15,000}$$

Expected Return: Project A

$$= 0.2(10\%) + 0.6(15\%) + 0.2(20\%)$$

$$= 15\%$$

Expected Return: Project B

$$= 0.2(5\%) + 0.6(15\%) + 0.2(25\%)$$

$$= 15\%$$

Standard Deviation: Project A

$$= [0.2(10\% - 15\%)^2 + 0.6(15\% - 15\%)^2$$

$$+ 0.2(20\% - 15\%)^2]^{1/2}$$

$$= (10\%)^{1/2}$$

$$= \underline{3.16\%}$$

Standard Deviation: Project B

$$= [0.2(3\% - 15\%)^2 + 0.6(15\% - 15\%)^2$$

$$+ 0.2(25\% - 15\%)^2]^{1/2}$$

$$= (40\%)1/2$$

$$= \underline{6.32\%}$$

We find that both investments have the same expected cash flow, $15,000, but Project B has a much higher standard deviation than does Project A, which indicates a higher level of risk. Given a risk averse investor, Project A is preferable to Project B.

D. Required rate of return

1. The required rate of return is the minimum rate necessary to compensate an investor for accepting the risk he associates with the purchase and ownership of an asset.

2. Two factors determine the required rate of return for the investor:

a. The risk-free rate of interest which recognizes the time value of money.

b. The risk premium which considers the riskiness (variability of returns) of the asset and the investor's attitude toward risk.

E. Relevant risk (Risk Premium)

1. Total variability can be divided into:

a. The variability of returns unique to the security (diversifiable or unsystematic risk).

b. The risk related to market movements (non-diversifiable or systematic risk).

2. By diversifying, the investor can eliminate the "unique" security risk. The systematic risk, however, cannot be diversified away.

3. Beta, a statistic that measures the systematic risk, is defined as the following ratio:

$$\text{Beta} = \frac{\text{covariance of the security's returns with the market}}{\text{variance of market returns}}$$

4. If a security's beta equals one, a 10 percent increase (decrease) in market returns will produce on average a 10 percent increase (decrease) in security returns.

5. A security having a higher beta is more volatile and thus more risky than a security having a lower beta value.

F. Capital asset pricing model-CAPM. The required rate of return for a given security can be expressed as equal to:

Required rate = risk-free rate + beta x (market return - risk-free rate)

or

$$R_j = R_f + \beta_j (R_m - R_f)$$

G. Security market line

1. Graphically illustrates the CAPM.

2. Designates the risk-return trade off existing in the market, where risk is defined in terms of beta according to the CAPM equation.

H. Criticism of CAPM

1. It relies totally on a security's sensitivity to the market (β) for measuring risk.

2. It is difficult to test empirically.

I. Arbitrage Pricing Theory

1. Security returns vary from expected returns due to unanticipated changes in important economic forces, such as: industrial production, inflation and interest rate structures.

2. $E(R_i) = R_f + (S_{i1})(RP_1) + (S_{i2})(RP_{i2}) + \ldots (S_{in})(RP_n)$

where $E(R_i)$ = the expected return for stock or portfolio i;

R_f = the risk-free rate;

S_{ij} = the sensitivity of stock i returns to unexpected changes in economic force j;

RP_i = the market risk premium associated with an unexpected change in the jth economic force; and

N = the number of relevant economic forces.

IV. Bond valuation

A. Nature of bond

1. A bond is a long-term promissory note which promises to pay the bondholder a predetermined, fixed amount of interest each year until maturity. At maturity, the principal will be paid to the bondholder.

2. A bond's par value is the amount that will be repaid by the firm when the bond matures, usually $1,000.

3. The bond has a <u>maturity date</u>, at which time the borrowing firm is committed to repay the loan principal.

4. The contractual agreement of the bond specifies a <u>coupon interest rate</u> which is expressed either as a percent of the par value or as a flat amount of interest which the borrowing firm promises to pay the bondholder each year. For example: A $1,000 par value bond specifying a coupon interest rate of 9 percent is equivalent to an annual interest payment of $90.

5. The only variable that can cause the value of a bond to increase or decrease is a change in the bondholder's required rate of return.

B. Procedure for valuing a bond

1. The value of a bond is simply the present value of the future cash flows discounted at the bondholder's required rate of return. This may be expressed as:

$$P_0 = \sum_{t=1}^{N} \frac{\$I_t}{(1+R_b)^t} + \frac{\$M}{(1+R_b)^N}$$

142

where I = the dollar interest to be received in each payment,

M = the par value of the bond at maturity,

R_b = the required rate of return for the bondholder,

N = the number of periods to maturity.

In other words, we are discounting the expected future cash flows to the present at the appropriate discount rate (required rate of return).

2. If interest payments are received semiannually (as with most bonds) the valuation equation becomes:

$$P_0 = \sum_{t=1}^{2N} \left(\frac{\frac{\$I_t}{2}}{1 + \frac{R_b}{2}} \right)^t + \left(\frac{\$M}{1 + \frac{R_b}{2}} \right)^{2N}$$

EXAMPLE

The Hendricks Corporation has bonds outstanding with a face (par) value of \$1,000; they are due in 10 years, with an 8 percent coupon rate. The required rate of return for the bondholder is 10 percent. What is the value of the bond today? Interest is paid semiannually.

The number of periods: 10 x 2 = 20.
Interest paid every 6 months: \$80/2 = \$40.
Required rate of return: 10%/2 = 5%.

$$P_0 = \sum_{t=1}^{20} \frac{\$40}{(1 + 0.05)^t} + \frac{\$1,000}{(1 + 0.05)^{20}}$$

= \$498.48 + \$377.00 = \$875.48

V. Preferred stock valuation

A. Owners of preferred stock receive dividends instead of interest.

B. Most preferred stocks are perpetuities (nonmaturing).

C. Value of preferred stock (P_0):

$$P_0 = \frac{\text{annual dividend}}{\text{required rate of return}} = \frac{D}{R_p}$$

143

VI. Common stock valuation

A. Although the bondholder and preferred stockholder are promised a specific amount each year, the dividend for common stock is based on the profitability of the firm and the management's decision either to pay dividends or retain profits for reinvestment.

B. The common dividend typically increases along with the growth in corporate earnings.

C. The earnings growth of a firm should be reflected in a higher price for the firm's stock.

D. In finding the value of a common stock (P_0), we should discount all future expected dividends (D_1, D_2, D_3 ..., D_∞) to the present at the required rate of return for the stockholder (R_c). That is:

$$P_0 = \frac{D_1}{(1 + R_c)^1} + \frac{D_2}{(1 + R_c)^2} \cdots + \frac{D_\infty}{(1 + R_c)^\infty}$$

E. If we assume that the amount of dividend is increasing by a constant growth rate each year,

$$D_t = D_0 (1 + g)^t$$

where g = the growth rate,

D_0 = the most recent dividend payment.

If the growth rate, g, is the same each year and is less than the required rate of return, R_c, the valuation equation for common stock can be reduced to

$$P_0 = \frac{D_1}{R_c - g} = \frac{D_0 (1+g)}{R_c - g}$$

EXAMPLE

Find the value of a stock that paid a $3 dividend last year. The stockholders' required rate of return is 15 percent and a 9 percent growth rate in earnings is anticipated in the indefinite future.

$$\frac{\$3(1 + 0.09)}{R_c - g} = \frac{\$3.27}{R_c - g}$$

$$= \frac{\$3(1 + 0.09)}{(0.15 - 0.09)} = \frac{\$3.27}{0.06} = \$54.50$$

VII. Measuring the expected rate of return

A. If the price of a security and the cash flows are already known, we can solve for the investor's expected rate of return on an investment using our previous present value equations.

B. Bondholder's expected rate of return

1. We solve for the bondholder's expected rate of return, R_b, by trial and error.

EXAMPLE

The market price is $754.70 for a 10-year bond that has a 6 percent coupon interest rate and a face value of $1000. Interest is paid annually. What is the investor's expected rate of return if the bond is purchased for $754.70? We can find the rate by solving for R_b in the following equation:

$$\$754.70 = \frac{\$60}{(1+R_b)^1} + \frac{\$60}{(1+R_b)^2} \ldots + \frac{\$60}{(1+R_b)^{10}} + \frac{\$1,000}{(1+R_b)^{10}}$$

We can solve for an unknown "R_b" in the equation above by trial and error. A rate that exceeds the coupon interest rate should be selected because the investor is not willing to pay the full par value of the bond. At 10 percent the present value of all cash flows is $754.70, computed as follows:

$60(6.145) + $1,000(0.386) = $754.70

Since the value obtained is precisely the market value, the expected rate of return is 10 percent.

C. Preferred stockholder's expected rate of return

1. If we know the market price of a preferred stock and the amount of the expected dividends, the expected rate of return from the investment can be determined as follows:

145

$$\text{expected rate of return} = \frac{\text{annual dividend}}{\text{market price of the stock}}$$

or

$$R_p = \frac{D}{P_o}$$

EXAMPLE

The market price for a company's preferred stock paying a $4 annual dividend is $40. The expected rate of return, R_p, is

$$R_p = \frac{\$4}{\$40} = 10\%$$

D. Common stockholder's expected rate of return

1. The expected rate of return for common stock can be calculated from the valuation equations discussed earlier.

2. Assuming that dividends are increasing at a constant annual growth rate (g), we can show that the expected rate of return for common stock, R_c, is

$$R_c = \begin{array}{c}\text{expected rate} \\ \text{of return}\end{array} = \frac{\text{dividend in year 1}}{\text{market price}} + \begin{array}{c}\text{growth} \\ \text{rate}\end{array}$$

$$= \frac{D_1}{P_0} = g$$

Since dividend - price is the "dividend yield," the

$$\text{Expected rate of return} = \begin{array}{c}\text{dividend} \\ \text{yield}\end{array} + \begin{array}{c}\text{growth} \\ \text{rate}\end{array}$$

EXAMPLE

The common stock of Narrow International Company is selling for $40. If the expected dividend at the conclusion of this year is $2 and if dividends and earnings are growing at an annual rate of 6 percent, the expected rate of return is

$$R_c = \frac{\$2}{\$40} + 6\% = 11\%$$

146

VIII. Historical performance of portfolio returns

    A. Data has been compiled on the actual returns for various portfolios of securities from 1926-1981.

    B. The following portfolios were studied.

        1. U.S. treasury bills
        2. U.S. government bonds
        3. Corporate bonds
        4. Common stocks

    C. Investors historically have received greater returns for greater risk-taking with the exception of the U.S. government bonds.

    D. When inflation is deducted from the returns the only true hedge against inflation has been a portfolio of common stocks.

Study Problems

1. Phillips Inc., is considering an investment in one of two common stocks. Given the information below, which investment is better, based on risk and return.

Common Stock A		Common Stock B	
Probability	Return	Probability	Return
0.10	-10%	0.30	5%
0.20	6	0.20	12
0.40	15	0.40	10
0.30	9	0.10	20

SOLUTION

Common Stock A
Expected Return

$$0.1(-10\%)+0.2(6\%)+0.4(15\%)+0.3(9\%)=-1\%+1.2\%+6\%+2.7\%=8.9\%$$

Standard Deviation

$$[(-10\%-8.9\%)^2(0.10) + (6\%-8.9\%)^2(0.2) + (15\%-8.9\%)^2(0.4)$$

$$+ (9\%-8.9\%)^2 (0.30)]^{1/2} = (35.721\% + 1.682\% + 14.884\% +$$

$$0.003\%)^{1/2} = 7.23\%$$

<u>Common Stock B</u>
Expected Return

$0.3(5\%)+0.2(12\%)+0.4(10\%)+0.10(20\%)=1.5\%+2.4\%+4\%+2\%=9.9\%$

Standard Deviation

$[(5\%-9.9\%)^2(0.3)+(12\%-9.9\%)^2(0.2)+(10\%-9.9\%)^2(0.4)+(20\%-9.9\%)^2(0.1)]^{1/2} = [(7.203\%+0.882\%+0.004\%+10.201\%)]^{1/2}=4.28\%$

Common stock B has both a higher expected return and a smaller standard deviation (less risk). Hence B is better.

2. Gents Clothiers, Inc. has bonds maturing in 6 years and pays 6% interest semiannually on a $1000 face value.

  a. If your required rate of return is 10 percent, what is the value of the bond?

  b. How would your answer change if the interest were paid annually?

SOLUTION

  a. Value of bond if interest is paid semiannually:

  1. Present value of interest payments:

$$= \$30 \begin{bmatrix} \text{TABLE VALUE} \\ \text{Appendix D} \\ \text{12 periods} \\ 5\% \end{bmatrix} = \$30(8.863)$$

$$= \$265.89$$

  2. Present value of principal:

$$= \$1,000 \begin{bmatrix} \text{TABLE VALUE} \\ \text{Appendix B} \\ \text{12 periods} \\ 5\% \end{bmatrix} = \$1,000(0.557)$$

$$= \$557$$

Present value of the interest	$265.89
Present value of the principal	557.00
Value of the bond	$822.89

b. Value of bond if interest is paid annually:

1. Present value of the interest payments:

$$= \$60 \begin{bmatrix} \text{TABLE VALUE} \\ \text{Appendix D} \\ 10\% \\ 6 \text{ years} \end{bmatrix} = \$60(4.355)$$

$$= \$261.30$$

2. Present value of the principal:

$$= \$1,000 \begin{bmatrix} \text{TABLE VALUE} \\ \text{Appendix B} \\ 10\% \\ 6 \text{ years} \end{bmatrix} = \$1,000(0.564)$$

$$= \$564$$

Present value of the interest	$261.30
Present value of the principal	564.00
Value of the bond	$825.30

3. Edge Manufacturing Corporation's bonds are selling in the market for $1,193.96. These 15-year bonds pay 8% interest (annually) on a $1,000 par value.

a. If they are purchased at the market price, what is the expected rate of return?

SOLUTION

Expected Rate of Return:

$$\$1,193.96 = \$80 \begin{bmatrix} \text{TABLE VALUE} \\ \text{Appendix D} \\ 15 \text{ years} \\ \text{at } R_b \end{bmatrix} + \$1,000 \begin{bmatrix} \text{TABLE VALUE} \\ \text{Appendix B} \\ 15 \text{ years} \\ \text{at } R_b \end{bmatrix}$$

where R_b is the expected rate of return to be solved for by trial and error. Guess a 6 percent rate of return. At 6 percent the present value of the interest and principal is equal to

$$\$80(9.712) + \$1,000(0.417) = \$1,193.96$$

The expected rate of return is 6 percent.

149

4. The market price is $865.60 for a 5-year, 12 percent bond ($1000 face value) that pays interest semiannually. What is the expected rate of return?

SOLUTION

$$\$865.60 = \$60 \begin{bmatrix} \text{TABLE VALUE} \\ \text{Appendix D} \\ 10 \text{ years} \\ \text{at } R_b \end{bmatrix} + \$1,000 \begin{bmatrix} \text{TABLE VALUE} \\ \text{Appendix B} \\ 10 \text{ years} \\ \text{at } R_b \end{bmatrix}$$

where R_b is the expected rate of return (to be solved by trial and error).

Try 8 percent:

$$\$60(6.710) + \$1,000(0.463) = \$865.60$$

The required rate of return is 8 percent (on a semiannual basis) or 16% (on an annual basis).

5. The preferred stock of Craft Company pays a $3 dividend. What is the value of the stock if your required rate of return is 8 percent?

SOLUTION

$$\text{Value of preferred stock} = \frac{\text{dividend}}{\text{required rate of return}}$$

$$P_0 = \frac{\$3}{0.08} = \underline{\$37.50}$$

6. Universal Machines' common stock paid $1.50 in dividends last year and is expected to grow indefinitely at an annual 6 percent rate. What is the value of the stock if you require a 12 percent return?

SOLUTION

$$\text{Value } (P_0) = \frac{\text{dividend in year 1}}{\text{required rate} - \text{growth rate}} = \frac{D_1}{R_c - g}$$

where $D_1 = D_0(1+g) = \$1.50(1+0.06)$

$$= \$1.59$$

$R_c = 12\%$

$g = 6\%$

$$P_0 = \frac{\$1.59}{0.12 - 0.06} = \$26.50$$

7. Texas Mining Company's common stock is selling for $35. The stock paid dividends of $2.50 last year and has a projected growth rate of 10 percent. If you buy the stock at the market price, what is the expected rate of return?

SOLUTION

Expected rate of return (R_c):

$$R_c = \frac{\text{dividend in year 1}}{\text{price}} + \text{growth} = \frac{D_1}{P_0} + g$$

where $D_1 = D_0 (1+g) = \$2.50(1 + 0.10) = \$2.75$

$P_0 = \$35$

$$R_c = \frac{\$2.75}{\$35.00} + 0.10 = 0.1785$$

$$= 17.85\%$$

8. Idalou Power Company's preferred stock is selling for $25 in the market and pays $2.50 in dividends.

a. What is the expected rate of return on the stock?

b. If your required rate of return is 12 percent, what is the fair value of the stock for you?

c. Should you acquire the stock?

SOLUTION

a. Expected rate of return $= \dfrac{\$2.50}{\$25.00} = 10\%$

b. Value of the stock to you $= \dfrac{\$2.50}{0.12} = \$20.83$

c. Since your required rate of return is higher than the expected rate of return, you should not acquire it.

9. BC Incorporated, has a beta of 0.65. If the expected market return is 10 percent and the risk free rate is 5 percent, what is the appropriate expected return of BC Incorporated?

SOLUTION

Expected return of BC Incorporated

= risk-free rate + Beta $\begin{bmatrix} \text{expected} & \text{risk-} \\ \text{market} & - & \text{free} \\ \text{return} & \text{rate} \end{bmatrix}$

= 5% + 0.65(10%-5%)

= 5% + 3.25% = 8.25%

10. The market price of International Electric Corporation is $40. The price at the end of one year is expected to be $45. Dividends for next year should be $2.50. What is the expected rate of return for a single holding period of one year?

    SOLUTION

    current price (P_0) = $\dfrac{\text{dividend in year 1}}{1 + \text{expected rate of return}}$ + $\dfrac{\text{price in year 1}}{1 + \text{expected rate of return}}$

    $\dfrac{\text{expected}}{\text{return}}$ = $\dfrac{\text{dividend in year 1 + price in year 1}}{\text{current price}}$ - 1

    $\dfrac{\text{expected}}{\text{return}}$ = $\dfrac{\$2.50 + \$45.00}{\$40.00}$ - 1 = 18.75%

11. Using the results of the Bowers, Bowers, and Logue study given below, calculate the investor's required rate of return for the following stocks:

Economic factor	1	2	3	4
Market risk premium (BBL)	-185.5%	144.5%	12.4%	-274.4%
Stock sensitivity factor				
A	-0.040	0.010	0.020	0.004
B	-0.020	0.030	0.040	0.005
C	-0.050	-0.010	0.009	0.006

Assume that the risk-free rate is 7.3%

SOLUTION

    A   E(R) = 7.3% - 185.5% (-0.040) + 144.5% (0.010)
                 + 12.4% (0.020) - 274.4% (0.004)
        = 15.32%

    B   E(R) = 7.3% - 185.5% (-0.020) + 144.5% (0.030)
                 + 12.4% (0.040) - 274.4% (0.005)
        = 14.47%

C $E(R) = 7.3\% - 185.5\%\,(-0.050) + 144.5\%\,(-0.010)$
$$+ 12.4\%\,(0.009) - 274.4\%\,(0.006)$$
$$= 13.60\%$$

TRUE-FALSE

_____ 1. The investor's required rate of return is the minimum rate necessary to attract an investor to purchase or hold a security.

_____ 2. Risk, as defined in this chapter, is the variation in returns about an expected value.

_____ 3. Time value of money can be represented by a risk-free rate of return only for risk-free securities.

_____ 4. A proxy for the risk-free rate is the Corporate AA Bond rate.

_____ 5. An investor's required rate of return is always greater then the expected rate of return.

_____ 6. By proper diversification, an investor can eliminate the market-related (systematic) risk.

_____ 7. A security having a beta of 1 will move up (or down) on average with the market by the same percentage.

_____ 8. The addition of a security with a beta of 0 provides no additional risk to a well-diversified portfolio.

_____ 9. The par value of a bond is essentially independent of the market value of a bond.

_____ 10. The only variable that can cause the value of a bond to increase or decrease is a change in the bond-holder's required rate of return.

_____ 11. An assumption necessary in the model for common stock valuation

$$P_0 = \frac{D_1}{R_c - g}$$

is that the amount of the dividend increases by a constant percent each year.

_____ 12. The annual return on common stock, historically has been greater than that of U.S. treasury bills.

_____ 13. A security with an expected return of 15.9% and a standard deviation of 9.8% is obviously better than a treasury bill of 8%.

_____ 14. In an efficient market place, the intrinsic value of a security will equal its market value.

_____ 15. If the market price of a security is larger than the value assigned to the security by an investor, then the expected rate is greater than the required rate of return.

MULTIPLE CHOICE

1. For a $1,000 par-value bond carrying an 8% coupon (interest paid quarterly) and having a 10% yield to maturity, the quarterly interest payments would be:

    a. $20.
    b. $30.
    c. $25.
    d. $50.
    e. $10.

2. The most recent dividend paid by Xeron on its common stock was $1.50 (annual). The required rate of return for the security is 6%. Growth is anticipated to be at 4% annually. The market price of the stock should be:

    a. $78.
    b. $100.
    c. $50.
    d. $150.
    e. $75.

3. Under the capital asset pricing model, the relevant risk is:

    a. Diversifiable risk.
    b. Systematic risk.
    c. Financial risk.
    d. Standard deviation.

4. The value of a security may be expressed as a function of:

    a. Expected cash flows.
    b. Riskiness of cash flows.
    c. The investor's required rate of return.
    d. a and b only.
    e. a, b, and c.

154

5. If the market is in equilibrium, the expected rate of return and the required rate of return:

    a.   Will be the same.
    b.   Will be different.
    c.   Have no relationship to each other.

6. If the expected return for a security is 15% and the risk-free rate is 6%, the risk premium is:

    a.   0%.
    b.   6%.
    c.   10%.
    d.   9%.
    e.   15%.

    expected return – risk-free rate = risk premium

7. In terms of the security market line, a security with a beta of 1.5 should provide a risk premium _____ times the risk premium existing for the market as a whole.

    a.   2.
    b.   1.
    c.   1.5.
    d.   2.5.
    e.   0.5.

    $\beta = 0$

8. If everything else is assumed to be constant, as the investor's required rate of return decreases, the value of a security:

    a.   Stays the same.
    b.   Increases.
    c.   Decreases.
    d.   Has no relationship to the investor's required rate of return.

13

Cost of Capital

Orientation: In Chapter 12 we considered the valuation of debt and equity instruments. The concepts advanced there serve as a foundation for determining the required rate of return for the firm and for specific investment projects. The objective in this chapter is to determine the required rate of return to be used in evaluating investment projects. This minimum required rate of return should result in acceptance of only those projects that will at worst leave the market value of the firm's stock unchanged and hopefully increase it.

I.   The concept of the cost of capital

    A.   Two reasons for computing a firm's cost of capital:

        1.   To determine the financial mix that has the lowest cost of capital.

        2.   To use as a criterion for accepting or rejecting a capital expenditure.

    B.   Defining the cost of capital:

        1.   The rate that must be earned in order to satisfy the required rate of return of the firm's investors.

        2.   The rate of return on investments at which the price of a firm's common stock will remain unchanged.

C. Type of investors and the cost of capital: Each type of capital used by the firm (debt, preferred stock, and common stock) should be incorporated into the cost of capital, with the relative importance of a particular source being based on the percentage of the financing provided by each source of capital.

II. Factors determining the cost of capital

A. General economic conditions. This includes the demand for and supply of capital within the economy, and the level of expected inflation. These are reflected in the riskless rate of return.

B. Market conditions. The security may not be readily marketable when the investor wants to sell; or even if a continuous demand for the security does exist, the price may vary significantly.

C. A firm's operating and financing decisions. Risk also results from the decisions made within the company. This risk is generally divided into two classes:

1. Business risk is the variability in returns on assets and is affected by the company's investment decisions.

2. Financial risk is the increased variability in returns to the common stockholders as a result of using debt and preferred stock.

D. Amount of financing required. The last factor determining the corporation's cost of funds is the amount of financing required, where the cost of capital increases as the financing requirements become larger. This increase may be attributable to one of two factors.

1. As increasingly larger security issues are floated in the market, additional flotation costs (costs of issuing the security) and underpricing will affect the percentage cost of the funds to the firm.

2. As management approaches the market for large amounts of capital relative to the firm's size, the investors' required rate of return may rise. Suppliers of capital become hesitant to grant relatively large amounts of funds without evidence of management's capability to absorb this capital into the business.

E. In summary. Generally as the level of risk rises a larger risk premium must be earned to satisfy a firm's investors. This, when added to the risk-free rate, equals the firm's cost of capital.

III. Assumptions of the cost of capital model

A. Constant business risk. We assume that any investment being considered will not significantly change the firm's business risk.

B. Constant financial risk. Management is assumed to use the same financial mix as it used in the past.

C. Constant dividend policy.

1. For ease of computation, it is generally assumed that the firm's dividends are increasing at a constant annual growth rate. Also, this growth is assumed to be a function of the firm's earning capabilities and not merely the result of paying out a larger percentage of the company's earnings.

2. We also implicitly assume that the dividend payout ratio (dividend/net income) is constant.

IV. Computing the weighted cost of capital. A firm's weighted cost of capital is a function of (1) the individual costs of capital, (2) the capital structure mix, and (3) the level of financing necessary to make the investment.

A. Determining individual costs of capital.

1. The <u>before-tax cost of debt</u> is found by trial-and-error by solving for k_d in

$$NP_O = \sum_{t=1}^{n} \frac{\$I_t}{(1 + k_d)^t} + \frac{\$M}{(1 + k_d)^N}$$

where NP_O = the market price of the debt, less flotation costs,

$\$I_t$ = the annual dollar interest paid to the investor each year,

$\$M$ = the maturity value of the debt

158

k_d = before-tax cost of the debt (before-tax required rate of return on debt)

N = the number of years to maturity.

The <u>after-tax cost of debt</u> is then calculated using

$$K_d = k_d(1 - t)$$

where   t = the corporation's <u>marginal</u> tax rate

K_d = after-tax cost of debt

2.   Cost of preferred stock (required rate of return on preferred stock), K_p, equals the dividend yield based upon the net price (market price less flotation costs) or

$$K_p = \frac{dividend}{net\ price} = \frac{D}{NP_o}$$

3.   Cost of Common Stock. There are three measurement techniques to obtain the required rate of return on common stock.

     a.   dividend-growth model

     b.   capital asset pricing model

     c.   risk-premium approach

4.   Dividend growth model

     a.   Cost of internally generated common equity, K_{ic}

$$K_{ic} = \frac{dividend\ in\ year\ 1}{market\ price} + \left(\begin{array}{c} annual\ growth \\ in\ dividends \end{array} \right)$$

$$K_{ic} = \frac{D_1}{P_o} + g$$

     b.   Cost of new common stock, K_{nc}

$$K_{nc} = \frac{D_1}{NP_o} + g$$

159

where NP_o = the market price of the common stock less flotation costs incurred in issuing new shares.

5. Capital asset pricing model

$$K_c = R_f + \beta_c (R_m - R_f)$$

where K_c = the cost of common

R_f = the risk-free rate

β_c = beta, measure of the stock's systematic risk

R_m = the expected rate of return on the market

6. Risk-Premium Approach

$$K_c = K_d + RP_c$$

where K_c = cost of common

K_d = cost of debt

RP_c = risk-premium of common stock

7. It is important to notice that the major difference between the equations presented here and the equations from Chapter 12 is that the _firm_ must recognize the flotation costs, incurred in issuing the security.

B. Selection of weights. The individual costs of capital will be different for each source of capital in the firm's capital structure. To use the cost of capital in investment analyses, we must compute a weighted or overall cost of capital.

1. It will be assumed that the company's current financial mix result from the financing of previous investments is relatively stable and that these weights will closely approximate future financing patterns.

2. In computing weights we can either use the current market values of the firm's securities or the book values as shown in the balance sheet. Since we will be issuing new securities at their _current_ market value, and not at book

(historical) values we should use the market value of the securities in calculating our weights.

V. Level of financing and the weighted average cost of capital. The weighted marginal cost of capital specifies the composite cost for each additional dollar of financing. The firm should continue to invest up to the point where the marginal internal rate of return earned on a new investment (IRR) equals the marginal cost of new capital.

A. Impact of a new common stock issue. Issuing new common stock will increase the firm's weighted cost of capital because external equity capital has a higher cost than internally generated common equity.

B. General effect of new financing on marginal cost of capital. Increases in the marginal cost of capital curve will occur at the dollar financing level where

$$\begin{matrix} \text{financing level} \\ \text{from all sources} \\ \text{where marginal} \\ \text{costs increase} \end{matrix} = \frac{\begin{matrix} \text{maximum level of financing to be} \\ \text{provided by a source at a} \\ \text{specified rate} \end{matrix}}{\begin{matrix} \text{percentage financing} \\ \text{provided by the source} \end{matrix}}$$

C. Procedure for determining the weighted marginal cost of capital curve

   1. Determine financial mix to be used.

   2. Calculate the levels of total financing at which the individual costs of capital increase.

   3. Calculate the costs of each source of capital for all levels of total financing.

   4. Compute the weighted marginal costs of capital for all levels of total financing.

   5. Construct a graph that compares the internal rates of return of available investment projects with the weighted marginal costs of capital.

D. Project acceptance. Investments with an internal rate of return exceeding the marginal cost of capital should be accepted.

161

Study Problems

1. A $1000 par-value bond will sell in the market for $1072 and carries a coupon interest rate of 9 percent. Issuance costs will be 7.5 percent. The number of years to maturity is 15 and the firm's tax rate is 46 percent. What is the after-tax cost for this security (K_d)?

SOLUTION

$$\$1,072(1 - 0.075) \text{ or } \$991.60 = \sum_{t=1}^{15} \frac{\$90}{(1 + k_d)^t} + \frac{\$1,000}{(1 + k_d)^t}$$

Try 10%: $\$923.54 = \$90(7.606) + \$1.000(0.239)$.
Try 9%: $\$1,000 = \$90(8.061) + \$1,000(0.275)$.

$$
\begin{array}{ll}
9\% & \$1,000.00 \\
    & \$\ \ 991.60
\end{array} \Big\} \ \$8.40 \Big\} \qquad \$76.46
$$
$$
\begin{array}{ll}
10\% & \$\ \ 923.54
\end{array}
$$

$$k_d = 0.09 + \frac{\$\ 8.40}{\$76.46}\ 0.01 = 9.11\%$$

$$k_d = 9.11\%(1 - 0.46) = 4.92\%$$

2. The current market price of ABC Company's common stock is $32.50. The firm expects to pay a dividend of $1.90, and the growth rate is projected to be 7 percent annually. The company is in a 40 percent tax bracket. Flotation costs would be 6 percent if new stock were issued. What is the cost of (a) internal and (b) external common equity?

SOLUTION

Let K_c = cost of internal common.

K_{nc} = cost of external (new) common.

D_1 = next dividend to be paid.

P_o = market price.

g = growth rate.

NP_o = market price less flotation costs.

(a) $K_c = \dfrac{D_1}{P_o} + g$

$$K_c = \frac{\$1.90}{\$32.50} + 0.07 = 12.85\%$$

(b) $K_{nc} = \frac{D_1}{NP_o} + g$

$$K_{nc} = \frac{\$1.90}{\$32.50(1 - 0.06)} + 0.07 = 13.22\%$$

3. Pharr, Inc.'s preferred stock pays a 16 percent dividend. The stock is selling for $62.75, and its par value is $40. Issuance costs are 5 percent and the firm's tax rate is 46 percent. What is the cost of this source of financing?

    SOLUTION

    $$K_p = \frac{D}{NP_o}$$

    $$K_p = \frac{\$40(0.16)}{\$62.75(1 - 0.05)} = \frac{\$6.40}{\$59.61} = 10.74\%$$

4. The current capital structure of Smithhart, Inc. is as follows:

    Bonds (7%, $1,000 par, 15 years) $ 750,000
    Preferred stock ($100 par, 7.25% dividend) 1,000,000

    Common stock:

Par value ($5 par)	$500,000	
Retained earnings	350,000	
Total		850,000
		$2,600,000

    The market price is $975 for the bonds, $60 for the preferred stock, and $42 for common stocks. Flotation costs are 9 percent for bonds and 5 percent for preferred stock. The firm's tax rate is 46 percent. Common stock will pay a $2.80 dividend which is not expected to grow. What is the weighted cost of capital using only internal common equity?

    SOLUTION

Source of Financing	Market Value	Weight
Bonds	$ 731,250[1]	13.22%
Preferred stock	600,000[2]	10.85
Common stock	4,200,000[3]	75.93
	$5,531,250	100.00%

163

[1]750 bonds at $975 value each

[2]10,000 shares at $60 value each

[3]100,000 shares at $42 value each

Cost of debt

$$\$975(1 - 0.09) \text{ or } \$887.25 = \sum_{t=1}^{15} \frac{\$70}{(1 + k_d)^t} + \frac{\$1,000}{(1 + k_d)^{15}}$$

From a trial-and-error method and interpolation, k_d equals 8.36%

$K_d = 8.36\% (1 - 0.46)$

$K_d = 4.51\%$

Cost of preferred stock

$$K_p = \frac{\$7.25}{\$60(1 - 0.05)} = 12.72\%$$

Cost of internal common equity

$$K_c = \frac{\$2.80}{\$42} + 0 = 6.67\%$$

Weighted Cost of Capital

Source of Financing	Cost	Weight	Weighted Costs
Bonds	4.51%	.1322	0.596%
Preferred stock	12.72	.1085	1.381
Common stock	18.45	.7593	14.009
			15.986%

5. Croweger Freight, Inc. maintains a capital mix consisting of 35 percent debt, 15 preferred stock, and 50 percent common equity. The company is considering several investments and needs a weighted marginal cost of capital curve developed to analyze the investments being considered. Retained earnings of $600,000 will be available for these investments. The company's financial analysts have computed the costs of capital for the various sources of financing as follows:

Source	Amount of Capital		Cost
Debt (after-tax)	$ 0	to $500,000	6.5%
	Over	$500,000	7.75%
Preferred stock	0	to $100,000	8.0%
	Over	$100,000	8.5%
Common stock	0	to $600,000	13.0%
	600,000	to $800,000	15.0%
	Over	$800,000	17.0%

Construct the weighted marginal cost of capital curve. (Note: The first level of common ($600,000) represents the internally generated common.)

SOLUTION

First compute the breaks in the curve.

Debt

$$\frac{\$500,000}{0.35} = \$1,428,571.40$$

Preferred stock

$$\frac{\$100,000}{0.15} = \$666,666.67$$

Common equity

$$\frac{\$600,000}{0.50} = \$1,200,000$$

$$\frac{\$800,000}{0.50} = \$1,600,000$$

Weighted Cost of Capital

Source	Amount of Financing	Weight	Cost	Weighted Cost
$0 to $666,666				
Bonds	$ 233,333.33	35%	6.5%	2.275%
Preferred Stock	100,000.00	15	8.0	1.200
Common Equity	333,333.34	50	13.0	6.500
	$ 666,666.67			9.975%
$666,666 to $1,200,000				
Bonds	$ 420,000.00	35%	6.5%	2.275%
Preferred Stock	180,000.00	15	8.5	1.275
Common Equity	600,000.00	50	13.0	6.500
	$1,200,000.00			10.05%

Source	Amount of Financing	Weight	Cost	Weighted Cost
$1,200,001 to $1,428,571				
Bonds	$ 500,000.00	35%	6.5%	2.275%
Preferred Stock	214,285.70	15	8.5	1.275
Common Equity	715,285.70	50	15.0	7.500
	$1,428,571.40			11.05%
$1,428,572 to $1,600,000				
Bonds	$ 560,000.00	35%	7.75%	2.7125%
Preferred Stock	240,000.00	15	8.5	1.2750
Common Equity	800,000.00	50	15.0	7.5000
	$1,600,000.00			11.4875%%
Over $1,600,000				
Bonds	$ 560,000.35	35%	7.75%	2.7125%
Preferred Stock	240,000.15	15	8.5	1.2750
Common Equity	800,000.50	50	17.0	8.5000
	$1,600,001.00			12.4875%%

Weighted Marginal
Cost of Capital Curve

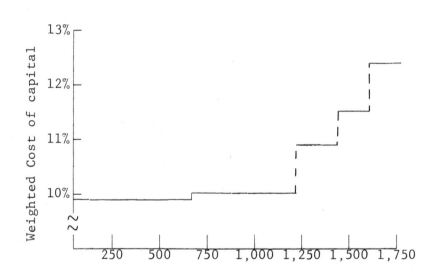

Level of financing ($ thousands)

6. If Croweger's weighted marginal cost of capital curve is the same as the one constructed in problem 5, which of the following investments should Croweger accept?

Investment	Cost	Internal Rate of Returns
A	$ 300,000	15.0%
B	925,000	17.0
C	600,000	10.0
D	500,000	12.5
E	750,000	19.0
Total	$3,075,000	

SOLUTION

First, rank the investments in order of the internal rate of return and then compare the cost of capital at that level of financing.

Investment	Cost	Internal Rate of Return	Weighted Cost of Capital
E	$ 750,000	19.0%	10.05
B	925,000	17.0	
Total	$1,675,000		12.4875
A	300,000	15.0	
Total	$1,975,000		12.4875
D	500,000	12.5	
Total	$2,475,000		12.4875
C	600,000	10.0	
Total	$3,075,000		12.4875

Investments E, B, A, and D would be accepted because the IRR of D is higher than the cost of capital at the level of financing required by the total cost of all the investments.

Self-Tests

True-False

_____ 1. The cost of capital may be defined as the rate of return on investments which causes the price of the firm's common stock to increase.

_____ 2. The level of expected inflation is reflected in the risk premium.

_____ 3. The cost of capital is an appropriate investment criterion only for investments of similar risk level to the existing assets.

_____ 4. Financial risk is the risk that the price of the security may vary significantly.

_____ 5. Only those projects exceeding the highest marginal cost of capital on a cost of capital curve should be accepted.

_____ 6. Investors generally assign a higher risk premium to a seldomly traded stock than they do to a frequently traded stock.

_____ 7. The dividend policy is not relevant to the cost of capital model.

_____ 8. The cost of preferred stock must be adjusted for taxes.

_____ 9. In computing a weighted cost of capital, it is assumed that the company's current capital structure is stable.

_____ 10. Issuance of any new security will cause the firm's weighted cost of capital to increase.

_____ 11. If the cost of capital rises as the level of financing increases, the weighted marginal cost of capital is the appropriate criterion for making investment decisions.

_____ 12. New common stock would be issued only if internal common equity does not provide sufficient equity capital for the amount of investments under consideration.

_____ 13. The only difference in the calculation of internal and external common equity is the price received by the firm from the market.

Multiple Choice

1. What is/are the reason(s) for computing a firm's cost of capital?

   a. To determine the capital structure that has the lowest cost.
   b. To assure the investors that their required rate of return is being met.
   c. To use the cost of capital as an investment criterion.
   d. b and c.
   e. a and c.
   f. a, b, and c.

2. The cost of capital may be defined as:

    a. The rate that must be earned in order to satisfy the
        required rate of return of the firm's investors.
    b. The rate of return on investments at which the price
        of the firm's common stock remains unchanged.
    c. The rate of return on investments which will
        increase the price of the firm's common stock.
    d. a and b.
    e. a and c.

3. What combination of the factors listed below is reflected
   in the risk premium?

                I.   Inflation
               II.   Business risk
              III.   Financial risk
               IV.   Financing level
                V.   Marketability of securities

    a. I, II, III, and V.
    b. II, III, IV, and V.
    c. II, III, and V.
    d. I, II, and III.
    e. All of the factors.

4. All of the following variables are needed in the computation of the cost of debt except:

    a. Market price of debt.
    b. Issuance cost.
    c. Tax rate for the firm.
    d. Growth rate.
    e. Maturity value.

5. Adjustment for taxes is required for which cost?

    a. Cost of preferred stock.
    b. Cost of debt.
    c. Cost of internal common equity.
    d. Cost of external common equity.

Appendix 13A

THE REQUIRED RATE OF RETURN FOR INDIVIDUAL PROJECTS

I.   Required rate of return for individual projects

    A.   The weighted marginal cost of capital, K_0, does not allow for varying levels of project risk. A return-risk line specifies the appropriate required rates of return for investments having different amounts of risk.

    B.   The return-risk line is defined as:

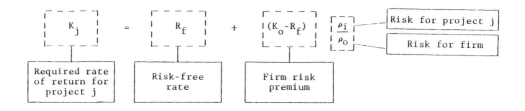

II. The effect of diversification

    A.   Diversification can be used to reduce risk relative to the expected return of a portfolio of assets or to increase the expected return relative to the riskiness of the portfolio of investments.

    B.   The ability to diversify occurs at two levels.

        1.   The firm can diversify its holdings in capital investments.

        2.   The firm's investors can diversify their own investments.

    C.   Perfect markets are assumed to exist whenever (1) information is readily available to all investors at no cost, (2) there are no transaction costs, (3) investment opportunities are readily accessible to all prospective investors, and (4) financial distress and bankruptcy costs are nonexistent.

    D.   Under these assumptions, the appropriate criterion for accepting or rejecting the jth project would be:

        1.   Accept project j if the expected returns exceed the required rate of return, K_j.

$$K_j = R_f + (R_m - R_f)\,\beta_j$$

where R_f = the risk-free rate.

R_m = the return on the market portfolio.

β_j = the volatility of the jth project returns relative to the investor's widely diversified portfolio.

This equation is the <u>capital asset pricing model</u> (CAPM).

E. Limitations of the capital asset pricing model.

   1. The difficulty in determining the relationship between the market returns and all the project returns.

   2. Bankruptcy costs are assumed to equal zero.

Study Problems

1. Hanoverian Manufacturing is evaluating several investments. Hanoverian's overall cost of capital is 12.75% and its average project's standard deviation is 6.5%. If the current risk-free rate is 10.5%, which projects should be accepted?

Project	Expected Return	Standard Deviation
I	19.00%	10.1%
II	17.50	9.8
III	10.88	3.9
IV	12.30	5.7
V	15.60	8.2

SOLUTION

The required rate of return for each project would be:

I. $K_j = 10.5\% + (12.75\% - 10.5\%)\left(\dfrac{10.1\%}{6.5\%}\right)$

   $K_j = 14\%$

II. $K_j = 10.5\% + (12.75\% - 10.5\%)\left(\dfrac{9.8\%}{6.5\%}\right)$

   $K_j = 13.89\%$

III. $K_j = 10.5\% + (12.75\% - 10.5\%)\left(\dfrac{3.9\%}{6.5\%}\right)$

   $K_j = 11.85\%$

171

IV. $K_j = 10.5\% + (12.75\% - 10.5\%) \left(\dfrac{5.7\%}{6.5\%}\right)$

$K_j = 12.47\%$

V. $K_j = 10.5\% + (12.75\% - 10.5\%) \left(\dfrac{8.2\%}{6.5\%}\right)$

$K_j = 13.34\%$

Project	Expected Return	Required Rate of Return	Decision
I	19.00%	14.00%	Accept
II	17.50	13.89	Accept
III	10.88	11.85	Reject
IV	12.30	12.47	Reject
V	15.60	13.34	Accept

2. The management of Capp Corporation is concerned about the effect of a new project on the riskiness of a diversified portfolio. Capp is currently considering the three investments shown below. The risk-free rate is 9%. If the expected return for the market is 12% and its standard deviation is 4%, which investments should be accepted?

Project	Expected Return	Standard Deviation	Correlation with Market Returns
A	19%	9.8%	0.730
B	12	6.7	0.870
C	14	8.0	0.785

SOLUTION

Using the following equation, we get:

$$\begin{bmatrix} \text{required} \\ \text{rate for} \\ \text{project} \\ j \end{bmatrix} = \begin{bmatrix} \text{risk-free} \\ \text{rate} \end{bmatrix} + \begin{bmatrix} \text{risk premium} \\ \text{for a widely} \\ \text{diversified} \\ \text{portfolio} \\ \overline{\text{standard de-}} \\ \text{viation of} \\ \text{the returns} \\ \text{for a widely} \\ \text{diversified} \\ \text{portfolio} \end{bmatrix} \begin{bmatrix} \text{correlation} \\ \text{of projects} \\ \text{returns with} \\ \text{portfolio} \\ \text{returns} \end{bmatrix} \begin{bmatrix} \text{standard} \\ \text{deviation} \\ \text{of the jth} \\ \text{project} \end{bmatrix}$$

The required rate for each project would be

A. $K_j = 9\% + \left(\dfrac{12\% - 9\%}{4\%}\right) (0.73)(9.8\%)$

172

$K_j = 14.37\%$

B. $K_j = 9\% + \left(\dfrac{12\% - 9\%}{4\%}\right)(0.87)(6.7\%)$

$K_j = 13.37\%$

C. $K_j = 9\% + \left(\dfrac{12\% - 9\%}{4\%}\right)(0.785)(8.0\%)$

$K_j = 13.71\%$

Project	Expected Return	Required Rate of Return	Decision
A	19%	14.37%	Accept
B	12	13.37	Reject
D	14	13.71	Accept

3. Wells Mining is considering the investments shown below. A diversified portfolio has an expected return of 10% and a standard deviation of 7%. The rate on government securities is 6.5%. If the capital asset pricing model is used, which projects should management accent?

Investment	Expected Return	Standard Deviation	Beta
A	13%	5.0%	1.35
B	17	8.0	1.78
C	18	8.5	1.83

SOLUTION

$K_j = R_f + (R_m - R_f)\,\beta_j$

where K_j = the required rate of return for investment j,

R_f = the risk-free rate,

R_m = the return on the diversified portfolio,

β_j = the beta for the jth investment,

A. $K_j = 6.5\% + (10\% - 6.5\%)(1.35)$

$K_j = 11.23\%$

B. $K_j = 6.5\% + (10\% - 6.5\%)(1.78)$

$K_j = 12.73\%$

C. $K_j = 6.5\% + (10\% - 6.5\%)(1.83)$

$K_j = 12.91\%$

Project	Expected Return	Required Rate of Return	Decision
A	13%	11.23%	Accept
B	17	12.73	Accept
C	18	12.91	Accept

Self-Tests

True-False

_____ 1. One limitation of the weighted cost of capital is that it does not allow for varying levels of project risk.

_____ 2. The return-risk line takes into account the risk of the project, but not the risk for the firm.

_____ 3. The capital asset pricing model (CAPM) includes the excess return-risk relationship of an individual firm.

_____ 4. Beta measures the volatility of the project returns relative to the investor's widely diversified portfolio.

_____ 5. If a project increases the probability of firm bankruptcy, the CAPM is the appropriate investment criterion.

Multiple Choice

1. Which of the following is a limitation of the return-risk equation?

   a. The assumption of no bankruptcy risk.
   b. The requirement that the existing financial mix remains constant
   c. The standardization of the risk premium relative to the riskiness of the firm's average project.

2. Which of the following is not an assumption of a perfect market?

   a. No transaction costs.
   b. No bankruptcy costs.
   c. No inflation premiums
   d. Free, readily available information.

3. An investment with a beta of 0.80 means that the returns of the investment:

    a. Are more volatile than the market returns.
    b. Are less volatile than the market returns.
    c. Have no correlation with the market returns.
    d. Are perfectly correlated with the market returns.

4. If the capital asset pricing model is used in investment decision making, what risk measure should be used?

    a. Total variability in returns.
    b. Beta.
    c. Standard deviation.
    d. Diversifiable risk.

14

Analysis and Impact of Leverage

Orientation: This chapter focuses on useful aids to the financial manager in his or her determination of the firm's proper financial structure. It includes the definitions of the different kinds of risk, a review of break-even analysis, the concepts of operating leverage, financial leverage, the combination of both leverages, and their effect on EPS (earnings per share).

I. Business risk and financial risk

    A. Risk has been defined as the likely variability associated with expected revenue streams.

        1. Focusing on the financial decision, the variations in the income stream can be attributed to:

            a. The firm's exposure to business risk.

            b. The firm's decision to incur financial risk.

    B. Business risk can be defined as the variability of the firm's expected earnings before interest and taxes (EBIT).

        1. Business risk is measured by the firm's corresponding expected coefficient of variation (i.e., the larger the ratio, the more risk a firm is exposed to).

2.   Dispersion in operating income does not cause business risk. It is the result of several influences, for example, the company's cost structure, product demand characteristics, and intra-industry competition. These influences are a direct result of the firm's investment decision.

C.   Financial risk is a direct result of the firm's financing decision. When the firm is selecting different financial alternatives, financial risk refers to the additional variability in earnings available to the firm's common shareholders and the additional chance of insolvency borne by the common shareholder caused by the use of financial leverage.

1.   Financial leverage is simply the financing of a portion of the firm's assets with securities bearing a fixed (limited) rate of return in hopes of increasing the ultimate return to the common shareholders.

2.   Financial risk is to a large extent passed on to the common shareholders who must bear almost all of the potential inconsistencies of returns to the firm after the deduction of fixed payments.

II.   Break-even analysis

A.   The objective of break-even analysis is to determine the break-even quantity of output by studying the relationships among the firm's cost structure, volume of output, and operating profit.

1.   The break-even quantity of output is the quantity of output (in units) that results in an EBIT level equal to zero.

B.   Use of the model enables the financial officer to:

1.   Determine the quantity of output that must be sold to cover all operating costs.

2.   Calculate the EBIT that will be achieved at various output levels.

C.   Some actual and potential applications of break-even analysis include:

1.   Capital expenditure analysis as a complementary technique to discounted cash flow evaluation models.

2. Pricing policy.

3. Labor contract negotiations.

4. Evaluation of cost structure.

5. The making of financial decisions.

D. Essential elements of the break-even model are:

1. Fixed costs are costs that do not vary in total amount as the sales volume or the quantity of output changes over some relevant range of output. For example, administrative salaries are considered fixed because these salaries are generally the same month after month. Other examples are:

   a. Depreciation.

   b. Insurance premiums.

   c. Property taxes.

   d. Rent.

   The total fixed cost is unchanged regardless of the quantity of product production or sales, although, over some relevant range, these costs may be higher or lower (i.e., in the long run).

2. Variable costs are costs that tend to vary in total as output changes. Variable costs are fixed per unit of output. For example, direct materials are considered a variable cost because they vary with the amount of products produced. Other variable costs are:

   a. Direct labor.

   b. Energy cost associated with the production area.

   c. Packaging.

   d. Freight-out.

   e. Sales commissions.

3. To implement the behavior of the break-even model, it is necessary for the financial manager to:

a. Identify the most relevant output range for his or her planning purposes.

b. Approximate all costs in the semifixed, semivariable range and allocate them to the fixed and variable cost categories.

4. Total revenue and volume of output

a. Total revenue from sales is equal to the price per unit multiplied by the quantity sold.

b. The volume of output is the firm's level from operations and is expressed as sales dollars or a unit quantity.

E. Finding the break-even point

1. The break-even model is just a simple adaptation of the firm's income statement expressed in the following format:

sales - (total variable costs + total fixed costs) = profit

a. Trial and error

(1) Select an arbitrary output level.

(2) Calculate the corresponding EBIT amount.

(3) When EBIT equals zero, the break-even point has been found.

b. Contribution margin analysis

(1) The difference between the unit selling price and the unit variable cost equals the contribution margin.

(2) Then, the fixed cost divided by the contribution margin equals the breakeven quantity in units.

c. Algebraic analysis

(1) Q_B = the break-even level of units sold,
    P = the unit sales price,

F = the total fixed cost for the period,

V = unit variable cost.

(2) Then,

$$Q_B = \frac{F}{P - V}$$

F. The break-even point in sales dollars:

1. Computing a break-even point in terms of sales dollars rather than units of output is convenient, especially if the firm deals with more than one product. Also, if the analyst cannot get unit cost data, he or she can compute a general break-even point in sales dollars by using the firm's annual report.

2. Since variable cost per unit and the selling price per unit are assumed constant, the ratio of total sales to total variable costs (VC/S) is a constant for any level of sales. So, if the break-even level of sales is denoted S*, the corresponding equation is:

$$S* = \frac{F}{1 - \frac{VC}{S}}$$

G. Limitations of break-even analysis:

1. The cost-volume-profit relationship is assumed to be linear.

2. The total revenue curve is presumed to increase linearly with the volume of output.

3. A constant production and sales mix is assumed.

4. The break-even computation is a static form of analysis.

III. Operating Leverage

A. Operating leverage is the responsiveness of a firm's EBIT to fluctuations in sales. Operating leverage results when fixed operating costs are present in the firm's cost structure. It should be noted here that fixed operating costs do not include interest charges incurred from the firm's use of debt financing.

B. The responsiveness of a firm's EBIT to fluctuating sales levels can be measured as follows:

$$\text{degree of operating leverage from the base sales level} = DOL_s = \frac{\% \text{ change in EBIT}}{\% \text{ change in sales}}$$

for example, if DOL_s equals five times, a 10% rise in sales over the coming period will result in a 50% rise in EBIT. (This means of measure also holds true for the negative direction.)

C. If unit costs are available, the DOL_s can be measured by the following formula:

$$DOL_s = \frac{Q(P - V)}{Q(P - V) - F}$$

D. If an analytical income statement is the only thing available, the following formula can be used to produce the same results:

$$DOL_s = \frac{\text{revenue before fixed costs}}{EBIT} = \frac{S - VC}{S - VC - F}$$

E. It should be noted here that the three formulas stated above all produce the same results. But, more important is the understanding that in this example a 1% change in sales will result in a 5% change in EBIT.

F. Implications of operating leverage:

   1. At each point above the break-even level the degree of operating leverage decreases (i.e., the greater the sales level, the lower the DOL_s).

   2. At the break-even level of sales the degree of operating leverage is undefined.

   3. Operating leverage is present anytime the percentage change in EBIT divided by the percentage change in sales is greater than one.

   4. The degree of operating leverage can be attributed to the business risk that a firm faces.

IV. Financial leverage

A. Financial leverage, as defined earlier, is the practice of financing a portion of the firm's assets

181

with securities bearing a fixed rate of return in hopes of increasing the ultimate return to the common stockholders. To see if financial leverage has been used to benefit the common shareholders, the discussion here will focus on the responsiveness of the company's earning per share (EPS) to changes in its EBIT. It should be noted here that not all analysts rely exclusively on this type of relationship. In fact, the weakness of such a contention will be examined in the following chapter.

B. The firm is using financial leverage and is exposing its owners to financial risk when:

$$\frac{\% \text{ change in EPS}}{\% \text{ change in EBIT}} \text{ is greater than } 1.00$$

C. A precise measure of the firm's use of financial leverage can be expressed in the following relationship:

$$\begin{array}{l}\text{degree of financial} \\ \text{leverage from the} \\ \text{base EBIT level}\end{array} = DFL_{EBIT} = \frac{\% \text{ change in EPS}}{\% \text{ change in EBIT}}$$

1. As was the case with operating leverage, the degree of financial leverage concept can be in the negative direction as well as in the positive direction.

2. You should also note that the greater the degree of financial leverage, the greater the fluctuations (positive or negative) in EPS.

D. An easier way of measuring the degree of financial leverage that produces the same results without computing percentage changes in EBIT and EPS is:

$$DFL_{EBIT} = \frac{EBIT}{EBIT - I}$$

where I is the sum of all fixed financing costs.

V. Combining operating and financial leverage

A. Since changes in sales revenues cause greater changes in EBIT, and if the firm chooses to use financial leverage, changes in EBIT turn into larger variations in both EPS and EAC (earnings available to common shareholders). Then, combining operating and financial leverage causes rather large variations in EPS.

B. One way to measure the combined leverage can be expressed as:

$$\text{degree of combined leverage from the base sales level} = DCL_s = \frac{\%\ \text{change in EPS}}{\%\ \text{change in sales}}$$

If the DCL_s is equal to 5.0 times, then it is important to understand that a 1% change in sales will result in a 5% change in EPS.

C. The degree of combined leverage is actually the product of the two independent leverage measures. Thus, we have:

$$DCL_s = (DOL_s) \times (DFL_{EBIT})$$

D. As you might have guessed, there is still another way to compute DCL_s. It is a more direct way in that no percentage fluctuations or separate leverage values have to be determined. You need only substitute the appropriate values into the following equation:

$$DCL_s = \frac{Q(P - V)}{Q(P - V) - F - I}$$

All variables have previously been defined.

E. Implications of combining operating and financial leverage

   1. The total risk exposure that the firm assumes can be managed by combining operating and financial leverage in different degrees.

   2. Knowledge of the various leverage measures that have been examined here aids the financial officer in his or her determination of the proper level of overall risk that should be accepted.

Study Problems

1. Columbia Products will earn $231,000 next year after taxes. Sales for Columbia will be $4,400,000. The firm operates in modern facilities near Columbia, South Carolina. The firm specializes in the production of furniture for lawyers' offices, accountants' offices, and college dormitories. The average unit sells for $220 and has an associated variable cost per unit of $165. Columbia experiences a 30 percent tax rate.

183

(a) What will fixed costs (in total) be next year for Columbia?

(b) Calculate Columbia's break-even point both in units and dollars.

(c) Generate the analytical income statement at the breakeven level of sales dollars.

SOLUTION

(a) All that we have to do here is use our knowledge of the break-even model and the analytical income statement model (both are discussed in detail in Chapter 14 of your text). The calculations follow:

$$\{(P \cdot Q) - [V \cdot Q + (F)]\} \ (1-T) = \$231,000$$

$$[(\$4,400,000) - (\$3,300,000) - F] \ (.7) = \$231,000$$

$$(\$1,100,000 - F) \ (.7) = \$231,000$$

$$\$770,000 - .7F = \$231,000$$

$$.7F = \$539,000$$

$$F = \underline{\$770,000}$$

(b)
$$Q_B = \frac{F}{P-V} = \frac{\$770,000}{\$55} = 14,000 \text{ units}$$

$$S* = \frac{F}{1 - \frac{VC}{S}} = \frac{\$770,000}{1 - .75} = \frac{\$770,000}{.25}$$

$$= \$3,080,000$$

We have shown that the firm will break even (i.e., EBIT= 0) when it sells 14,000 units. With a selling price of $220 per unit the break-even sales level is $3,080,000.

(c) The analytical income statement at the break-even level of sales would appear as follows:

Sales	$3,080,000
Variable costs	2,310,000
Revenue before fixed costs	$ 770,000
Fixed costs	770,000
EBIT	$ -0-

2. Woody's Carry-Out Pizza expects to earn $16,000 next year before interest and taxes. Sales will be $130,000. The store is the only pizza parlor near the fraternity-row district of Gardiner University. The owner, Eric Nemeth, makes only one variety and size of pizza (the House Special) and it sells for $10. The variable cost per pizza is $6. Woody's Carry-Out Pizza experiences a 48% tax rate.

    (a) What are the pizza parlor's fixed costs expected to be next year?

    (b) Calculate the parlor's break-even point in units and dollars.

SOLUTION

    (a) To compute fixed costs:

$$S - (VC + FC) = EBIT$$
$$\$130,000/\$10 = 13,000 \text{ units sold}$$
$$\$130,000 - [(13,000)(\$6) + X] = \$16,000$$
$$\$130,000 - \quad \$78,000 - X \quad = \$16,000$$
$$X \quad = \$36,000$$

    (b) First, the break-even point in units:

$$Q_B = \frac{F}{P - V} = \frac{\$36,000}{\$10 - \$6} = 9,000 \text{ units}$$

Then, the break-even point in dollars:

$$S^* = \frac{F}{1-VC/S} = \frac{\$36,000}{1 - \dfrac{\$78,000}{\$130,000}} = \$90,000$$

3. The ESM Corporation projects that next year its fixed costs will total $120,000. Its only product sells for $17 per unit, of which $9 is a variable cost. The management of ESM is considering the purchase of a new machine that will lower the variable cost per unit to $7. The new machine, however, will add to fixed costs through an increase in depreciation expense.

    (a) How large can the addition to fixed costs be in order to keep the firm's break-even point in units produced and sold unchanged?

SOLUTION

    (a) Compute the present level of break-even output:

$$X = \frac{F}{P - V}$$

$$\frac{\$120,000}{17-9} \quad \frac{\$120,000}{8} = 15,000 \text{ units}$$

Compute the new level of fixed costs at the break-even output:

$$F + (7)(15,000) = (17)(15,000)$$

$$F + 105,000 = 255,000$$

$$F = \$150,000$$

Compute the addition to fixed costs:

$$\$150,000 - \$120,000 = \underline{\$30,000 \text{ addition}}$$

4. The management of ESM Corporation decided not to purchase the new piece of equipment. Using the existing cost structure, calculate the degree of operating leverage at 35,000 units of output.

SOLUTION

$$\text{DOL at 35,000 units} = \frac{35,000(\$17 - \$9)}{35,000(\$17 - \$9) - \$120,000}$$

$$= \frac{\$280,000}{\$160,000} = 1.75 \text{ times}$$

This indicates, for example, that a 10% increase in sales for the ESM Corporation will result in a 17.5% increase in EBIT, provided the assumptions of cost-volume-profit analysis hold.

5. The Moose Hobby Company manufactures a full line of gold-plated model airplanes. The average selling price of a finished unit is $25. The associated variable cost is $15 per unit. Fixed costs for the company average $70,000 per year.

   (a) What would be the company's profit or loss at the following units of production sold? 5,000; 7,000; 9,000 units.

   (b) Find the degree of operating leverage for the production and sales given in part (a) above.

SOLUTION

(a) The company's profit or loss:

	@ 5,000 units	@ 7,000 units	@ 9,000 units
Sales (P X Q)	$125,000	$175,000	$225,000
- VC (VC/unit X Q)	75,000	105,000	135,000
- FC	70,000	70,000	70,000
Profit	($ 20,000)	-0-	$ 20,000

(b) The degree of operating leverage at the different levels of output

$$DOL_S = \frac{Q(P-V)}{Q(P-V) - F}$$

DOL at 5,000 units $= \dfrac{5,000(\$25-\$15)}{5,000(\$25-\$15) - \$70,000}$

$$= \frac{\$50,000}{-20,000} = -2.5 \text{ times}$$

DOL at 7,000 units $= \dfrac{7,000(\$25-\$15)}{7,000(\$25-\$15) - \$70,000}$

$$= \frac{\$50,000}{0} = \text{undefined}$$

DOL at 9,000 units $= \dfrac{9,000(\$25-\$15)}{9,000(\$25-\$15) - \$70,000}$

$$= \frac{\$90,000}{\$20,000} = 4.5 \text{ times}$$

6. An analytical income statement for the D. A. Bauer Corporation is shown below. It is based on an output level of 69,000 units.

Sales	$1,035,000
Variable costs	552,000
Revenue before fixed costs	$ 483,000
Fixed costs	183,000
EBIT	$ 300,000
Interest expense	80,000
Earnings before taxes	$ 220,000
Taxes	110,000
Net Income	$ 110,000

(a) Calculate the degree of operating leverage at this output level.

(b) Calculate the degree of financial leverage at this level of output.

(c) Determine the combined leverage effect at this output level.

SOLUTION

(a) $$\text{DOL at 69,000 units} = \frac{69,000(\$15-\$8)}{69,000(\$15-\$8) - \$183,000}$$

$$= 1.61 \text{ times}$$

(b) $$\text{DFL at EBIT of } \$300,000 = \frac{\$300,000}{\$300,000 - \$80,000}$$

$$= 1.364 \text{ times}$$

(c)

$$\text{Combined leverage effect} = \frac{69,000(\$15-\$8)}{69,000(\$15-\$8)-\$183,000-\$80,000}$$

$$= 2.195 \text{ times}$$

Notice that the combined leverage effect is the product of the degrees of operating and financial leverage. A 1% increase in sales for D. A. Bauer Corporation would be magnified into a 2.195% increase in net income because of the combined leverage effect.

7. You are supplied with the following analytical income statement for C. J. Omlette Shoppe. It reflects last year's operations.

Sales	$75,000
Variable costs	37,000
Revenue before fixed cost	$38,000
Fixed costs	19,000
EBIT	$19,000
Interest Expense	7,000
Earnings before taxes	$12,000
Taxes	6,000
Net Income	$ 6,000

(a) What is the degree of operating leverage at this level of output?

(b) What is the degree of financial leverage?

(c) What is the degree of combined leverage?

(d) If sales should increase by 30%, by what percent would earnings before interest and taxes increase?

(e) What is C. J.'s break-even point in sales dollars?

SOLUTION

(a) The degree of operating leverage:

$$\text{DOL at } \$75{,}000 = \frac{\text{Revenue before fixed costs}}{\text{EBIT}} = \frac{S-VC}{S-VC-F}$$

$$= \frac{\$38{,}000}{\$19{,}000} = 2 \text{ times}$$

(b) The degree of financial leverage:

$$\text{DFL at } \$19{,}000 \text{ EBIT} = \frac{\text{EBIT}}{\text{EBIT} - I} = \frac{\$19{,}000}{\$19{,}000-\$7{,}000}$$

$$= 1.58 \text{ times}$$

(c) The degrees of combined leverage:

$$\text{DCL}_S = (\text{DOL}_S)(\text{DFL}_{EBIT}) = (2)(1.58) = 3.16 \text{ times}$$

(d) An increase in sales of 30% would result in a 60% increase in EBIT.

(e) Break-even level in sales dollars:

$$S^* = \frac{F}{1 - VC/S} = \frac{\$19{,}000}{1 - \dfrac{\$37{,}000}{\$75{,}000}} = \$37{,}500$$

8. Delphi Parts produces three different lines of boating accessories for several Florida boat manufacturers. The product lines are numbered. Their sales mix and contribution margin ratios appear in the chart below.

PRODUCT LINE	% OF TOTAL SALES	CONTRIBUTION MARGIN RATIO
1	17	44%
2	53	30%
3	30	22%

Forecasted sales for the coming year are $1,200,000. The firm's fixed costs are $300,000.

(a) Prepare a table showing sales, total variable costs, and the total contribution margin (dollars) associated with each line.

(b) What is the aggregate contribution margin ratio indicative of this mix?

(c) What is the breakeven point in dollars for this particular sales mix?

SOLUTION

(a)

Product	1	2	3	Total
Sales	204,000	636,000	360,000	1,200,000
VC*	114,240	445,200	280,800	840,240
Contr. Margin	89,760	190,800	79,200	359,760

(b)

Contr. Margin Ratio	44%	30%	22%	30.0%

(c) $S* = FC/(1 - VC/S) = 300,000/.300$

$S* = \$1,000,000$

9. If Delphi (see problem 14-8) decides to change the sales mix for the next year to 40%, 33%, and 27% for products 1, 2, and 3, respectively, how will this affect their breakeven point in dollars? Which mix do you think they would prefer?

SOLUTION

Product Line	% Total Sales	Contr. Margin Ratio
1	40	44%
2	33	30%
3	27	22%

Overall Contr. Ratio Margin = $.40(44) + .33(30) + .27(22)$

$= 33.4\%$

$S* = 300,000/.334 = \$898,204$

This second mix would be preferred since the overall contribution margin ratio is higher and the breakeven point in dollars is now lower. The contribution to fixed costs is higher with the second mix.

Self-Test

TRUE-FALSE

_____ 1. Dispersion in operating income causes business risk.

_____ 2. Your firm adds to its facilities a completely automated product line. This will have no effect on the break-even point (in units of output).

_____ 3. Variable costs are fixed per unit of output but vary in total as output changes.

_____ 4. Your firm expects a 7% increase in sales for the next year. The degree of operating leverage will decrease for your firm.

_____ 5. If the degree of operating leverage increases and if all else remains unchanged, the degree of combined leverage will decrease.

_____ 6. When the firm uses more financial leverage, its stockholders expect a greater return.

_____ 7. The break-even model enables the financial officer to determine the quality of output that must be sold to cover all operating costs.

_____ 8. If EBIT were to remain constant while the firm incurred additional interest expense, the degree of financial leverage would increase.

_____ 9. If future sales are expected to increase, then decreasing the degree of operating leverage would be a wise decision.

_____ 10. Financial risk can be defined as the variability of the firm's expected earnings before interest and taxes (EBIT).

_____ 11. The incurrence of fixed operating costs in the firm's income stream is referred to as financial leverage.

_____ 12. Break-even analysis is a long-run concept since all costs are variable in the long-run.

_____ 13. Operating leverage is the responsiveness of the firm's EBIT to fluctuations in profit.

_____ 14. Earnings per share is the most appropriate criterion for all financing decisions.

_____ 15. The decision to use financial leverage by the firm magnifies its variation in earnings per share, compared to the use of no financial leverage.

_____ 16. Variable costs are fixed per unit of output.

_____ 17. Fixed costs per unit vary with units of output.

_____ 18. Combining operating and financial leverage magnifies variations in earnings per share.

_____ 19. A firm faces a greater chance of insolvency with an increase in the use of financial leverage (other factors held constant).

_____ 20. The decision to use debt or preferred stock in the financial structure of a corporation means that those who own the common shares are exposed to financial risk.

_____ 21. The contribution margin is the difference between the unit selling price and the unit fixed cost.

MULTIPLE CHOICE

1. Which of the following is <u>not</u> a limitation of break-even analysis?

    a. The price of the product is assumed to be constant.
    b. In multiple product firms, the product mix is assumed to be constant.
    c. It provides a method for analyzing operating leverage.
    d. Variable costs per unit are assumed to be constant.

2. Which of the following is not considered a fixed cost?

    a. Depreciation.
    b. Rent.
    c. Electricity.
    d. Administrative salaries.

3. At each point above the break-even level the degree of operating leverage

   a. Increases; that is, the greater the sales level, the lower the DOL_s.
   b. Decreases; that is, the greater the sales level, the lower the DOL_s.
   c. Increases; that is, the greater the sales level, the greater the DOL_s.
   d. Decreases; that is, the greater the sales level, the greater the DOL_s.

4. The greater the degree of financial leverage, the greater the fluctuation in

   a. Variable costs.
   b. Administrative salaries.
   c. Earnings per share.
   d. None of the above.

5. At the break-even level of sales the degree of operating leverage is

   a. zero.
   b. undefined.
   c. a positive number.
   d. not enough information is given.

6. An operating leverage factor of 8.00 indicates that if sales increase by

   a. 1%, EBIT will increase by 1%.
   b. 1%, EBIT will increase by 8%.
   c. 8%, EBIT will fall by 1%.
   d. 8%, EBIT will rise by 8%.

7. In the context of break-even point in sales dollars, if the variable cost per unit rises and if all other variables remain constant, the break-even level of sales will

   a. Fall.
   b. Rise.
   c. Stay the same.
   d. Either a or c.

8. The combined effect of financial and operating leverage is

   a. The sum of the degree of financial leverage and the degree of operating leverage.
   b. The product of the two degrees.
   c. The product of the degrees minus the sum of the degrees.
   d. None of the above.

9. The firm is exposing itself to financial risk when its % change in EPS ÷ % change in EBIT is:

   a. less than 1.
   b. greater than 1.
   c. equal to 1.
   d. between 0 and 1.

10. Given that the degree of operating leverage is 10 and sales over the coming period are expected to increase by 5%, then % change in EBIT would be:

    a. 2%.
    b. 5%.
    c. 2.5%.
    d. none of the above.

11. A firm that incurs a low level of fixed operating costs might prudently use:

    a. a low degree of financial leverage.
    b. a high degree of financial leverage.
    c. a low degree of combined leverage.
    d. none of the above.

12. As the firm's sales revenue increases over time,

    a. it can lessen its business risks.
    b. it can lessen its operating leverage.
    c. both a and b.
    d. none of the above.

13. A combined leverage measure of 6.5 indicates that:

    a. a 1% increase in sales would increase EPS by 6.5%.
    b. a 1% increase in sales would increase EBIT by 6.5%.
    c. a 1% increase in EPS would increase sales by 6.5%.
    d. a 1% increase in EBIT would increase sales by 6.5%.

14. The practice of financing a portion a firm's assets with securities bearing a fixed rate of return in hopes of increasing the ultimate return to shareholders refers to:

   a. Operating leverage.
   b. Financial leverage.
   c. Breakeven sales level.

15. The selling price of a product is $25 and the unit variable cost is $17. If a firm's fixed costs are $20,000, what is the breakeven level in units:

   a. 800 units.
   b. 2000 units.
   c. 2500 units.
   d. 4300 units.

16. Business risk is the residual effect of:

   a. The company's cost structure.
   b. Product demand characteristics.
   c. Intra-industry competitive position.
   d. All of the above.
   e. None of the above.

17. The breakeven model assumes that if sales increase by 10% variable costs:

   a. Remain unchanged.
   b. Rise by 10%.
   c. Rise by 20%.
   d. The breakeven model makes no assumptions about variable costs and sales.

15

Planning the Firm's Financing Mix

Orientation: This chapter concentrates on the way the firm arranges its sources of funds. The cost of capital-capital structure argument is highlighted. A moderate view on the effect of financial leverage use on the composite cost of capital is adopted. Later, techniques useful to the financial officer faced with the determination of an appropriate financing mix are described.

I.   Introduction

    A.   A distinction can be made between the terms financial structure and capital structure.

        1.   Financial structure is the mix of all items that appear on the right-hand side of the firm's balance sheet.

        2.   Capital structure is the mix of the long-term, sources of funds used by the firm.

        3.   In this chapter we do <u>not</u> dwell on the question of dealing with an appropriate maturity composition of the firm's sources of funds. Our main focus is on capital structure management i.e., determining the proper proportions relative to the total in which the permanent forms of financing should be used.

    B.   The <u>objective</u> of capital structure management is to mix the permanent sources of funds in a manner that will maximize the company's common stock price. This will minimize the firm's composite cost of capital. This proper mix of funds sources is referred to as the <u>optimal capital structure</u>.

II. Capital structure theory

A. The cost of capital-capital structure argument may be characterized by this question:

1. Can the firm affect its overall cost of funds, either favorably or unfavorably, by varying the mixture of financing sources used?

B. The argument deals with the postulated effect of the use of financial leverage on the overall cost of capital of the company.

C. If the firm's cost of capital can be affected by the degree to which it uses financial leverage, then capital structure management is an important subset of business financial management.

D. The analytical discussion in Chapter 15 revolves around a simplified version of the basic dividend valuation model. Recall that the basic dividend valuation model can be expressed as:

$$P_0 = \sum_{t=1}^{\infty} \frac{D_t}{(1 + K_c)^t}$$

where $P_0 =$ the current price of the firm's common stock,

$D_t =$ the cash dividend per share expected by investors during period t,

$K_c =$ the cost of common equity capital.

1. If it is assumed that (1) cash dividends will <u>not</u> change over the infinite holding period and that (2) the firm retains none of its current earnings, then the cash dividend flowing to investors can be viewed as a level payment over an infinite holding period.

2. Under these conditions, the basic dividend valuation model reduces to the equation noted below, where E_t represents earnings per share during the time period t:

$$P_0 = \frac{D_t}{K_c} = \frac{E_t}{K_c}$$

197

3. The various capital structure theories discussed in Chapter 15 use the above equation in the context of a partial equilibrium analysis in order to assess the impact of leverage use on common stock price.

III. Capital structure theory: The independence hypothesis

A. According to this position, made famous by Professors Franco Modigliani and Merton H. Miller, in a setting in which business income is not subject to taxation (and, thus, the deductibility of interest expense is irrelevant for valuation purposes) the firm's composite cost of capital, K_0, and common stock price, P_0, are both <u>independent</u> of the degree to which the firm chooses to use (or avoid) financial leverage.

B. This means that the total market value of the firm's outstanding securities (taken to be the market value of debt plus the market value of common stock) is <u>unaffected</u> by the manner in which the right-hand side of the balance sheet is arranged.

C. The independence hypothesis rests upon what is called the <u>net operating income</u> (NOI) <u>approach to valuation</u>. When corporate income is not taxed, this methodology arrives at the market value of the firm by capitalizing (discounting) the firm's expected net operating income stream. The division of that income stream to investors (either debt or equity) is a mere detail that does not affect enterprise value.

D. In this framework, the use of a greater degree of financial leverage may result in greater earnings and dividends, but the firm's cost of common equity will rise at precisely the same rate as the earnings and dividends. This means that the firm's common stock price is unaffected by the use of financial leverage over all degrees of leverage use.

E. This viewpoint is illustrated in Figures 15.1 and 15.2. Figure 15.1 shows that the weighted cost of capital, K_0, is independent of the degree of financial leverage used. The use of more debt would cause the cost of common equity to rise, resulting in exactly the same overall cost of capital that persisted before more debt was, in fact, used. Figure 15.2 shows that stock price, P_0, is not influenced by the degree of financial leverage used.

IV. Capital structure theory: The dependence hypothesis

A.   This position is at the opposite pole from the previously outlined independence hypothesis. The dependence hypothesis suggests that both the weighted cost of capital, K_0 and the firm's common stock price, P_0, are affected by the firm's use of financial leverage.

B.   At this extreme, no matter how modest or excessive the firm's use of debt financing, both its cost of debt capital, K_d, and cost of equity capital, K_c, will not be affected by capital structure adjustments.

C.   So, the cost of debt is less than the cost of common equity, which implies that greater financial leverage use will lower the firm's weighted cost of capital, K_0, indefinitely. Further, greater use of debt financing will have a favorable effect on the firm's stock price.

D.   The dependence hypothesis rests upon what is called the net income (NI) approach to valuation. Both the NOI model and the NI model are illustrated at the end of this Study Guide chapter in the first study problem. You should be familiar with their structure, assumptions, and implications.

E.   The dependence hypothesis viewpoint is shown in Figures 15.3 and 15.4. Notice in Figure 15.3 that the firm's cost of capital, K_0 decreases as the debt-to-equity ratio increases. Figure 15.4 shows that according to this position, the common stock price rises with increased leverage use. The implication is that the firm should use as much financial leverage as is possible.

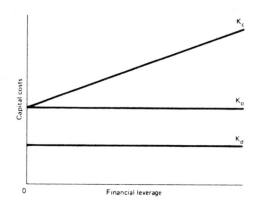

Figure 15.1
Capital Costs and Financial Leverage: No Taxes
The Independence Hypothesis (NOI Theory)

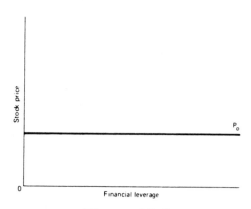

Figure 15.2
Stock Price and Financial Leverage: No Taxes
The Independence Hypothesis (NOI Theory)

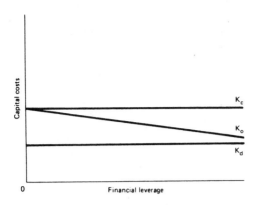

Figure 15.3
Capital Costs and Financial Leverage: No Taxes
The Dependence Hypothesis (NI Theory)

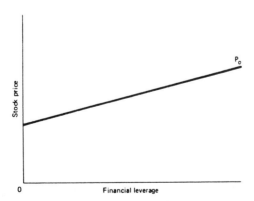

Figure 15.4
Stock Price and Financial Leverage: No Taxes
The Dependence Hypothesis (NI Theory)

V. Capital structure theory: A moderate position

   A. The moderate position on capital structure impor-
      tance admits to the facts that (1) interest expense
      is tax deductible in the world of corporate activity
      and (2) the probability of the firm's suffering
      bankruptcy costs is directly related to the com-
      pany's use of financial leverage.

   B. When interest expense is tax deductible, the _sum_ of
      the cash flows that the firm could pay to _all_
      contributors of corporate capital (debt investors
      and equity investors) is affected by its financing
      mix. This is _not_ the case when an environment of
      corporate taxation is presumed.

      1. A dollar amount labeled the _tax shield on_
         interest may be calculated as:

         Tax shield = $r_d(M)(t)$

         where r_d = the interest rate paid on
                         outstanding debt,

                 M = the principal amount of the debt,

                 t = the firm's tax rate.

      2. The moderate position presents the view that
         the tax shield must have value in the market-
         place. After all, the government's take is
         decreased and the investor's take is increased
         because of the deductibility of interest
         expense.

      3. Therefore, according to this position, finan-
         cial leverage affects firm value and it must
         also affect the cost of corporate capital.

   C. To use too much financial leverage, however, would
      be imprudent. It seems reasonable to offer that the
      probability that the firm will be unable to meet the
      financial obligations contained in its debt con-
      tracts will increase the more the firm uses leverage-
      inducing instruments in its capital structure
      (debt). The likelihood of firm failure, then,
      carries with it certain costs (bankruptcy costs)
      that rise as leverage use increases. There will be
      some point at which the expected cost of default
      will be large enough to outweigh the tax shield
      advantage of debt financing. At that point the firm
      will turn to common equity financing.

D. Figure 15.5 depicts the moderate view on capital
    structure importance. This view of the cost of
    capital-capital structure argument produces a
    saucer-shaped or U-shaped average cost of capital
    curve. In Figure 15.5 the firm's optimal range of
    financial leverage use lies between points A and B.
    It would be imprudent for the firm to use additional
    financial leverage beyond point B because (1) the
    average cost of capital would be higher than it has
    to be and (2) the firm's common stock price would be
    lower than it has to be. Therefore, we can say that
    the degree of financial leverage use signified by
    point B represents the firm's <u>debt capacity</u>.

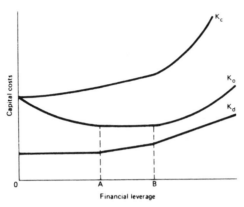

Figure 15.5
Capital Costs and Financial Leverage: The Moderate
View Which Considers Taxes and Financial Distress

E. We conclude that the determination of the firm's
    financing mix <u>is</u> centrally important to both the
    financial manager and the firm's owners.

VI. Basic tools of capital structure management

A. Recall that the use of financial leverage has two
    effects on the earnings stream flowing to the firm's
    common stockholders: (1) the added variability in
    the earnings per share (EPS) stream that accompanies
    the use of fixed-charge securities and (2) the level
    of EPS at a given earnings before interest and taxes
    level (EBIT) associated with a specific capital
    structure. The first effect is quantified by the
    degree of financial leverage measure discussed in
    Chapter 14. The second effect is analyzed by means
    of what is generally referred to as <u>EBIT-EPS</u>
    analysis.

B. The objective of EBIT-EPS analysis is to find the EBIT level that will equate EPS regardless of the financing plan chosen (from among two plans) by the financial manager.

1. A graphic analysis or an algebraic analysis can be used.

2. By allowing for sinking fund payments, the analysis can focus upon uncommitted earnings per share (UEPS).

3. Study problems 2 and 3 at the end of this chapter illustrate the nature of EBIT-EPS analysis.

4. EBIT-EPS analysis considers only the level of the earnings stream and ignores the variability (riskiness) in it. In other words, this tool of capital structure management disregards the implicit costs of debt financing. Therefore, it must be used with caution and in conjunction with other basic tools of capital structure management.

C. Comparative leverage ratios provide another tool of capital structure management. This involves the computation of various balance sheet leverage ratios and coverage ratios. Information for the latter comes essentially from the income statement. The ratios that would exist under alternative financing plans can then be computed and examined for their suitableness to management.

D. The use of industry norms in conjunction with comparative leverage ratios can aid the financial manager in arriving at an appropriate financing mix. Industry norms can be thought of as standards for comparison. We recognize that industry groupings contain firms whose basic business risk may differ widely. Nevertheless, corporate financial analysts, investment bankers, commercial loan officers, and bond rating agencies rely on industry classes in order to compute such "normal" ratios. Since so many observers are interested in industry standards, the financial officer must be too.

E. Finally, the financial officer can study the projected impact of capital structure decisions on corporate cash flows. This is often called cash flow analysis or the study of company-wide cash flows. This involves the preparation of a series of cash budgets under (1) different economic conditions and (2) different rent capital structures. The net cash flows under these different situations can be examined to determine if the financing requirements expose the firm to such a high degree of default risk that it is unbearable. According to this tool, the appropriate level of financial leverage use is reached when the chance of running out of cash is exactly equal to that which management will assume. An underlying assumption is that management's risk-bearing preferences are conditioned by the investing marketplace.

VII. A glance at actual capital structure management

A. The opinions and practices of financial executives reinforce the major topics covered in this chapter. Most senior financial officers, for example, <u>do</u> believe there is an optimum capital structure for the corporation.

B. <u>Target debt ratios</u> are widely used by financial officers. Surveys indicate that the firm's actual target debt ratio is affected by several factors including (1) the firm's ability to adequately meet its financing charges, (2) maintaining a desired bond rating, (3) providing an adequate borrowing reserve, and (4) exploiting the perceived advantages of financial leverage. In practice the firm's <u>own management group and staff of analysts</u> seem to be the most important influence on actually setting the target debt ratio.

C. In this chapter we defined <u>debt capacity</u> as the maximum proportion of debt that the firm can include in its capital structure and still maintain its lowest composite cost of capital. Executives operationalize this concept in different ways. The most popular approach is to define the firm's debt capacity as a target percent of total capitalization (i.e., total long-term debt divided by the sum of all long-term debt, preferred equity, and common equity).

D. In the opinion of your authors, the single most important factor that should affect the firm's financing mix is the underlying nature of the business in which it operates. This means the firm's <u>business risk</u> must be carefully assessed. Recall that business risk was defined in Chapter 14. This means the firm's capital structure cannot be properly designed without a thorough understanding of its commercial (business) strategy.

1.   The Columbia Camera Company has $10,000,000 of net operating earnings. In its capital structure, $14,500,000 worth of debt is outstanding, with an interest of 12 percent. The debt is selling in the marketplace at its book value. Parts (a) and (b) assume that there is no tax on corporate income.

(a)   According to the NOI valuation method, compute the total value of the firm and the implied equity-capitalization rate. Assume an implied overall capitalization rate, k_0, of 20 percent.

(b)   Compute the total value of the firm and the implied overall capitalization rate, k_0, according to the dependence hypothesis, (NI theory) capitalization model. Assume an equity-capitalization rate, k_c, of 16 percent.

(c)   Now allow for the existence of a federal tax on corporate income at a 53 percent rate. Calculate the value of the firm's tax shield.

SOLUTION

(a)
0	Net operating earnings	$10,000,000
k_0	Overall capitalization rate	0.20
V^0	Total value of the firm	$50,000,000
B	Market value of debt	−14,500,000
S	Market value of stock	$35,500,000

$$k_c = \frac{0 - I}{K} = \frac{\$10,000,000 - \$1,740,000}{\$35,500,000} = 23.27\%$$

where   I = interest expense

(b)
$$
\begin{aligned}
0 &= \$10,000,000 \\
I &= \underline{\quad 1,740,000} \\
E &= \$\ 8,260,000 \\
k_c &= \quad\quad 0.25 \\
S &= \overline{\$33,040,000} \\
B &= \underline{\quad 14,500,000} \\
V &= \$47,540,000
\end{aligned}
$$

$$k_0 = \frac{O}{V} = \frac{\$10,000,000}{\$47,540,000} = 21.03\%$$

(c)   Tax shield = $r_d(M)(t)$

$$
\begin{aligned}
&= (0.12)(14,500,000)(0.53) \\
&= \underline{\$922,200}
\end{aligned}
$$

2. E. Wrok and Associates, Inc., are planning to open a small manufacturing corporation. The company will manufacture a full line of solar-energized home products. The investors of the company have proposed two financing plans. Plan I is an all common equity alternative. Under this plan 200,000 common shares will be sold to net the firm $20 per share. Financial leverage is stipulated in Plan II and 100,000 shares will be sold. A debt issue with a 30-year maturity period will be privately placed. The interest rate on the debt issue will be 18 percent while the principal borrowed will amount to $2,000,000. The corporate tax rate is 50 percent.

(a) Find the EBIT indifference level associated with the two financing proposals.

(b) Prepare an analytical income statement that proves EPS will be the same regardless of the plan chosen at the EBIT level found in part (a).

(c) If a detailed financial analysis projects that long-term EBIT will always be close to $100,000 annually, which plan would be chosen? Why?

SOLUTION

(a) In the following equation, E = EBIT.

$$\frac{(E - \$0)(1 - 0.5) - 0}{200,000} = \frac{(E - \$360,000)(1 - 0.5) - 0}{100,000}$$

$$\frac{0.5E}{200,000} = \frac{0.5E - \$180,000}{100,000}$$

$$\$50,000E = 100,000E - \$36,000,000,000$$

$$E = \underline{\$720,000}$$

(b) Analytical Income Statement

	With C/S Financing	Financing With C/S and Debt
EBIT	$720,000	$720,000
Less: Interest Expense	0	360,000
Earnings before taxes	$720,000	$360,000
Less: Taxes @ 50%	360,000	180,000
Earnings available to common	$360,000	$180,000
C/S Outstanding	200,000	100,000
EPS	$1.80	$1.80

(3) Plan II, because at any level above the indifference point, the more heavily levered financing plan will generate a higher EPS.

3. Albina's Ice Cream Factory's capital structure for the past year of operations is shown below:

First Mortgage bonds at 15%	$ 4,000,000
Debentures at 17%	3,500,000
Common stock (1,500,000 shares)	10,500,000
Retained earnings	2,000,000
Total	$20,000,000

The federal income tax rate is 50%. Albina's Ice Cream Factory, home-based in San Antonio, wants to raise an additional $1,500,000 to open new facilities in Houston and Dallas. The firm can accomplish this via two alternatives. That is, it can sell a new issue of 20-year debentures with 18 percent interest; alternatively, 30,000 new shares of common stock can be sold to the public to net the ice cream factory $50 per share. A recent study performed by an outside consulting organization projected Albina's Ice Cream's long-term EBIT level at approximately $13,575,000.

(a) Find the indifference level of EBIT (with regard to earnings per share) between the suggested financing plans.

(b) Which alternative do you recommend that Albina's Ice Cream Factory pursue?

SOLUTION

(a) In the following equations, E = EBIT

$$\frac{(E - \$1,195,000)(0.5)}{1,530,000} = \frac{(E - \$1,465,000)(0.5)}{1,500,000}$$

$$\frac{0.5E - \$597,500}{153} = \frac{0.5E - \$732,500}{150}$$

$$75E - \$89,625,000 = 76.5E - \$112,072,500$$

$$E = \underline{\$14,965,000} \text{ indifference level of EBIT}$$

(b) The consulting firm projected Albina's Ice Cream Factory's long-term EBIT at $13,575,000. Since this projected level of EBIT is less than the indifference level of $14,965,000, the earnings per share of the firm will be greater if the common stock is issued.

4. Carlton Sprinklers is considering a plan to increase its financial leverage. The plan being considered by management is to sell $5 million of bonds that would mature in 20 years. The interest rate on the bonds would be 12%. The bonds would have a sinking fund provision requiring that one-twentieth of the principal be retired each year. The management of Carlton feels that the upcoming year will be their toughest ever and could serve as a worst case scenario. Carlton usually carries an operating cash balance of $1 million. Cash collections for the coming year are expected to be $5 million. Miscellaneous cash receipts will be $300,000. Wages and salaries will be $1.2 million. Raw materials costs will be $1.5 million. The firm expects $750,000 in non-discretionary cash outflows and all taxes are included. The firm is in the 34% marginal tax bracket.

(a) At present, Carlton is unleveraged. What will be the total fixed financial charges that the firm must pay next year?

(b) If the bonds are issued, what is your forecast of the expected cash balance at the end of the next year?

(c) Should Carlton's management consider issuing the bonds?

SOLUTION

(a) FC = Interest + Sinking Fund
    FC = 600,000 + 250,000
    FC = $850,000

(b) $CB_r = CB_o + NCF_r - FC$

    $CB_o = 1,000,000$;
    $FC = 850,000$; and
    $NCF_r = 5,300,000 - 3,450,000 = 1,850,000$.

    so, $CB_r = 1,000,000 + 1,850,000 - 850,000$
    $= \underline{2,000,000}$

(c) The above analysis suggests that Carlton could cover its cash obligations, if it issued the bonds.

TRUE-FALSE

_____ 1. Capital structure is the mix of all items that appear on the right-hand side of the firm's balance sheet.

_____ 2. The major influence on the maturity structure of the financing plan is the nature of the assets owned by the firm.

_____ 3. The optimal capital structure can be defined as the mix of permanent sources of funds that minimize the company's common stock price.

_____ 4. The EBIT-EPS analysis measures the variability (riskiness) of the earnings stream thereby recognizing the implicit costs of debt financing.

_____ 5. According to cash flow analysis, the appropriate level of financial leverage use is reached when the chance of running out of cash is exactly equal to that which management will assume.

_____ 6. In computing the firm's tax bill the interest expense is assumed not to be tax deductible.

_____ 7. Inputs to the coverage ratios generally come from the firm's balance sheet.

_____ 8. According to the moderate position of capital structure theory, financial leverage affects firm value but not the cost of corporate capital.

_____ 9. Above a critical level of EBIT the firm's earnings per share will be lower if greater degrees of financial leverage are employed.

_____ 10. Industry norms, used with other tools of capital structure management can be helpful in determining an appropriate financing mix.

_____ 11. If capital structures consist only of debt instruments and common equity and both k_c and k_d are the same, then a change in the capital structure would not affect the firm's stock price.

_____ 12. Whether or not corporate income is taxed, the sum of the cash flows made to all contributors of corporate financial capital is not affected by the firm's financing mix.

_____ 13. In practice, as more financial leverage is used, it will increase the firm's value indefinitely and lower its cost of capital continuously.

_____ 14. The EBIT-EPS analysis chart tells us that EPS will be greater than zero, if the EBIT level just covers the plan's financing cost.

_____ 15. At a point below the EBIT indifference level, the financing plan involving less leverage will generate a higher EPS.

_____ 16. Capital structure is equal to the financial structure less current liabilities.

_____ 17. According to NOI theory the real cost of debt includes the change in the cost of common equity brought about by the use of the debt.

_____ 18. NOI theory suggests that cost of capital and the stock price are independent of the degree to which the company chooses to leverage.

_____ 19. Debt capacity is the maximum proportion of debt that a company can include in its capital structure without affecting the cost of common equity.

_____ 20. A sinking fund is a real cash reserve used to buy back common equity in the event of a hostile take-over.

MULTIPLE CHOICE

1. According to the dependence hypothesis

   a. Regardless of the amount of debt financing used by the firm, its cost of debt and equity capital are unaffected.
   b. Greater use of debt financing results in a favorable effect on the firm's stock price.
   c. a and b.
   d. None of the above.

2. The firm's capital structure would consist of

   a. Long-term debt.
   b. Common equity.
   c. Preferred equity.
   d. Only b and c.
   e. All of the above.

3. A firm will turn to common equity financing when

    a. The stock market is looking favorable.
    b. The expected cost of default is greater than the tax advantage of debt financing.
    c. It reaches optimal capital structure.
    d. Only a and b.

4. The objective of capital structure management is to

    a. Minimize the composite cost of capital.
    b. Determine the optimal capital structure.
    c. Maximize the common stock price.
    d. All of the above.

5. The implicit cost of debt is the change in the cost of common equity brought on by using _____.

    a. Operating leverage.
    b. Financial leverage.
    c. Stock options.
    d. All of the above.

6. Which of the following assumptions does capital structure theory not include?

    a. Corporate income is not subject to any tax.
    b. Transaction costs of selling securities are prevalent.
    c. The expected values of all investors' forecasts of the future levels of EBIT for each firm are identical.
    d. The capital structures consist only of stocks and bonds.

7. According to the independence hypothesis:

    a. The firm's cost of capital and stock price is unaffected by the degree of financial leverage.
    b. The firm's total market value is affected by the manner in which the right-hand side of the balance sheet is arranged.
    c. Both a and b.
    d. None of the above.

8. Which of the following is not a limitation of EBIT-EPS analysis?

    a. It disregards the explicit cost of debt financing.
    b. It ignores the level of the firm's earnings stream.
    c. Both a and b are limitations.
    d. None of the above.

9. Which of the following is not true about capital structure theory (moderate position)?

   a. Firm's bankruptcy cost is related to its use of financial leverage.
   b. The sum of the cash flows that the firm could pay to all contributors of corporate capital is not affected by its financing mix.
   c. Financial leverage affects the firm's value.
   d. a and c.

10. Which of the following is <u>not</u> a basic tool of capital structure management?

   a. EBIT-EPS analysis.
   b. Comparative leverage ratios.
   c. Use of industry norms.
   d. None of the above.

11. According to the NOI approach, a 10% increase in earnings and dividends per share caused by a financing mix change will:

   a. Cause the firm's cost of common equity to rise by 10%.
   b. Cause the cost of common equity to fall by some percentage less than 10%.
   c. Cause the cost of common equity to rise by some percentage less than 10%.
   d. Cause no change in the cost of common equity.

12. The dependence hypothesis suggests that:

   a. The use of more debt will not change the cost of common equity.
   b. The use of more debt will decrease the overall cost of capital.
   c. Both a and b.
   d. Neither a or b.

13. Which of the following is/are a way of analyzing capital structure:

   a. EBIT-EPS analysis.
   b. Comparative leverage ratios.
   c. Analysis of cash flows.
   d. a and b.
   e. All of the above.

16

Dividend Policy and Internal Financing

Orientation: In determining the firm's dividend policy, two issues are important. The dividend payout ratio (percentage of earnings paid out in dividends) must be decided as well as the manner in which dividends are to be paid out over time, i.e., the stability of the dividend payment. These issues must be resolved to maximize the value of the firm's common stock. In doing so, the financial manager should consider the investment opportunities available to the firm and any preference that the company's investors have for dividend income or capital gains. Also, stock dividends, stock splits, or stock repurchases can be used to supplement or replace cash dividends.

I.   The tradeoffs in setting a firm's dividend policy

    A.   If a company pays a large dividend, it will thereby:

        1.   Have a low retention of profits within the firm.

        2.   Need to rely heavily on a new common stock issue for equity financing.

    B.   If a company pays a small dividend, it will thereby:

        1.   Have a high retention of profits within the firm.

        2.   Will not need to rely heavily on a new common stock issue for equity financing. The profits retained for reinvestment will provide the needed equity financing.

II. The importance of a firm's dividend policy depends on the impact of the dividend decision on the firm's stock price. That is, given a firm's capital-budgeting and borrowing decisions, what is the impact of the firm's dividend policies on the stock price?

III. Three views about the importance of a firm's dividend policy.

A. View 1: Dividends do not matter

1. Assume that the dividend decision does not change the firm's capital budgeting and financing decisions.

2. Assume perfect markets which means:

   a. There are no brokerage commissions when investors buy and sell stocks.

   b. New securities can be issued without incurring any flotation cost.

   c. There is no income tax; personal or corporate.

   d. Information is free and equally available to all investors.

   e. There are no conflicts of interest between management and stockholders.

3. Under the foregoing assumptions, it may be shown that the market price of a corporation's common stock is unchanged under different dividend policies. If the firm increases the dividend to its stockholders, it has to offset this increase by issuing new common stock in order to finance the available investment opportunities. If on the other hand, the firm reduces its dividend payment, it has more funds available internally to finance future investment projects. In either policy the present value of the resulting cash flows to be accrued to the current investors is independent of the dividend policy. By varying the dividend policy, only the type of return is affected (capital gains versus dividend income), not the total return.

B. View 2: High dividends increase stock value

1. Dividends are more predictable than capital gains because management can control dividends, while they cannot dictate the price of the stock. Thus, investors are less certain of receiving income from capital gains than from dividend income. The incremental risk associated with capital gains relative to dividend income should therefore cause us to use a higher required rate in discounting a dollar of capital gains than the rate used for discounting a dollar of dividends. In so doing, we would give a higher value to the dividend income than we would the capital gains.

2. Criticisms of view 2.

   a. Since the dividend policy has no impact on the volatility of the company's overall cash flows, it has no impact on the riskiness of the firm.

   b. Increasing a firm's dividend does not reduce the basic riskiness of the stock; rather, if dividend payment requires management to issue new stock, it only transfers risk <u>and</u> ownership from the current owners to new owners.

C. View 3: Low dividends increase value

Stocks that allow us to defer taxes (low dividends-high capital gains) will possibly sell at a premium relative to stocks that require us to pay taxes currently (high dividends-low capital gains). Only then will the two stocks provide comparable after-tax returns, which suggests that a policy to pay low dividends will result in a higher stock price. That is, high dividends hurt investors, while low dividends-high retention help the firm's investors.

D. Additional thoughts about the importance of a firm's dividend policy.

1. Residual dividend theory: Because of flotation costs incurred in issuing new stock, firms must issue a larger amount of securities in order to receive the amount of capital required for investments. As a result, new equity capital will be more expensive than capital raised through retained earnings. Therefore, financing investments internally (and decreasing dividends) instead of issuing new stock may be

216

favored. This is embodied in the residual dividend theory, where a dividend would be paid only when any internally generated funds remain after financing the equity portion of the firm's investments.

2. The clientele effect: If investors do in fact have a preference between dividends and capital gains, we could expect them to seek out firms that have a dividend policy consistent with these preferences. They would in essence "sort themselves out" by buying stocks which satisfy their preferences for dividends and/or capital gains. In other words, there would be a "clientele effect," where firms draw a given clientele, given the stated dividend policy. However, unless there is a greater aggregate demand for a particular policy than is being satisfied in the market, dividend policy is still unimportant, in that one policy is as good as the other. The clientele effect only tells us to avoid making capricious changes in a company's dividend policy.

3. Information effect.

    a. We know from experience that a large, unexpected change in dividends can have significant impact on the stock price. Despite such "evidence," it is not unreasonable to hypothesize that dividend policy only appears to be important, because we are not looking at the real cause and effect. It may be that investors use a change in dividend policy as a signal about the firm's "true" financial condition, especially its earning power.

    b. Some would argue that management frequently has inside information about the firm that it cannot make available to the investors. This difference in accessibility to information between management and investors, called information asymmetry, may result in a lower stock price than would be true if we had conditions of certainty. Dividends become a means in a risky market place to minimize any "drag" on the stock price that might come from differences in the level of information available to managers and investors.

217

4. Agency costs: Conflicts between management and stockholders may exist, and the stock price of a company owned by investors who are separate from management may be less than the stock value of a closely-held firm. The difference in price is the cost of the conflict to the owners, which has come to be called agency costs. A firm's dividend policy may be perceived by owners as a tool to minimize agency costs. Assuming the payment of a dividend requires management to issue stock to finance new investments, then new investors will be attracted to the company only if management provides convincing information that the capital will be used profitably. Thus, the payment of dividends indirectly results in a closer monitoring of management's investment activities. In this case, dividends may provide a meaningful contribution to the value of the firm.

5. Expectations theory: As the time approaches for management to announce the amount of the next dividend, investors form expectations as to how much the dividend will be. When the actual dividend decision is announced, the investor compares the actual decision with the expected decision. If the amount of the dividend is as expected, even if it represents an increase from prior years, the market price of the stock will remain unchanged. However, if the dividend is higher or lower than expected, the investors will reassess their perceptions about the firm and the value of the stock.

E. The empirical evidence about the importance of dividend policy

1. The results: To test the relationship between dividend payments and security prices, we could compare a firm's dividend yield (dividend/stock price) and the stock's total return; the question being, "Do stocks that pay high dividends provide higher or lower returns to the investors?" Such tests have been conducted using a variety of the most sophisticated statistical techniques available. Despite the use of these extremely powerful analytical tools involving intricate and complicated procedures, the results have been mixed. However, over long periods of time, the results

have given a slight advantage to the low-dividend stocks; that is, stocks that pay lower dividends appear to have higher prices. The findings are far from conclusive, however, owing to the relatively large standard errors of the estimates.

2. Reasons for inconclusive results.

   a. To be accurate, we would need to know the amount of dividends investors _expect_ to receive. Since these expectations cannot be observed, we can only use historical data, which may or may not relate to expectations.

   b. Most empirical studies have assumed a linear relationship between dividend payments and stock prices. The actual relationship may be nonlinear, possibly even with discontinuities in the relationship.

F. Conclusions about the importance of dividend policy

   1. As a firm's investment opportunities increase, the dividend payout ratio should decrease.

   2. The firm's dividend policy appears to be important; however, appearances may be deceptive. The real issue may be the firm's _expected_ earnings power and the riskiness of these earnings.

   3. If dividends influence stock price, it probably comes from the investor's desire to minimize and/or defer taxes and from the role of dividends in minimizing agency costs.

   4. If the expectations theory has merit, which we believe it does, it behooves management to avoid surprising the investors when it comes to the firm's dividend decision.

IV. Dividend policy decisions

A. Other practical considerations

   1. Legal restrictions

      a. A corporation may not pay a dividend

219

        (1)   If the firm's liabilities exceed its assets.

        (2)   If the amount of the dividend exceeds the accumulated profits (retained earnings).

        (3)   If the dividend is being paid from capital invested in the firm.

   b.   Debtholders and preferred stockholders may impose restrictive provisions on management, such as common dividends not being paid from earnings prior to the payment of interest or preferred dividends.

2. Liquidity position: The amount of a firm's retained earnings and its cash position are seldom the same. Thus, the company must have adequate _cash_ available as well as retained earnings to pay dividends.

3. Absence or lack of other sources of financing: All firms do not have equal access to the capital markets. Consequently, companies with limited financial resources may rely more heavily on internally generated funds.

4. Earnings predictability: A firm that has a stable earnings trend will generally pay a larger portion of its earnings in dividends. If earnings fluctuate significantly, a larger amount of the profits may be retained to ensure that enough money is available for investment projects when needed.

5. Ownership control: For many small firms, and certain large ones, maintaining the controlling vote is very important. These owners would prefer the use of debt and retained profits to finance new investments rather than issue new stock.

6. Inflation: Because of inflation, the cost of replacing equipment has increased substantially. Depreciation funds tend to become insufficient. Hence, greater profit retention may be required.

B. Alternative dividend policies

1. Constant dividend payout ratio: The percentage of earnings paid out in dividends is held

constant. Therefore, the dollar amount of the dividend fluctuates from year to year.

2. Stable dollar dividend per share: Relatively stable dollar dividend is maintained. The dividend per share is increased or decreased only after careful investigation by the management.

3. Small, regular dividend plus a year-end extra: Extra dividend is paid out in prosperous years. Management's objective is to avoid the connotation of a permanent dividend increase.

C. Bases for stable dividends

1. Investors may use the dividend policy as a surrogate for information that is not easily accessible. The dividend policy may be useful in assessing the company's long-term earnings prospects.

2. Many investors rely on dividends to satisfy personal income need. If dividends fluctuate from year to year, investors may have to sell or buy stock to satisfy their current needs, thereby incurring expensive transaction costs.

3. Legal listings stipulate that certain types of financial institutions may only invest in companies that have a consistent dividend payment.

4. Conclusion: An investor who prefers stable dividends will assign a lower required rate of return (a higher P/E ratio) for a stock paying a stable dividend. This results in a higher market price for the stock.

V. Dividend payment procedures

A. Dividends are generally paid quarterly.

B. The declaration date is the date on which the firm's board of directors announces the forthcoming dividends.

C. The date of record designates when the stock transfer books are to be closed (who is entitled to the dividend).

D.   Brokerage firms terminate the right of ownership to the dividend four working days prior to the date of record. This date is called the <u>ex-dividend date</u>.

E.   Dividend checks are mailed on the <u>payment date</u>.

VI. Stock dividends and stock splits

A.   Both a stock dividend and a stock split involve issuing new shares of stock to current stockholders.

B.   The investors' percentage ownership in the firm remains unchanged. The investor is neither better nor worse off than before the stock split/dividend.

C.   On an economic basis there is no difference between a stock dividend and a stock split.

D.   For accounting purposes the stock split has been defined as a stock dividend exceeding 25 percent.

E.   Accounting treatment

    1.   For a stock dividend, the dollar amount of the dividend is transferred from retained earnings to the capital accounts.

    2.   In the case of a split, the dollar amounts of the capital accounts do not change. Only the number of shares is increased while the par value of each share is decreased proportionately.

F.   Rationale for a stock dividend or split

    1.   The price of stock may not fall precisely in proportion to the share increase; thus, the stockholders' value is increased.

    2.   If a company is encountering cash problems, it can substitute a stock dividend for a cash dividend. Investors will probably look beyond the dividend to determine the underlying reasons for conserving cash.

VII. Stock repurchases

A.   A number of benefits exists justifying stock repurchases instead of dividend payment. Included in these are:

1. To provide an internal investment opportunity.

2. To modify the firm's capital structure.

3. To impact earnings per share, thus increasing stock price.

B. Share repurchase as a dividend decision

1. A firm may decide to repurchase its shares, increasing the earnings per share which should be reflected in a higher stock price.

2. The investor's choice

    a. For tax purposes the investor may prefer the firm to repurchase stock in lieu of a dividend. Dividends are taxed as ordinary income, whereas any price appreciation resulting from the stock repurchase would be taxed as a capital gain.

    b. The investor may still prefer dividend payment because

        (1) Dividends are viewed more dependable than stock repurchases.

        (2) The price the firm must pay for its stock may be too high.

        (3) Riskiness of the firm's capital structure may increase, lowering the P/E ratio and thus the stock price.

C. Financing or investment decision

1. A stock repurchase effectively increases the debt-equity ratio towards higher debt, thus repurchase is viewed as a financing decision.

2. Buying its own stock at depressed prices, a firm may consider the repurchase as an investment decision. However, this action is not a true investment opportunity, as the extreme result would mean the company would consume itself.

D. The repurchase procedure

1. A public announcement should be made detailing the amount, purpose and procedure for the stock repurchase.

2. Open market purchase - at the current market price.

3. Tender offer - more formal and at a specified price.

4. Negotiated basis - repurchasing from specific large shareholders.

Study Problems

1. The Harvestor Corporation has the following capital structure:

Common Stock ($5 par; 300,000 shares)	$1,500,000
Paid in Capital	2,500,000
Retained Earnings	4,000,000
Total Net Worth	$8,000,000

(a) If the company issues a 20 percent stock dividend, how would the new capital structure appear? The market price per share for the stock is $10.

(b) How would the capital accounts appear after a two-for-one split?

SOLUTION

(a)

Decrease in retained earnings ($10 x 60,000 shares)	$600,000
Increase in par value of common stock ($5 x 60,000 shares)	300,000
Remainder to increase capital surplus	$300,000

The new capital structure after a 20 percent stock dividend:

Common Stock ($5 par; 360,000 shares)	$1,800,000
Paid in Capital	2,800,000
Retained Earnings	3,400,000
Total Net Worth	$8,000,000

(b) The new capital structure after a two-for-one split:

Common Stock ($2.50 par; 600,000 shares)	$1,500,000
Capital Surplus	2,500,000
Retained Earnings	4,000,000
Total Net Worth	$8,000,000

2. The Mansville Corporation's capital structure is as follows:

Common Stock ($4 par; 5,000,000 shares outstanding)	$20,000,000
Paid in Capital	1,000,000
Retained Earnings	9,000,000
Total Net Worth	$30,000,000

The firm's earnings after taxes are $2 million, of which the company paid out 25 percent in cash dividends. The price of the firm's common stock was $8.

(a) If the firm declares a 20 percent stock dividend, how would the capital structure appear?

(b) If the firm declares a 30 percent stock dividend, what would be the end result on the capital structure? (Hint: Stock dividends in excess of 25 percent should be calculated on the basis of book value less retained earnings instead of market value.)

(c) If a 20 percent stock dividend is assumed, what would be the earnings per share and dividends per share?

SOLUTION

(a) Capital structure after a 20 percent stock dividend:

Increase in the shares outstanding:

20% x 5,000,000 shares = 1,000,000 shares

Increase in the par value:

$4 x 1,000,000 = $4,000,000

Increase in the capital surplus account:

($8 - $4) x 1,000,000 = $4,000,000

Result:

Common Stock (6,000,000 shares)	$24,000,000
Capital Surplus	5,000,000
Retained Earnings	1,000,000
Total Net Worth	$30,000,000

(b) Capital structure after a 30 percent stock dividend:

Increase in shares outstanding:

30% x 5,000,000 = 1,500,000 shares

Increase in par value:

1,500,000 shares x $4 par value $6,000,000

Increase in capital surplus:

$1,000,000 x 30%   300,000

Amount transferred from
    retained earnings: $6,300,000

Revised capital structure:

Common Stock ($4 par value; 6,500,000 shares)	$26,000,000
Paid in Capital	1,300,000
Retained Earnings	2,700,000
Total Net Worth	$30,000,000

(c) Earnings per share after a 20 percent stock dividend:

$$\frac{\text{Earnings}}{\text{Number of Shares}} = \frac{\$2,000,000}{6,000,000} = \$0.33$$

Dividends per share after a 20 percent stock dividend:

$$\frac{\text{Dividends}}{\text{Number of Shares}} = \frac{\$500,000}{6,000,000} = \$0.083$$

3. Philips Limited treats dividends as a residual variable in its financial decisions (see residual dividend theory). Net income has been forecasted for the upcoming year to be $600,000, which may be used for reinvesting in the firm or for paying dividends. The firm has only equity in its capital structure and its cost of internally generated equity capital is 10 percent. If, however, new common stock were issued, flotation costs would raise this cost to 11 percent. If the firm considers the 10 percent cost of internal equity to be the opportunity cost of retained earnings,

(a) (1) How much in dividends should be paid if the company has $500,000 in projects with expected returns exceeding 10 percent?

226

(2) How much should the dividend be if $600,000 in investments are available having expected returns greater than 10 percent?

(b) How much should be paid in dividends if the firm has $1 million in projects whose expected returns exceed 11 percent?

(c) How would your answer change in part (b) if the firm's optimal debt-equity mix is 40 percent debt and 60 percent common and the cost of capital remains the same?

SOLUTION

(a) (1) According to the residual dividend theory, the firm should pay dividends only when it has exhausted its investments whose returns exceed the firm's cost of capital. Therefore, the firm should pay $100,000 in dividends ($600,000 income available for investing less $500,000 investments).

(2) The firm should use all of the $600,000 for investing in the projects and should not pay any dividends.

(b) If the firm has investment opportunities with returns exceeding the cost of capital, the firm should undertake these investments. In this example, the cost of capital increases (to 11%) when new equity is issued. Since the returns on the available investment projects (totaling $1 million) exceed the cost of equity capital, the firm should use up its internally generated funds ($600,000) and raise the remaining $400,000 by issuing new common stock. Therefore, no dividends would be paid.

(c) We would need $400,000 in new debt, i.e., 40 percent of $1 million. The remaining $600,000 (which is 60 percent of the needed capital) will be supplied by internally generated funds. No dividend will be paid.

4. Beardsell Products and Voltas Products are identical firms in terms of (1) being in the same industry, (2) producing the same products, (3) being subject to the same risks, and (4) having equivalent earnings per share. Beardsell pays a constant cash dividend, whereas Voltas follows a constant percentage payout ratio of 50 percent. However, Voltas' common stock price has been lower than

Beardsell's in spite of Voltas' dividend being substantially larger than Beardsell's in certain years. Given the data below:

	Beardsell Products			Voltas Products		
Year	EPS	Dividend	Market Price	EPS	Dividend	Market Price
1984	$2.50	$0.65	9	$2.50	$1.25	6 3/4
1985	-0.25	0.65	8 3/4	-0.25	0	6 1/2
1986	3.00	0.65	9 1/4	3.00	1.50	9
1987	2.00	0.65	9	2.00	1.00	10

(a) What might account for the differences in the market prices of the two companies?

(b) What might both companies do in order to enhance the market prices of their respective shares?

SOLUTION

(a) The dissimilarity between market prices might be a function of the different dividend policies, with a lower capitalization rate, and, accordingly, a higher price being assigned to Beardsell as a result of the stable dividend stream.

(b) It appears that neither company would appear to be growth-oriented. If both firms are valued in terms of their dividend yield, which seems to be the case, higher dividend payouts might produce higher prices.

5. The Maple Syrup Company is considering two dividend policies for the years 1986 and 1987. The firm will be liquidated in 1987. One dividend plan would pay a dividend of $2.30 in 1986 and a liquidating dividend of $37.03 in 1987. The alternative plan would pay a dividend of $6.90 in 1986 and a final dividend of $31.74 in 1987. The required rate of return for the common stockholders is 15 percent. If perfect capital markets are assumed, what would be the effect of each dividend policy on the price of common stock?

SOLUTION

Under perfect market conditions, the effect of each dividend policy is determined by finding the present value of the dividend stream for each dividend plan.

Plan 1: Present value calculations

	Year 1986	Year 1987
Dividends	$2.30	$37.03

$$\text{Present Value} = \frac{\$2.30}{(1.15)} + \frac{\$37.03}{(1.15)^2} = \$30$$

Plan 2:

	Year 1986	Year 1987
Dividends	$6.90	$31.74

$$\text{Present Value} = \frac{\$6.90}{(1.15)} + \frac{\$31.74}{(1.15)^2} = \$30$$

We find that both plans have the same present value. The common stockholders should be indifferent about both plans.

6. Rexall Corporation is considering five investment opportunities. The required investment outlays and expected rates of return for these investments are shown below. The cost of capital for the firm is 13 percent. Investments are to be financed with 30 percent debt and 70 percent equity. Internally generated funds available for reinvestment equal $1 million.

(a) Which investments should be accepted?

(b) According to the residual dividend theory, what amount should be paid out in dividends?

Investment	Cost	Internal Rate of Return
A	$200,000	20%
B	300,000	15
C	900,000	14
D	100,000	10
E	400,000	7

SOLUTION

(a) The data given in the problem is shown graphically:

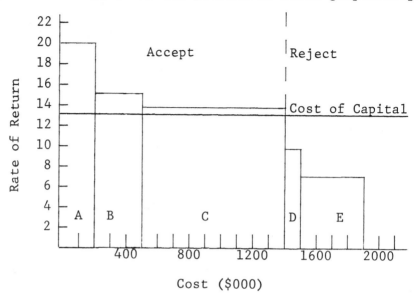

Cost ($000)

Investments A, B, and C should be accepted because their expected returns exceed the firm's cost of capital.

        Total cost of three projects:
          $200,000 + $300,000 + $900,000   = $1,400,000
        Equity financing: $1,400,000 x 70%   =   980,000
        Debt financing: $1,400,000 - $980,000 =   420,000

        Internally generated funds available: $1,000,000
        Less equity necessary for projects: 980,000
        Funds available for dividend payment: $ 20,000

7. International Computers Inc., a new firm, is financed only by common stock. The firm's life is limited to 2 years (1986 and 1987), at the end of which the firm will be liquidated. At the beginning of 1986 the firm's assets are $5 million and 200,000 shares are outstanding. Cash available for reinvestment or dividend payment for 1986 is $1 million. The expected return on investment is 15 percent. At the end of 1986 an additional investment of $500,000 will be required. This may be financed by retaining $500,000 of the 1986 profits or issuing new stock or a combination of both. In fact, management is considering one of two plans:

230

Plan A: The $500,000 investment would be financed entirely by internal financing with the investors receiving $500,000 in dividends.

Plan B: Investors would receive $600,000 in dividends, with the investment in 1986 being financed $400,000 internally and a $100,000 new stock issue.

The proposed dividend plans for 1986 are shown below:

	Plan A	Plan B
Internally generated cash flow	$1,000,000	$1,000,000
Dividend for 1986	500,000	600,000
Cash available for reinvestment	$ 500,000	$ 500,000
Amount of investment in 1986	500,000	500,000
External financing required	0	$ 100,000

Assume perfect markets, and demonstrate that under either dividend plan the market price of the firm's stock remains the same, i.e., the dividend policy of the firm is irrelevant from the investor's point of view.

SOLUTION

The solution to this problem is obtained by following two steps:

(1) Calculating the amount and timing of the dividend stream for the original investors, and

(2) Determining the present value of the dividend stream under each plan.

For step 1, see Table 16.1, below.

Table 16.1

Number of Original Shares Outstanding Equals 200,000

	Plan A	Plan B
Year: 1986		
Dividends	$ 500,000	$ 600,000
	($2.50 per share)	($3 per share)
Year: 1987		
Total Dividends		
A. Original Investment		
Old Investors	$5,000,000	$5,000,000
New Investors	0	100,000
B. Retained Earnings*	500,000	400,000
C. Profits for 1987**	825,000	825,000
Total Dividend to	$6,325,000	$6,325,000
All Investors		
Less Dividend to New Investors:		
A. Original Investment	0	(100,000)
B. Profits for New Investors	0	(15,000)
(15% of $100,000)		
Dividends Available to	$6,325,000	$6,210,000
Original Investors		
Amount Per Share	$ 31.625	$ 31.05

*The portion of the 1986 profits that were reinvested in the firm at the conclusion of 1986.

**Profits for 1987 equal 15 percent of $5,500,000, the asset base in 1987.

For step 2, the present value of the dividend streams discounted at 15 percent must be determined:

Plan A:
$$\frac{\$2.50}{(1.15)^1} + \frac{\$31.625}{(1.15)^2} = \$26.09$$

Plan B:
$$\frac{\$3.00}{(1.15)^1} + \frac{\$31.05}{(1.15)^2} = \$26.09$$

We see that under both plans, the market price of International Computers is the same.

Self-Tests

TRUE-FALSE

_____ 1. If dividend policy is treated as a passive residual, dividends are paid only if the firm has any remaining capital after financing attractive investments.

_____ 2. In practice, the firm should invest retained earnings as long as the required rate of return exceeds the expected rate of return from the investment.

_____ 3. The greater the ability of a firm to borrow, the less is its ability to pay a cash dividend.

_____ 4. If a firm has sporadic investment opportunities, it might be expected to pay out more dividends.

_____ 5. A stock dividend results in a recapitalization of retained earnings.

_____ 6. In a stock split, the only accounting change is the shifting of amounts from retained earnings to the common stock (par) account.

_____ 7. The introduction of flotation costs to the "dividend irrelevance" concept favors the retention of earnings in the firm.

_____ 8. The only wealth-creating activity under "perfect market" conditions for an all-equity firm is the management's investment decisions.

_____ 9. Dividend income and capital gains from the sale of stock are taxed at the same personal income tax rate. Thus, there is no advantage to capital gains over dividend income for the investor.

_____ 10. An "expected" change in the dividend policy of a firm may not affect the price of the firm's stock when the change is actually announced.

_____ 11. A stock repurchase increases the debt-to-equity ratio.

_____ 12. Stock repurchases offer an attractive investment alternative any time prices are depressed.

_____ 13. The "bird-in-the-hand" theory assigns a higher value to capital gains than to dividend income.

_____ 14. A firm's dividend policy affects the variability of the firm's overall cash flows, even when we do not allow the dividend policy to impact investment decisions.

_____ 15. Stocks that allow us to defer taxes will not sell at a premium.

MULTIPLE CHOICE

1. Which of the following is not an assumption of the "dividend irrelevance" theory?

   a. No taxes.
   b. Efficient capital markets.
   c. No flotation costs.
   d. Costless information.

2. An argument for the relevance of dividends would be:

   a. Informational content.
   b. Resolution of uncertainty.
   c. Preference for current income.
   d. All of the above.
   e. None of the above.

3. An advantage of a stock dividend is that it:

   a. May help to conserve cash.
   b. Tends to increase the market price.
   c. Keeps the price of the stock within a desired trading range.
   d. All of the above.

4. When the assumption of no taxes is removed from the "dividend irrelevance" theory:

   a. There is a preference for the retention of earnings.
   b. There is a preference for paying out dividends.
   c. The preference depends on the individual investor's tax status, but generally there is a preference for retention of earnings.

5. The following factors may influence the dividend policy that a firm undertakes:

   a. The liquidity of the firm.
   b. Capital structure.
   c. Legal restrictions.
   d. a and c.
   e. a and b.

6. Advantages of a stock repurchase may be:

   a. A means to modify capital structure.
   b. To impact earnings per share.
   c. The elimination of a particular minority group.
   d. All of the above.

7. A firm may not legally pay dividends if:

   a. Its liabilities exceed its assets.
   b. The dividend is being paid from capital invested in the firm.
   c. Debtholders' contracts are not satisfied.
   d. All of the above.
   e. a and b.

8. For tax purposes, a corporation may exclude _____% of the dividend income received from another corporation.

   a. 0.
   b. 10.
   c. 50
   d. 80.
   e. 100.

9. When real-world considerations are taken into account, the amount of a firm's dividend payment depends on the following factors:

   a. Profitability of investment opportunities.
   b. Investor's preference for capital gains or dividend income.
   c. Debt-to-equity ratio.
   d. Trading range of the firm's stock.
   e. a and b.

10. Small-sized firms generally use retained earnings for investment purposes because:

    a. They do not have easy access to the capital markets.
    b. Ownership control is an important factor.
    c. Their earnings fluctuate widely.
    d. Inflation has greater impact on small companies.
    e. None of the above
    f. a and b.

11. Which one of the following dividend policies is the most popular?

    a. Constant dividend payout ratio.
    b. Stable dividend (dollar) per share.
    c. Small, regular dividend plus a year-end extra.

12. The ex-dividend date is

    a. The same as the date of record.
    b. Four working days prior to date of record.
    c. Eight days prior to the payment date.
    d. Five days after the declaration date.
    e. None of the above.

13. Properly viewed, a stock repurchase should be used as:

    a. A dividend decision.
    b. An investment decision.
    c. A refinancing decision.
    d. Both a and c.
    e. All of the above.

17

Raising Funds in the Capital Market

Orientation: This chapter considers the market environment in which long-term capital is raised. The underlying rationale for the existence of security markets is presented, investment banking services and procedures are detailed, private placements are discussed, and security market regulation is reviewed.

I.   The mix of corporate securities sold in the capital market.

   A.   When corporations raise cash in the capital market, what type of financing vehicle is most favored? The answer to this question is corporate bonds. The corporate debt markets clearly dominate the corporate equity markets when new (external) funds are being raised.

   B.   We know from our discussion on the cost of capital (Chapter 13) and planning the firm's financing mix (Chapter 15) that the U.S. tax system inherently favors debt as a means of raising capital. Over the 1972-82 period, bonds and notes accounted for about 73 percent of new corporate securities sold for cash.

II.   Why financial markets exist

   A.   Financial markets consist of institutions and procedures that facilitate transactions in all types of financial claims.

B. Some economic units spend more during a given period of time than they earn. Some economic units spend less than they earn. Accordingly, a mechanism is needed to facilitate the transfer of savings from those economic units that have a savings surplus to those that have a savings deficit. Financial markets provide such a mechanism.

C. The function of financial markets, then, is to allocate savings in an economy to the ultimate demander (user) of the savings.

D. If there were no financial markets, the wealth of an economy would be lessened. Savings could not be transferred to economic units, such as business firms, which are most in need of those funds.

III. Financing business: The movement of funds through the economy.

A. In the _financing process_, financial institutions play a major role in bridging the gap between savers and borrowers in the economy.

B. In a normal year the household sector is the largest net supplier of funds to the financial markets. We call the household sector, then, a _savings-surplus_ sector.

C. In contrast, the nonfinancial business sector is a _savings-deficit_ sector. In recent years the federal government has become a "quasi-permanent" savings deficit sector.

D. All in all, within the domestic economy, the non-financial business sector is dependent on the household sector to finance its investment needs.

E. The financial market system includes a complex network of intermediaries that assist in the trans-fer of savings among economic units. Chapter 17 in your text highlights the investment activity of two important intermediaries: life insurance companies and pension funds.

F. The _movement of savings_ through the economy occurs in three distinct ways:

1. The direct transfer of funds.

2. Indirect transfer using the investment banker.

238

3.   Indirect transfer using the financial inter-
      mediary.

IV. Components of the U.S. financial market system.

A.   <u>Public offerings</u> can be distinguished from <u>private placements</u>.

1.   The public (financial) market is an impersonal market in which both individual and institutional investors have the opportunity to acquire securities.

a.   A public offering takes place in the public market.

b.   The security-issuing firm does not meet (face-to-face) the actual investors in the securities.

2.   In a private placement of securities only a limited number of investors has the opportunity to purchase a portion of the issue.

a.   The market for private placements is more personal than its public counterpart.

b.   The specific details of the issue may actually be developed on a face-to-face basis among the potential investors and the issuer.

B.   <u>Primary markets</u> can be distinguished from <u>secondary markets</u>.

1.   Securities are first offered for sale in a primary market. For example, the sale of a new bond issue, preferred stock issue, or common stock issue takes place in the primary market. These transactions increase the total stock of financial assets in existence in the economy.

2.   Trading in currently existing securities takes place in the secondary market. The total stock of financial assets is unaffected by such transactions.

C.   The <u>money market</u> can be distinguished from the <u>capital market</u>.

1.   The money market consists of the institutions and procedures that provide for transactions in

short-term debt instruments which are generally issued by borrowers who have very high credit ratings.

    a.   "Short-term" means that the securities traded in the money market have maturity periods of not more than 1 year.

    b.   Equity instruments are not traded in the money market.

    c.   Typical examples of money market instruments are (1) U.S. Treasury bills, (2) federal agency securities, (3) bankers' acceptances, (4) negotiable certificates of deposit, and (5) commercial paper.

2.   The capital market consists of the institutions and procedures that provide for transactions in long-term financial instruments. This market encompasses those securities that have maturity periods extending beyond 1 year.

B.   <u>Organized security exchanges</u> can be distinguished from <u>over-the-counter</u> markets.

1.   Organized security exchanges are tangible entities whose activities are governed by a set of bylaws. Security exchanges physically occupy space and financial instruments are traded on such premises.

    a.   Major stock exchanges must comply with a strict set of reporting requirements established by the Securities and Exchange Commission (SEC). These exchanges are said to be <u>registered</u>.

    b.   The New York Stock Exchange, the American Stock Exchange, and the Midwest Stock Exchange collectively account for over 90% of the annual dollar transactions on the registered stock exchanges.

    c.   Organized security exchanges provide several benefits to both corporations and investors. They (1) provide a continuous market, (2) establish and publicize fair security prices, and (3) help businesses raise new financial capital.

d. A corporation must take steps to have its securities <u>listed</u> on an exchange in order to directly receive the benefits noted above. Listing criteria differ from exchange to exchange.

2. Over-the-counter markets include all security markets <u>except</u> the organized exchanges. The money market is a prominent example. Most corporate bonds are traded over-the-counter.

V. Using an investment banker

A. The investment banker is a financial specialist who acts as an intermediary in the selling of securities. He or she works for an investment banking firm (house).

B. Three basic functions are provided by the investment banker:

1. He or she assumes the risk of selling a new security issue at a satisfactory (profitable) price. This is called <u>underwriting</u>. Typically, the investment banking house, along with the underwriting syndicate, actually buys the new issue from the corporation that is raising funds. The syndicate (group of investment banking firms) then sells the issue to the investing public at a higher (hopefully) price than it paid for it.

2. He or she provides for the <u>distribution</u> of the securities to the investing public.

3. He or she <u>advises</u> firms on the details of selling securities.

C. Several distribution methods are available for placing new securities into the hands of final investors. The investment banker's role is different in each case.

1. In a <u>negotiated purchase</u> the firm in need of funds contacts an investment banker and begins the sequence of steps leading to the final distribution of the securities that will be offered. The price that the investment banker pays for the securities is "negotiated" with the issuing firm.

241

2. In a <u>competitive-bid purchase</u> the investment banker and underwriting syndicate are selected by an auction process. The syndicate willing to pay the greatest dollar amount per new security to the issuing firm wins the competitive bid. This means that it will underwrite and distribute the issue. In this situation, the price paid to the issuer is not negotiated; instead, it is determined by a sealed-bid process much on the order of construction bids.

3. In a <u>commission</u> (or <u>best-efforts</u>) offering the investment banker does <u>not</u> act as an underwriter. He or she attempts to sell the issue in return for a fixed commission on each security that is actually sold. Unsold securities are simply returned to the firm hoping to raise funds.

4. In a privileged <u>subscription</u> the new issue is not offered to the investing public. It sold to a definite and limited group of investors. Current stockholders are often the privileged group.

5. In a <u>direct sale</u> the issuing firm sells the securities to the investing public without involving an investment banker in the process. This is not a typical procedure.

D. The negotiated purchase is most likely to be the distribution method used by the private corporation. It consists of several steps.

1. The security-issuing firm selects an investment banker.

2. A series of pre-underwriting conferences takes place. Discussions center on (1) the amount of capital to be raised, (2) the possible receptiveness of the capital markets to a specific mode of financing, and (3) the proposed use of the new funds. These conferences are consummated by the signing of a <u>tentative underwriting agreement</u>. The approximate price to be paid for each security is identified in this agreement.

3. An underwriting syndicate is formed. The syndicate is a temporary association of investment bankers formed to purchase the security issue from the corporation. The syndicate's objective is to resell the issue at a profit.

4.   Most new public issues must be registered with the SEC before they can be sold to final investors. This involves filing a lengthy technical document called a <u>registration statement</u> with the SEC. This document aims to disclose relevant facts about the issuing firm and the related security to potential investors. Another document, the <u>prospectus</u>, is also filed with the SEC for examination. It is a shortened version of the official registration statement. Once both documents are approved, the prospectus becomes the official advertising vehicle for the security offering.

5.   A selling group is formed to distribute the new securities to final investors. Securities dealers who are part of the selling group are permitted to purchase a portion of the new issue at a price to the public. A <u>selling group agreement</u> binds the syndicate and the members of the selling group.

6.   A due diligence meeting is held to finalize all details prior to taking the offering to the public. The price at which the issuing firm will sell the new securities to the syndicate is settled. Usually, the offering is made to the public on the day after this meeting.

7.   The syndicate manager (from the investment banking house that generated the business) is permitted to mitigate downward price movements in the secondary market for the subject offering. This is accomplished by the syndicate managers placing buy orders for the security at the agreed upon public offering price.

8.   A contractual agreement among the syndicate members terminates the syndicate. In the most pleasant situations this agreement is made when the issue has been fully subscribed (sold).

VI. Private placements

A.   Each year billions of dollars of new securities are privately (directly) placed with final investors. In a private placement a small number of investors purchases the entire security offering. Most private placements involve debt instruments.

B.   Large financial institutions are the major investors in private placements. These include (1) life insurance firms, (2) state and local retirement funds, and (3) private pension funds.

C.   The advantages and disadvantages of private placements as opposed to public offerings must be carefully evaluated by the financial manager.

    1.   The advantages include (1) greater speed than a public offering in actually obtaining the needed funds, (2) lower flotation costs than are associated with a public issue, and (3) increased flexibility in the financing contract.

    2.   The disadvantages include (1) higher interest costs than are ordinarily associated with a comparable public issue, (2) the imposition of several restrictive covenants in the financing contract, and (3) the possibility that the security may have to be registered some time in the future at the lender's option.

VII. Flotation costs

A.   The firm raising long-term capital typically incurs two types of flotation costs: (1) the underwriter's spread and (2) issuing costs. The former is typically the larger.

    1.   The underwriter's spread is the difference between the gross and net proceeds from a specific security issue. This absolute dollar difference is usually expressed as a percent of the gross proceeds.

    2.   Many components comprise issue costs. The two most significant are (1) printing and engraving and (2) legal fees. For comparison purposes, these, too, are usually expressed as a percent of the issue's gross proceeds.

B.   SEC data reveal two relationships about flotation costs.

    1.   Issue costs (as a percent of gross proceeds) for common stock exceed those of preferred stock, which exceed those of bonds.

    2.   Total flotation costs per dollar raised decrease as the dollar size of the security issue increases.

VIII. Regulation

    A.   The primary market is governed by the Securities Act of 1933.

        1.   The intent of this federal regulation is to provide potential investors with accurate and truthful disclosure about the firm and the new securities being sold.

        2.   Unless exempted, the corporation selling securities to the public must register the securities with the SEC.

        3.   Exemptions follow from a variety of conditions. For example, if the size of the offering is small enough (less than $500,000), the offering does not have to be registered. If the issue is already regulated or controlled by some other federal agency, registration with the SEC is not required. Railroad issues and public utility issues are examples.

        4.   If not exempted, a registration statement is filed with the SEC containing particulars about the security-issuing firm and the new security.

        5.   A copy of the prospectus, a summary registration statement, is also filed. It will not yet have the selling price of the security printed on it; it is referred to as a _red herring_ and called that until it is approved by the SEC.

        6.   If the information in the registration statement and prospectus is satisfactory to the SEC, the firm can proceed to sell the new issue. If the information is not satisfactory, a _stop order_ is issued which prevents the immediate sale of the issue. Deficiencies have to be corrected to the satisfaction of the SEC before the firm can sell the securities.

        7.   The SEC does _not_ evaluate the investment quality of any issue. It is concerned, rather, with the presentation of complete and accurate information upon which the potential investor can act.

    B.   The secondary market is regulated by the Securities Exchange Act of 1934. This federal act created the SEC. It has many aspects.

1. Major security exchanges are required to register with the SEC.

2. Insider trading must be reported to the SEC.

3. Manipulative trading that affects security prices is prohibited.

4. Proxy procedures are controlled by the SEC.

5. The Federal Reserve Board was given the responsibility of setting margin requirements. This affects the proportion of a security purchase that can be made via credit.

C. The Securities Act Amendments of 1975 touched on three important issues.

1. Congress mandated the creation of a national market system (NMS). Implementation details of the NMS were left to the SEC. Agreement on the final form of the NMS is yet to come.

2. Fixed commissions (also called fixed brokerage rates) on public transactions in securities were eliminated.

3. Financial institutions, like commercial banks and insurance firms, were prohibited from acquiring membership on stock exchanges where their purpose in so doing might be to reduce or save commissions on their own trades.

D. In March, 1982, the SEC adopted "Rule 415." This process is now known as a shelf registration or a shelf offering.

1. This allows the firm to avoid the lengthy, full registration process each time a public offering of securities is desired.

2. In effect, a master registration statement that covers the financing plans of the firm over the coming two years is filed with the SEC. After approval, the securities are sold to the investing public in a piecemeal fashion or "off the shelf."

3. Prior to each specific offering a short statement about the issue is filed with the SEC.

TRUE-FALSE

_____ 1. A share of IBM common stock is a real asset.

_____ 2. Capital formation in underdeveloped countries might be assisted if those countries' financial market systems were more extensively developed.

_____ 3. General Motors is a typical example of a financial intermediary.

_____ 4. The Money Market is housed at 11 Wall Street, New York City.

_____ 5. Common stocks are money market instruments.

_____ 6. Price quotations on organized security exchanges have been facilitated by the existence of NASDAQ.

_____ 7. The Banking Act of 1933 separated the activities of commercial banking and investment banking.

_____ 8. In a negotiated purchase, the price the investment banker pays the security-issuing firm for the new issue is negotiated between these parties.

_____ 9. Underwriting syndicates are prohibited by the Securities Act of 1933.

_____ 10. Life insurance companies are major purchasers of privately placed securities.

_____ 11. Secondary markets reduce the risk of investing in financial claims.

_____ 12. Equity instruments are traded in the money market.

_____ 13. The capital market includes those securities that have maturity periods extending beyond one year.

_____ 14. Trading in currently existing securities takes place in the primary market.

_____ 15. When new funds are being raised in a typical year, corporate equity markets are favored over corporate debt markets, in terms of dollar volume.

_____ 16. The U.S. tax system favors debt as a method of raising capital in comparison to equity instruments.

_____ 17. A life insurance company is an example of a financial intermediary.

_____ 18. "Crowding out" refers to the use of debt vs. the use of common stock to raise new funds.

_____ 19. Flotation costs for debt generally exceed those of common stock.

_____ 20. In general, flotation costs are inversely related to the size of the security issue.

_____ 21. Inventories represent a category of financial assets.

MULTIPLE CHOICE

1. Which of the following is <u>not</u> a benefit provided by the existence of organized security exchanges?

    a. A continuous market.
    b. Helping business raise new capital.
    c. Keeping long-term bond prices below 8%.
    d. Establishing and publicizing fair security prices.

2. What is it called when an investment banker agrees to sell only as many securities as he or she can at an established price?

    a. A private placement.
    b. A direct placement.
    c. A privileged subscription.
    d. A best-efforts agreement.
    e. An upset agreement.

3. Which of the following security distribution methods is least profitable to the investment banker?

    a. Negotiated purchase.
    b. Competitive-bid purchase.
    c. Commission basis.
    d. Privileged subscription.
    e. Direct sale.

4. A prospectus resembles most closely

    a. A registration statement.
    b. A red herring.
    c. A selling group agreement.
    d. A letter of credit.

5. The purpose of financial markets is to

   a. Lower bond yields.
   b. Allocate savings efficiently.
   c. Raise stock prices.
   d. Employ stock brokers.

6. The maturity boundary dividing the U.S. money and capital markets is

   a. An arbitrary classification system.
   b. Set by the Federal Reserve Board.
   c. Periodically reviewed and altered by the SEC.
   d. Determined by the U.S. Treasury.

7. Flotation costs are highest on

   a. Bonds.
   b. Preferred stock.
   c. Common stock.

8. Insider trading is regulated by

   a. The Banking Act of 1933.
   b. The Glass-Steagall Act of 1933.
   c. The Securities Act of 1933.
   d. The Securities Exchange Act of 1934.

9. Which of the following methods for the distribution of securities bypasses the use of an investment banker?

   a. Negotiated purchase.
   b. Competitive-bid purchase.
   c. Direct sales.
   d. Best-efforts basis.
   e. Privileged subscriptions.

10. The difference between the gross and net proceeds from a given security issue expressed as a percent of the gross proceeds is known as:

    a. Issue costs.
    b. Flotation costs.
    c. Underwriter's spread.
    d. Legal fees.

11. Which of the following is generally not an advantage of private placements?

    a. Speed.
    b. Reduced flotation costs.
    c. Financing flexibility.
    d. Interest costs.

12. Which of the following is <u>not</u> an example of a money market instrument?

    a. U.S. Treasury bills.
    b. Common stock.
    c. Federal agency securities.
    d. Commercial paper.

13. An agreement which obligates the investment banker to underwrite securities that are not accepted by privileged investors is known as a:

    a. Privileged subscription.
    b. Standby agreement.
    c. Negotiated purchase.
    d. Best-efforts basis.

14. The demand for funds by the federal government puts upward pressure on interest rates causing private investors to be pushed out of the financial markets. This is called:

    a. The big squeeze.
    b. The efficient market hypothesis.
    c. The crowding out effect.
    d. Liquidity preference.
    e. Government intervention.

15. Insurance companies invest in the "long-end" of the securities market. In which of the following instruments would an insurance company be <u>least</u> likely to invest <u>most</u> of its funds in:

    a. Mortgages.
    b. Corporate Bonds.
    c. Commercial Paper.
    d. Corporate Stocks.

16. Which of the following is/are NYSE listing requirements:

    a. Profitability.
    b. Market Value.
    c. Public Ownership.
    d. All of the above.
    e. None of the above.

18

Term Loans and Leases

<u>Orientation</u>: The first section of this chapter provides an overview of the major sources of term loans and their characteristics. The second section of the chapter provides an overview of lease financing, including a discussion of leasing arrangements, the accounting treatment of financial leases, the lease versus purchase decision, and the potential benefits from leasing.

I.   Term loans

    A.   In general, term loans have maturities from 1 to 10 years and are repaid in periodic installments over the life of the loan. Term loans are usually secured by a chattel mortgage on equipment or a mortgage on real property. The principal suppliers of term credit include commercial banks, insurance companies, and to a lesser extent pension funds.

        1.   The <u>maturities</u> of term loans are usually as follows:

            a.   Commercial banks: 1 to 5 years.

            b.   Insurance companies: 5 to 15 years.

            c.   Pension funds: 5 to 15 years.

        2.   The collateral backing term loans is usually as follows:

a.   Shorter maturity loans are usually secured with a chattel mortgage on machinery and equipment or securities such as stocks and bonds.

b.   Longer maturity loans are frequently secured by mortgages on real estate.

3.   In addition to collateral, the lender on a term loan agreement will very often place <u>restrictive covenants</u> which are designed to maintain the borrower's financial condition on a par with that which existed at the time the loan was made.

    a.   <u>Working capital restrictions</u> involve maintaining a minimum, current ratio that reflects the norm for the borrower's industry, as well as the lender's desires.

    b.   <u>Additional borrowing restrictions</u> prevent the borrower from increasing the amount of debt financing outstanding without the lender's approval.

    c.   A third covenant that is very popular requires that the borrower supply <u>periodic financial statements</u> to the lender.

    d.   Term loan agreements often include a provision that requires that the lender approve major personnel changes and insure the lives of "key" personnel with the lender as the beneficiary.

4.   Term loans are generally repaid in periodic installments in accordance with <u>repayment schedules</u> established by the lender. Each installment includes both an interest and a principal component.

II. Leasing

A.   There are three major lease agreements: direct leasing, sale and leaseback, and leveraged leasing.

1.   In a <u>direct lease</u> the firm acquires the services of an asset it did not previously own. Direct leasing is available through a number of financial institutions, including manufacturers, banks, finance companies, independent leasing

companies, and special-purpose leasing companies. Basically, direct leasing involves the purchase of the asset by the lessor from a vendor and leasing the asset to the lessee.

2. A _sale and leaseback_ arrangement occurs when a firm sells land, buildings, or equipment that it already owns to a financial institution and simultaneously enters into an agreement to lease the property back for a specified period under specific terms. The lessee firm receives cash in the amount of the sales price of the asset sold and the use of the asset over the term of the lease. In return, the firm must make periodic rental payments throughout the term of lease to the lessor.

3. In a _leveraged lease_ a third participant is added who finances the acquisition of the asset to be leased for the lessor. From the lessee's standpoint, this lease is no different from the two lease arrangements discussed above. But with a leveraged lease, specific consideration is given to the financing arrangement used by the lessor in acquiring the asset to be leased.

B. The accounting profession through _Financial Accounting Statement No. 13_ requires the capitalization or any lease that meets one or more of the following criteria:

1. The lease transfers ownership of the property to the lessee by the end of the lease term.

2. The lease contains a bargain repurchase option.

3. The lease term is equal to 75% or more of the estimated economic life of the leased property.

4. The present value of the minimum lease payments equals 90% of the excess of the fair value of the property over any related investment tax credit retained by the lessor.

C. The _lease versus purchase_ decision requires a standard capital budgeting type of analysis, as well as an analysis of two alternative "packages" of financing. Two models are used to evaluate the lease versus purchase decision.

1. The first model computes the net present value of the purchase option which can be defined as follows:

$$NPV\ (P) = \sum_{t=1}^{n} \frac{ACF_t}{(1 + K)^t} - IO$$

where ACF_t =   the annual after-tax cash flow resulting from the purchase in period t,

      K =   the firm's cost of capital applicable to the project being analyzed and the particular mix of financing used to acquire the project,

    IO =   the initial cash outlay required to purchase the asset in period zero (now),

     n =   the productive life of the project.

2.   In the second model a net advantage to lease (NAL) over purchase equation is used which indicates the more favorable (least expensive) method of financing. The equation used to arrive at NAL is as follows:

$$NAL = \sum_{t=1}^{n} \frac{O_t(1-T) - R_t(1-T) - TI_t - TD_t}{(1 + r)^t}$$

$$- \frac{V_n}{(1 + K_s)^n} + IO$$

where O_t =   any operating cash flows incurred in period t which are incurred only where the asset is purchased. Most often this consists of maintenance expenses and insurance that would be paid by the lessor.

    R_t =   the annual rental for period t.

    T =   the marginal tax rate on corporate income.

    I_t =   the tax deductible interest expense foregone in period t if the lease option is adopted. This level of interest expense was set equal to that which would have been paid on a loan equal to the full purchase price of the asset.

254

D_t = depreciation expense in period t for the asset.

V_n = the after-tax salvage value of the asset expected in year n.

K_s = the discount rate used to find the present value of V_n. This rate should reflect the risk inherent in the estimated V_n. For simplicity, the after-tax cost of capital is often used as a proxy for this rate.

IO = the purchase price of the asset which is not paid by the firm in the event the asset is leased.

r = the before-tax rate of interest on borrowed funds. This rate is used to discount the relatively certain after-tax cash flow savings accruing through leasing the asset.

If NAL were positive, there would be a positive cost advantage to lease financing. If NAL were negative, then purchasing the asset and financing with a debt plus equity package would be the preferred alternative. However, we would lease or purchase the asset in accordance with the value of NAL in only two circumstances:

a. If NPV (P) were positive, then the asset should be acquired through the preferred financing method as indicated by NAL.

b. If NPV (P) were negative, then the asset's services should be acquired via the lease alternative only if NAL is positive and greater in absolute value than NPV(P). That is, the asset should be leased only if the cost advantage of leasing (NAL) is great enough to offset the negative NPV(P). In effect, if a positive NAL were to more than offset a negative NPV(P), then the net present value through lease would be positive.

D. Over the years a number of potential benefits have been offered for lease financing. Some of the more frequently cited advantages are enumerated and commented upon here.

1. **Flexibility and convenience**. It is often argued that lease financing is more convenient than other forms of financing because smaller amounts of funds can be raised at lower cost. In addition, it is often argued that lease payment schedules can be made to coincide with cash flows generated by the asset. These may or may not be real advantages. It depends on the actual circumstances faced by the lessee firm.

2. **Lack of restrictions**. It has been argued that leases require fewer restrictions on the lessee than do debt agreements.

3. **Avoiding the risk of obsolescence**. This argument is generally conceded to be fallacious because the lessor includes his or her estimated cost of obsolescence in the lease patents.

4. **Conservation of working capital**. Here it is argued that leasing involves no down payment. However, the borrower might obtain the same effect by borrowing the down payment.

5. **100% financing**. The lease involves 100% financing but purchasing the asset would surely involve some equity. As we noted above, the down payment could be borrowed to produce 100% financing via a loan. In addition, it is not clear that 100% lease financing is desirable because it represents 100% non-owner financing. Finally the lease agreement does _not_ entitle the lessee to the asset's salvage value. Thus, the lease provides 100% financing for the "use value" of the asset but not its "salvage value."

6. **Tax savings**. The difference in tax shelters between leasing and other forms of financing can only be evaluated by using a net advantage of lease model as we discussed earlier.

7. **Ease of obtaining credit**. Lease financing _may_ be more or less difficult to obtain than other forms of financing. This advantage (or disadvantage) can only be evaluated on a case-by-case basis.

Study Problem

1. Palmer Industries, which has a 50% tax rate, wants to acquire a $200,000 piece of equipment. The equipment would be depreciated over a 5-year life on a straight-line basis. At the end of the 5-year period the equipment is expected to have a zero salvage value. Palmer has two alternatives available to it with regard to how the equipment is to be financed. It can borrow the $200,000 at 10% interest and repay the loan in 5 equal annual installments or lease the equipment for 5 annual rental payments of $55,000 each (payable at the beginning of the year). Palmer usually finances its assets by using 40% debt and 60% equity. Maintenance services are estimated to be $4,000 under the leasing contract and net cash flows from the equipment are estimated to be $100,000 per year before depreciation and taxes.

Required :

(a) Compute the annual installments, principal, interest, and remaining balance for a loan equal to the full purchase price of the asset (i.e., $200,000).

(b) Assuming Palmer's after-tax cost of capital is 12%, compute the net present value of the purchase alternative.

(c) Provided that Palmer has a target debt ratio of 100% for projects like this, compute the net advantage to leasing (NAL) the equipment.

(d) Which method of financing should be used by Palmer? Why?

SOLUTION:

(a)

Year	Installment	Interest	Principal	Remaining Balance
0				$200,000
1	$52,757	$20,000	$32,757	167,243
2	52,757	16,724	36,033	131,210
3	52,757	13,121	39,636	91,574
4	52,757	9,157	43,600	47,974
5	52,757	4,797	47,960	14*

*Difference due to rounding.

(b) Initial outlay (I0) = $200,000.

Calculating annual net cash flows:

	Book Profits	Cash Flow
Annual cash flow	$100,000	$100,000
Less depreciation	(40,000)	--
Earnings before taxes	60,000	100,000
Less taxes (50%)	(30,000)	(30,000)
Annual after-tax cash flow		$ 70,000

$$\text{Net present value} = \$70,000 \sum_{t=1}^{5} \frac{1}{(1 + 0.12)^t} - \$200,000$$

$$= \$70,000 \, (3.605) - \$200,000$$

$$= \underline{\$52,350}$$

Thus, the equipment's purchase through normal financing is justified, as the net present value is greater than zero.

(c) The net advantage to leasing is computed as follows:

$$NAL = \sum_{t=1}^{n} \frac{O_t(1-T) - R_t(1 - T) - TI_t - TD_t}{(1 + r)^t} - \frac{V_n}{(1 + k_s)^n} + IO$$

Solving for NAL's component parts,

$$\sum_{t=1}^{n} \frac{O_t(1 - T)}{(1 + r)^t} = 4,000(1 - 0.50)\,(3.791) = \$7,582$$

Note that the rental payments are made at the beginning of each year.

$$\sum_{t=0}^{n-1} \frac{R_t(1 - T)}{(1 + r)^t} = 55,000(0.5)\,(3.791) = \$104,252.50$$

$$(1.10) = \$114,677.75$$

$$\sum_{t=1}^{n} T(I_t) = \frac{0.5(20,000)}{(1.10)} + \frac{0.5(16,724)}{(1.10)^2} + \frac{0.5(13,121)}{(1.10)^3}$$

$$+ \frac{.05(9,157)}{(1.10)^4} + \frac{0.5(4,797)}{(1.10)^5}$$

$$= \$9,090.91 + 6,910.74 + 4,929.00 + 3,127.12$$

$$+ 1,489.28$$

$$= \$25,547.05$$

$$\sum_{t=1}^{n} \frac{TD_t}{(1 + r)^t} = 0.5(40,000)\ (3.791) = \$75,820.00$$

$$\frac{V_n}{(1 + k_s)^n} = 0$$

$$IO = \$200,000$$

$$NAL = \$7,582.00 - 114,677.75 - 25,547.05$$

$$- 75,820.00 - 0 + 200,000$$

$$= -\$8,462.80$$

(d) The leasing alternative should not be selected by Palmer since the NAL is negative and the NPV(P) is positive. Hence, the net present value of acquiring the asset's services by leasing equals

$$\$52,350 - \$8,462.80 = \$43,887.20$$

Self-Tests

TRUE-FALSE

_____ 1. One of the primary economic reasons for borrowing is the inability of a firm to utilize all of the tax benefits associated with the leasing of an asset.

_____ 2. A lease payment is deductible as an expense for federal income tax purposes.

_____ 3. If leases are capitalized on the balance sheet, it permits easier analysis of the contractual obligations of the firm.

_____ 4. Over the years the accounting treatment of leases has changed toward greater disclosure.

_____ 5. Under a sale and leaseback arrangement, a company acquires the use of an asset that it did not own previously.

_____ 6. The distinguishing feature between a financial lease and an operating lease is cancellability.

_____ 7. A chattel mortgage is a lien on real property.

_____ 8. Insurance company term loans are generally competitive with bank term loans.

_____ 9. The working capital requirement is probably the most commonly used and most comprehensive provision in a term loan agreement.

_____ 10. The interest rate on a term loan is generally higher than the rate on a short-term loan to the same borrower.

MULTIPLE CHOICE

1. Which of the following distinguishes a bank term loan from trade credit?

   a. A final maturity of one year or more.
   b. Credit is extended under an informal loan agreement.
   c. Credit is extended under a formal loan agreement.
   d. a and b only.
   e. a and c only.

2. Rarely will a bank make a term loan that has a final maturity of more than:

   a. 5 years.
   b. 10 years.
   c. 20 years.
   d. 25 years.
   e. None of the above.

3. The interest rate on a term loan is <u>not</u> set by:

   a. Periodic negotiations between the borrower and the lender over the term of the loan.
   b. A fixed rate effective over the life of the loan.
   c. A variable rate that is adjusted in keeping with changes in the prime rate.
   d. All of the above.
   e. None of the above.

4. The important protective covenants of a loan agreement may be classified as follows:

   a. General provisions.
   b. Routine provisions.
   c. Specific provisions.
   d. All of the above.
   e. a and c only.

5. Which of the following is a source of equipment financing?

   a. Commercial bank.
   b. Finance company.
   c. Seller of the equipment.
   d. All of the above.

19

Long-Term Debt, Preferred Stock, and Common Stock

Orientation: This chapter examines detailed variations of the three major sources of long-term and permanent funds for the firm: long-term debt, preferred stock, and common stock. Key terminology is introduced. The major sources of financing are described and their usefulness to the corporation is discussed.

I.   Bonds or long-term debt

   A.   Certain terms are common to the practice of finan-
        cing long-term needs through bond issues. Some of
        the key definitions of these terms are noted below.

        1.   The coupon interest rate determines the fixed
             return on a long-term debt contract. A coupon
             interest rate of 9 percent on a $1,000 par
             value bond indicates that the investment will
             receive $90 in interest receipts annually.

        2.   When a debt issue is offered to the public, a
             trustee is designated by the issuing corpora-
             tion to act on behalf of the bond investors.
             The formal agreement is actually between the
             firm and the trustee who acts for the bond-
             holders. The contract between the firm and the
             trustee is called the bond indenture.

             a.   The trustee's job is to see that the terms
                  of the indenture are actually carried out.

             b.   The indenture contains the terms of the
                  bond issue and any restrictive provisions
                  placed on the firm.

3. Do not confuse the coupon interest rate with the <u>yield to maturity</u> on the bond. The yield to maturity is the discount rate that equates the present value of the interest and principal payments with the current market price of the bond. From our discussions of capital budgeting techniques, it is clear that this discount rate is nothing more than the internal rate of return for this bond.

B. The rate of return that investors demand on bond issues is determined by several factors, including the size of the issue, the issue's maturity, the issue's riskiness or rating, the restrictive requirements of the issue, and the current riskless interest rate.

C. There are a number of different debt instruments.

1. A <u>debenture</u> is an unsecured or general credit bond. Specific property is not pledged as collateral for these long-term promissory notes.

   a. The investor in a debenture obtains his or her protection from both the general credit worthiness of the firm and the bond indenture.

2. <u>Subordinated debentures</u> have a lower claim on assets in the event of liquidation than do other senior debtholders.

3. <u>Income bonds</u> represent a departure from the other forms of debt.

   a. Interest on these promissory notes is paid to investors only when it is earned.

   b. Although interest may be passed, it is generally allowed to accumulate for some period of time and it must be paid prior to the payment of any common stock dividends.

4. A <u>mortgage bond</u> is secured by a lien on specific assets of the firm.

   a. In the mortgage, a preference in a specific asset is granted by the borrower to a class of creditors.

263

b. In the event of default of a provision contained in the bond indenture, a trustee can seize the pledged property, sell it, and use the proceeds to settle the lender's claim.

c. It is possible to sell more than one class of mortgage bonds using the same property as collateral. Thus, first-mortgage bonds and second-mortgage bonds could be sold pledging the same fixed asset. In the event of default, however, the holders of the first-mortgage bonds must be paid in full prior to any distribution of proceeds to the second-mortgage bondholders.

d. A mortgage may be either closed-end, open-end, or limited open-end.

e. With a closed-end mortgage, additional bonds with equal rank against the same security may not be issued.

f. With an open-end mortgage, additional bonds under an existing lien may be issued.

g. With a limited open-end mortgage, a limited amount of additional bonds may be issued with equal rank against the same security.

5. Collateral trust bonds are another form of secured, long-term financing.

a. This type of financing is secured by a pledge of stocks and/or bonds by the borrowing company to the trustee.

b. If default occurs, the securities are sold by the trustee and the proceeds are used to pay the bondholders.

6. Equipment trust certificates, which are actually a hybrid between debt and lease financing, are used extensively by railroads to acquire needed equipment.

a. According to this method, a manufacturer builds the equipment to meet the firm's specifications. The equipment is then sold to a trustee.

b. The trustee sells equipment trust certificates to pay the manufacturer. The trustee then leases the equipment to the firm.

c. The lease payments are used by the trustee to pay a fixed return to investors in the certificates. The annual installments provide for retirement of the certificates well within the economic life of the assets being used. When the certificates are retired, title to the assets passes to the firm (railroad or airline).

7. Pollution Control Revenue Bonds are actually a corporate obligation disguised as a municipal bond.

a. Debt service funds for the bond comes directly from a lease or payment pledge agreement between the municipality and a corporation, many times a public utility.

b. Their popularity stems from the fact that their tax-free status as a municipal obligation reduces the yield that investors demand.

8. Industrial Development Bonds which were extremely popular in the 50's and 60's are almost identical to Pollution Control Revenue Bonds.

a. In this case the local government attempts to attract new industry by constructing a plant and then leasing it to the incoming firm.

b. Since the bonds were issued by a municipality they were tax free and thus resulted in lower financing costs for the firm.

9. While Floating Rate or Variable Rate Bonds have been popular in Europe for years, it was not until 1974 that they finally appeared in this country.

a. To issuers like banks and finance companies whose revenues go up when interest rates rise and decline as interest rates fall, this type of debt eliminates some of the risk and variability in earnings that accompany interest rate savings.

    b.   While all floating rate bonds are a bit different most have an initial period during which a minimum rate is guaranteed after which the rate is then tied to the 91-day Treasury-bill rate.

    c.   The most common issuer is a bank, bank holding company, or finance company.

10.   <u>Eurobonds</u> are not so much a different type of security as they are securities, in this case bonds, issued in a different country, in this case a European country.

    a.   The reason we have given them special attention is due to their extreme popularity in recent years.

    b.   The primary attraction to borrowers aside from favorable rates in the Eurodollar market is its relative lack of regulation (as Eurodollar bonds are not registered with the S.E.C.); less rigorous disclosure requirements and the speed with which they may be issued.

11.   <u>Junk</u> or low-rated bonds are bonds rated BB or below.

    a.   Originally the term junk bonds was used to describe bonds issued by "fallen angels" or firms with sound financial histories that were facing severe financial problems.

    b.   Today the term "junk bonds" refers to any bond with a low rating.

    c.   In recent years junk bonds have been effectively used to finance corporate buyouts.

12.   <u>Zero</u> and <u>low</u> bonds allow the issuing firm to issue bonds at a substantial discount from their $1,000 face value with a zero or very low coupon.

    a.   The disadvantages are, when the bond matures, the issuing firm will face an extremely large nondeductible cash outflow, much greater than the cash inflow they experienced when the bonds were first issued.

    b.   Discount bonds are not callable and can only be retired at maturity.

    c.   On the other hand, annual cash outflows associated with interest payments do not occur with zero coupon bonds.

D.   Retiring debt

    1.   Bonds may be retired at maturity at which time the bondholder receives the par value of the bond or the bonds can be retired prior to maturity.

    2.   A call provision entitles the corporation to repurchase or "call" the bonds from their holders at stated prices over specified periods.

    3.   A sinking fund allows for the periodic repayment of debt, thus reducing the total amount of debt outstanding.

E.   Bond refunding

    1.   It is possible to analyze the profitability of refunding a bond issue prior to its maturity as a capital-budgeting decision.

    2.   The decision carries with it an initial cash outlay, which is followed by interest savings in the future, if new bonds are marketed with a lower interest rate. A complete example will be given in the study problems.

    3.   In analyzing a refunding operation, most analysts favor discounting the projected savings not at the firm's cost of capital, but at the after-tax cost of borrowing on the new bonds. This is because in a refunding decision, as opposed to a normal investment decision, the costs and benefits are known with complete certainty.

II. Preferred stock

A.   Preferred stock is a hybrid form of financing that combines features of debt and common stock.

1. Preferred stockholders' claims on assets come after those of creditors but before those of common shareholders.

2. Although preferred stock carries a stipulated dividend, the actual payment of a dividend is discretionary. The omission of a payment does not result in the default of the obligation.

3. Preferred stockholders are usually limited to the specified dividend yield and do not ordinarily share in any residual earnings.

B. Almost all preferred stocks have a cumulative feature that provides for unpaid dividends in any one year to be carried forward.

1. The accrued preferred stock dividends must be paid before the company can meet the dividend obligation of the common shareholders.

2. There is no guarantee or obligation that the preferred stock dividends in arrears will be paid.

   a. If the preferred stock dividends are in arrears and the company wishes to pay a common dividend, the company may choose not to clear up the arrearage but make an exchange offering to preferred stockholders instead.

C. To further provide protection for the preferred shareholder, protective provisions in addition to the cumulative feature are common to preferred stock.

1. Many times in the event of nonpayment of dividends, the preferred stockholder will be provided with voting rights.

D. Although preferred stock does not have a set maturity associated with it, issuing firms generally provide for some method of retirement.

1. Most preferred stock has a call provision that allows the issuing firm to replace the preferred stock if interest rates fall.

2. Sinking fund provisions are also common to preferred stock. They allow the firm to periodically set aside an amount of money for the retirement of its preferred stock.

III. Common stock

    A. The common stockholders of a corporation are its residual owners. They assume the ultimate risk associated with ownership.

        1. In the event of liquidation, these stockholders have a residual claim on the assets of the company (i.e., after the claims of all creditors and preferred stockholders are settled in full).

        2. Common stock has no maturity date. It can be liquidated by the owner's selling the stock in the secondary market.

    B. Common stockholders are entitled to share in the earnings of the company only if cash dividends are paid.

        1. Stockholders prosper from the market-value appreciation of their stock and the dividends paid (if the stock pays dividends).

        2. Creditors can take legal action if contractual interest and principal are not met, but stockholders have no legal recourse if the company defaults on dividend payments.

    C. The common stockholders of a company are the residual owners and thus are entitled to elect the board of directors.

        1. In most large corporations the average stockholder has very little power over who manages and how the company is managed.

            a. Each stockholder is entitled to one vote for each share of stock he or she owns.

            b. Most stockholders vote by proxy, which is a form by which the stockholder assigns his or her rights to another person.

                (1) If minority stockholders can accumulate enough proxy votes, they can exercise limited control or influence over the board of directors of the company.

                (2) In most proxy contests the existing management wins because it has both

the organization and the use of the company's financial resources to fight the unhappy stockholders.

2. Depending on the corporate charter, the board of directors is elected either under a majority voting system or under a cumulative voting system.

   a. Under the majority voting system, each stockholder has one vote for each share of stock he or she owns. The stockholder must vote for each director position that is open.

   b. Under the cumulative voting system, a stockholder is able to accumulate his or her votes and cast them for less than the total number of directors being elected.

   c. A cumulative voting system, in contrast to the majority system, permits minority interests a possible chance to elect a certain number of directors.

D. A preemptive right entitles a common stockholder to maintain his or her proportional ownership by offering the stockholder an opportunity to purchase, on a pro rata basis, any new stock being offered or any securities being converted into common stock.

E. The rights offering

1. An offering of securities to existing share-holders prior to selling all or part of the issue to the general public is called a <u>rights offering</u>.

2. When a firm elects to sell new common stock by means of the privileged subscription method, each stockholder receives in the mail one <u>right</u> for each share of stock owned.

   a. The specific terms of the offering spell out the number of rights needed to buy one new share of stock, the subscription price of the stock, and the expiration date of the offering.

   b. The existing stockholder may exercise his or her rights and buy additional shares, sell his or her rights for cash, or simply do nothing.

270

3. The market value of a right is determined by three major factors: (1) the current market price of the stock, (2) the subscription price of the new shares, and (3) the number of rights needed to buy one new share.

4. To determine how many shares must be sold to raise the desired funds the desired funds are divided by the subscription price:

$$\frac{\text{new shares}}{\text{to be sold}} = \frac{\text{desired funds to be raised}}{\text{subscription price}}$$

5. The number of rights needed to purchase one share of stock can be determined as follows:

$$\frac{\text{number of rights needed to}}{\text{purchase one share of stock}} = \frac{\text{original number of shares outstanding}}{\text{new shares to be sold}}$$

6. When the stock is selling ex-rights, the theoretical market value of one right can be determined by using the following relationship:

$$R = \frac{P_{ex} - S}{N}$$

where   R = value of one right,

P_{ex} = the ex-rights price of the stock,

S = the subscription price,

N = the number of rights needed to purchase one share of stock.

7. Alternatively, when the stock is selling rights-on, that is, prior to the ex-rights date, the value of a right can be determined from the following equation:

$$R = \frac{P_{on} - S}{N + 1}$$

where P_{on} = the rights-on price of the stock.

Study Problems

1. This problem illustrates the major principles involved in determining whether or not an existing bond issue should be refunded. First, the financial characteristics of the

271

existing (old) bond issue are listed and then the financial data related to the proposed (new) issues are presented.

Bonds currently outstanding:

Principal amount outstanding:	$20,000,000
Coupon rate:	7%
Years to maturity:	15
Unamortized bond discount:	$ 300,000
Unamortized flotation costs:	$ 120,000
Call premium:	5%

Proposed issue of bonds:

Principal amount outstanding:	$20,000,000
Coupon rate:	6%
Years to maturity:	15
Proceeds to the firm after flotation costs:	$20,000,000
Issue expense:	$ 100,000
Corporate income tax rate:	50%

Both issues will be outstanding simultaneously for a period of 30 days. Using the net-present-value method (on an after-tax basis), determine whether or not the firm should refund the old bond issue.

SOLUTION

Step 1: Calculate the <u>initial outlay</u>.

1. Determine the difference between the inflow from the new issue and the outflow from retiring the old issue.

Cost of calling old bonds (1.05 x $20 million)	$21,000,000
Proceeds, after flotation costs, from new issue	20,000,000
Difference between inflows and outflows	$ 1,000,000

2. Determine total issuing and overlap expenses

Issuing expense on new bonds	$100,000	
Interest expense on old bonds during overlap period ($1,400,000/12)	116,667	$ 216,667

3. Add: the item above to determine $ 1,216,667
   the gross initial outlay

4. Determine tax deductible expenses
   incurred:

   Interest expenses during $ 116,667
     overlap period
   Unamortized flotation costs   420,000
     and discount on the old
     bonds
   Call premium (i.e., call   1,000,000
     price less par value)
                                   ─────────
                                   $1,536,667

5. Less: tax savings
   Marginal tax rate (50% x $ 768,334
   total tax deductible expenses)   ─────────

6. Equals:
   Net <u>initial</u> cash flow $ 448,333
                                               ═════════

Step 2:   Calculate the <u>annual cash benefit</u> from elimin-
          ating the old bonds through refunding.

1. Determine annual interest expenses
   7% interest on $20,000,000 $ 1,400,000

2. Determine expenses incurred
   Annual interest expense $1,400,000
   Annual amortization of flota-   28,000
     tion costs and discount on
     old bond ($420,000/15)
   Total annual tax deductible $1,428,000
     expense

3. Less: Annual tax savings
   Marginal tax rate (50% x total $ 714,000
     annual tax deductible expenses)   ─────────

4. Equals:
   Annual cash benefit from elimination
     of old bonds $ 686,000
                                               ═════════

Step 3:   Calculate the <u>annual cash outflow</u> from issuing
          the new bonds.

1. Determine the annual interest expense
   6% on $20,000,000 $ 1,200,000

273

2. Determine expenses incurred
    Annual interest expense $1,200,000
    Annual amortization of bond   -0-
      discount
    Annual amortization of   6,667
      issuing expenses
      ($100,000/15)
    Total annual tax deductible $1,206,667
      expenses

3. Less: annual tax savings
    Marginal tax rate (50%) total $ 603,334
      annual tax deductible expenses

4. Equals: annual net cash
    Annual net cash outflow from $ 596,666
      issuing bonds

Step 4: Calculate the annual net cash benefit from the
         refunding decision.

1. Add benefits:
    Annual cash benefits from eliminating $ 686,000
      the old bonds
2. Less costs:
    Annual cash outflows from issuing $ 596,666
      the new debt

3. Equals:
    Annual net cash benefits $ 89,334

Step 5: Calculate the present value of the annual net
         cash benefits.

1. Discount the 15-year $89,334 annuity
    back to present at the after-tax cost
    of borrowing on the new bonds (6%)(1 - 0.5)

    $89,334(11.938) = $ 1,066,469

Step 6: Calculate the refunding decision's net present
         value.

1. Present value of annual net cash $ 1,066,469
      benefits

2. Less: present value of initial outlay   448,333

3. Equals: net present value $ 618,136

The positive net present value of $618,136 indicates that
the refunding should be undertaken.

2. F. Beamer Construction, Inc., a regional contracting firm, currently has 600,000 shares of common stock outstanding. The company will issue another 100,000 shares through a rights offering. The market price of the firm's common stock is $80 per share. The subscription price to the new issue has been set at $73 per share.

(a) Compute the number of rights needed to buy one new share at the subscription price of $73.

(b) Compute the value of a right.

(c) What will be the theoretical value of one share of stock when it goes ex-rights?

(d) Prior to the rights being exercised but after the stock goes ex-rights, some adverse economic news startles the market and the price of Beamer stock drops to $78 per share. Determine the price of one right under these conditions.

SOLUTION

(a) The ratio of old or existing common shares to the new shares that will be sold determines the number of rights needed to buy one new share:

$$\frac{600,000}{100,000} = 6$$

(b)
$$R + \frac{P_{on} - S}{N + 1} = \frac{80 - 73}{6 + 1} = \frac{7}{7} = \$1 \text{ (value of one right)}$$

(c) Theoretically, the value of the common stock will fall by the value of one right:

$$P_{ex} = P_{on} - R_O = 80 - 1 = \$79$$

(d)
$$R = \frac{P_{ex} - S}{N} = \frac{78 - 73}{6} = \$0.833$$

3. You own six shares of Beamer Construction common stock (see problem 2). Demonstrate that you will neither gain nor lose any monetary return if you exercise your rights and the stock sells at its theoretical value after the rights have been exercised.

SOLUTION

The value of six old shares at the current market price: $6(80) = \$480$

275

The cost of exercising the rights is the = 73
    subscription price:

The value of your seven shares (what you = $553
    could have received had you sold your
    old shares plus your out-of-pocket
    subscription price cost)

The average value of your seven shares to you, then, is $533/7 - $79 per share. Notice that this is the theoretical value of the stock when it goes ex-rights. This analysis, of course, ignores any transaction fees.

Self-Tests

TRUE-FALSE

_____ 1. The call privilege on a bond issue will be most costly to the issuing firm when the general level of interest rates is low and is expected to rise.

_____ 2. The generally accepted discount rate to be used in the analysis of a bond-refunding operation is the after-tax cost of borrowing on the refunded bond.

_____ 3. Collateral trust bonds are actually a form of lease financing used to a large degree by the railroad industry.

_____ 4. Most preferred stock issues have a noncumulative feature.

_____ 5. The cumulative feature allows a preferred stockholder to accumulate his or her votes and cast them for one or more directors.

_____ 6. Preferred stockholders do not ordinarily share in the residual earnings of a company.

_____ 7. Sinking-fund arrangements are commonly found with preferred stock issues.

_____ 8. Unlike common stock dividends, preferred stock dividends carry a legal obligation and must be paid or the company will default.

_____ 9. Proxy contests usually result in the victory of the dissatisfied stockholders.

_____10. A preemptive right entitles the common and preferred stockholders to maintain their proportional ownership in the corporation.

_____11. A collateral trust bond is a bond secured by common stock or other bonds.

_____12. One way to obtain a continuous source of debt financing is through a sinking fund.

_____13. Like common stock, preferred stock pays a dividend that varies with earnings.

MULTIPLE CHOICE

1. What is the name for a bond secured by a lien on designated assets of the firm?

    a. Debenture.
    b. Income bond.
    c. Bankers' acceptance.
    d. Mortgage bond.

2. Which of the following bonds offers investors the most protection?

    a. Debentures.
    b. Subordinated debentures.
    c. Income bonds.
    d. First-mortgage bonds.
    e. Second-mortgage bonds.
    f. A second-mortgage bond in which the mortgage is open-ended.

3. A bond not secured by a mortgage will share equally in bankruptcy with:

    a. Common stock.
    b. Preferred stock.
    c. First-mortgage bonds.
    d. Unsecured general creditors.

4. A participating feature allows preferred stockholders to:

    a. Participate in the election of the corporate board of directors.
    b. Convert their preferred stock into common stock.
    c. Receive some residual earnings of the corporation.

5. In a rights offering of common stock the subscription price is:

    a. Set equal to the current market price of the stock.
    b. Set below the current market price of the stock.
    c. Set above the current market price of the stock.
    d. None of the above.

6. In calculating the value of one right when the stock is selling rights-on, the analyst needs to know the number of rights needed to buy one share of stock and:

    a. The length of the rights offering period.
    b. The transactions costs involved.
    c. The price/earnings ratio of the firm's stock.
    d. The subscription price per share to the stock issue.

7. A bond indenture:

    a. Contains the provisions of the security agreement.
    b. States the bond's current ratings.
    c. States the yield to maturity of the bond.
    d. All of the above.

8. A firm will refund an outstanding bond issue:

    a. To increase trading in the bond issue.
    b. Because interest rates have increased.
    c. To alter the firm's debt-to-equity ratio.
    d. To issue the bonds with a lower coupon rate.

9. Which of the following bonds provides the least protection to bondholders?

    a. Equipment certificates.
    b. Mortgage Bonds.
    c. Income bonds.
    d. Treasury bonds.

20

Convertibles and Warrants

Orientation: The purpose of this chapter is to explain the use or convertibles and warrants and to describe the terminology associated with them and their valuation.

I.   A convertible security is a bond or preferred stock that can be exchanged for a stated number of common shares at the option of the holder.

    A.   The conversion ratio is the stated number of shares that the security can be converted into.

    B.   The conversion price is the face value of the security divided by the conversion ratio.

    C.   The conversion value equals the conversion ratio times the market price of the stock when one converts.

    D.   The security value of a convertible is the price the convertible debenture (or preferred stock) would sell for in the absence of its conversion feature.

    E.   The conversion premium is the difference between the market price of the convertible and the higher of the security value and the conversion value.

    F.   The conversion parity price is the price the investor in effect buys the company's stock for. It is the ratio of the market price of the convertible bond to the conversion ratio.

G. There are several reasons generally given for issuing convertibles:

1. As a sweetening to long-term debt to make the security attractive enough to ensure a market for it.

2. As a method of delayed common stock financing.

    a. No dilution of earnings occurs at time of issuance.

    b. Companies expect them to be converted sometime in the future.

    c. Less dilution of earnings occurs in the future because the conversion price is greater than the common stock price at time of issuance.

3. Convertibles are also issued as a source of temporarily inexpensive funds.

4. In addition, convertibles are also issued to financing mergers to avoid tax liabilities.

H. There are two ways in which a company can stimulate conversion:

1. Include an acceleration clause, which period-ically increases the conversion price and results in a lower conversion ratio over time.

2. Force conversion by calling the convertible.

I. The value of the security is twofold.

1. The value of the common stock when one converts is the first component.

2. The value of the bond or preferred stock provides a cushion or a floor value in case the stock does not rise significantly (Provided interest rates do not increase).

$$\text{security value} = \sum_{t=1}^{N} \frac{\$I}{(1+i)^t} + \frac{\$M}{(1+i)^N}$$

where I = annual dollar interest paid to the investor each year,

i = market yield to maturity on straight bond of same company,

N = number of years to maturity,

M = maturity value or par value of the debt.

EXAMPLE:

Suppose that a company had a convertible outstanding (face $1,000) with 20 years to maturity at an 8% rate. If the company wanted to issue a straight bond 20 years to maturity, a 10% yield would be required to attract investors. What is the current floor value or market price of the bond?

$$SV = \sum_{t=1}^{20} \frac{\$80}{(1.10)^t} + \frac{\$1,000}{(1.10)^{20}}$$

$$= \$80(8.514) + \$1,000(0.149) = \$830.12$$

J. The market price of a convertible security is frequently above its conversion value; this difference is called the <u>premium</u>.

K. Unless the conversion feature is considered worthless, the security will sell for a premium-over-security value (i.e., above the value of the security solely as a bond or preferred stock).

L. In comparing the two premiums, one finds an inverse relationship between them. In the extremes, the security is selling either as a common stock or a bond equivalent.

II. Warrants are a "sweetener" added to a bond or debt issue. Warrants entitle the holder to purchase a specified number of shares of stock at a stated price.

A. The exercise price can be either fixed or "stepped up" over time.

B. A warrant usually has a fixed expiration date.

C. A detachable warrant can be sold separately in the market-place.

D. A nondetachable warrant can only be exercised by the bondholder and cannot be sold on its own.

E. Warrants are issued for two major reasons:

1. Warrants are attached to debt issues as sweeteners to increase the marketability of these issues.

2. Warrants provide an additional cash inflow when they are exercised. Convertible securities do not.

F. The minimum price of a warrant is equal to the price of the common stock less the exercise price times the exercise ratio.

G. The premium on a warrant is the amount above the minimum price for which the warrant sells.

Study Problems

1. Corporation X is about to issue a convertible bond with face value of $1,000 for $1,000 each. The conversion ratio is 20. The current market price of the common stock is $35. The coupon rate of this bond will be 10%. If Corporation X had chosen to finance a straight bond, the effective yield to investors would have been 12%. The number of years to maturity of the convertible is 20 years. What is the conversion premium?

SOLUTION

$(20)($35) = 700 conversion value

$$SV = \sum_{t=1}^{20} \frac{$100}{(1.12)^t} + \frac{$1,000}{(1.12)^{20}}$$

$$= $100(7.469) + $1,000(0.104)$$

$$= $746.90 + $104.00 = $850.90$$

$$\begin{array}{c} \text{Conversion} \\ \text{premium} \end{array} = \begin{pmatrix} \text{market price of} \\ \text{the convertible} \end{pmatrix} = \begin{pmatrix} \text{higher of the sec-} \\ \text{urity value and} \\ \text{conversion value} \end{pmatrix}$$

$$= $1,000 - $850.90$$

$$= $149.10$$

2. The L. Turner Corporation has a warrant that allows the purchase of one share of common stock at $20 per share. The warrant is currently selling at $15, and the common stock is priced at $30 per share. Determine the minimum price and the premium of the warrant.

SOLUTION

$$\text{minimum price} = \left(\begin{array}{c}\text{price of}\\\text{common stock}\end{array}\right) - \left(\begin{array}{c}\text{exercise}\\\text{price}\end{array}\right) \text{ X } \begin{array}{c}\text{exercise}\\\text{ratio}\end{array}$$

$$= (30 - \$20) \text{ x } 1.0$$

$$= \$10$$

$$\text{premium} = \left(\begin{array}{cc}\text{market price of} & \text{minimum price}\\\text{warrant} & - \quad \text{of warrant}\end{array}\right)$$

$$= (\$15 - \$10)$$

$$= \$5$$

Self-Tests

TRUE-FALSE

_____ 1. The only time a firm receives any proceeds from issuing convertibles is when the convertibles are initially issued.

_____ 2. At the time of issuance a convertible security is always priced lower than its conversion value.

_____ 3. An overhanging issue increases the firm's financing flexibility.

_____ 4. The conversion ratio is the ratio of the market price of the convertible security to the conversion price.

_____ 5. The conversion parity price is the price the investor in effect buys the company's stock for when he or she purchases the convertible.

_____ 6. Warrants usually sell for less than their minimum price.

_____ 7. The value of a convertible is determined by its value as a straight bond or preferred stock and its conversion value.

_____ 8. The exercise ratio on a warrant is the number of warrants needed to purchase one share of common stock.

_____ 9. A company can force conversion on a convertible by calling it or through the use of step-up conversion prices.

283

_____10. The stock price/exercise price ratio is one of the most important factors in determining the size of the warrant premium.

_____11. A major reason for issuing warrants is to increase the marketability of the common stock.

_____12. When the convertible security is issued, the firm receives the proceeds from the sale less flotation costs.

_____12. Once the convertible owner trades his convertibles in for common stock, he can retrade the stock back for the convertibles if he desires.

MULTIPLE CHOICE

1. Convertible bonds:

   a. Prohibit the issuance of more common stock.
   b. Can never be called.
   c. Are often an indirect way of selling common stock.
   d. Have no advantages to the investor over straight debt.

2. If a warrant carries a right to one share of common stock and is exercisable at $20 per common share while the market price of a share is $30, the minimum price of the warrant:

   a. Is $10.00.
   b. Is $5.00.
   c. Is $1.00.
   d. Cannot be determined.

3. A convertible's security value:

   a. Will equal its face value.
   b. Changes with interest-rate movement and changes in financial risk.
   c. Will remain constant.
   d. None of the above.

4. The call price of a convertible security is:

   a. The net proceeds received by the issuing company at time of issuance.
   b. Always greater than the face of the bond.
   c. Equal to the conversion value.
   d. None of the above.

284

5. Nondetachable warrants:

   a. Sell for more than detachable warrants in the market.
   b. Sell for less than detachable warrants in the market.
   c. Can never be sold alone in the market.
   d. None of the above.

6. The conversion premium is:

   a. The difference between the market price of the convertible and the common stock.
   b. The product of the conversion ratio and the conversion price.
   c. The difference between the market price of the convertible and the higher of either its bonds or conversion value.
   d. None of the above.

7. Most warrants:

   a. Are nondetachable.
   b. Have an exercise price set above the prevailing market price of the underlying security.
   c. Have an expiration date equal to that of the underlying common stock.
   d. a and c.

APPENDIX 20A

FUTURES AND OPTIONS

I.   Futures and options can be used by the financial manager
     to reduce the risks associated with interest and exchange
     rate and commodity price fluctuations.

     A.   A futures contract is a contract to buy or sell a
          stated commodity (such as soybeans or corn) or a
          financial claim (such as U. S. Treasury bonds) at a
          specified price at some future specified time.

          1.   A futures contract is a specialized form of a
               forward contract distinguished by: (1) an
               organized exchange, (2) a standardized contract
               with limited price changes and margin require-
               ments, (3) a formal clearinghouse and (4) daily
               resettlement of contracts.

               a.   An organized exchange provides a central
                    trading place and encourages confidence in
                    the futures market by allowing for effec-
                    tive regulation of trading.

               b.   Standardized contracts lead to greater
                    liquidity in the secondary market for that
                    contract, which in turn draws more traders
                    into the market.

               c.   The futures clearinghouse serves to
                    guarantee that all trades will be honored.
                    This is done by having the clearinghouse
                    interpose itself as the buyer to every
                    seller and the seller to every buyer.

               d.   Under the daily resettlement process
                    maintenance margins must be maintained.
                    Since the maintenance margin is equal to
                    the maximum possible daily fluctuation for
                    that contract, the trader can never lose
                    more than is in his margin account in any
                    one day.

          2.   For the financial manager financial futures
               provide an excellent way of controlling risk in
               interest rates, foreign exchange rates, and
               stock fluctuations.

     B.   There are two basic types of options: puts and
          calls. A call option gives its owner the right to
          purchase a given number of shares of stock or some
          other asset at a specified price over a specified

time period. A put gives its owner the right to sell a given number of shares of common stock or some other asset at a specified price over a given time period.

1. The popularity of options can be explained by their leverage, financial insurance, and investment alternative expansion features.

   a. The leverage feature allows the financial manager the chance for unlimited capital gains with a very small investment.

   b. When a put with an exercise price equal to the current stock price is purchased, it insures the holder against any declines in the stock price over the life of the put. This is the financial insurance feature of options and can be used by portfolio managers to reduce risk exposure in portfolios.

   c. From the point of view of the investor, the use of puts, calls, and combinations of them can materially increase the set of possible investment alternatives available.

2. Recently, four new variations of the traditional option have appeared: the stock index option, the interest rate option, the foreign exchange option and the Treasury bond futures option.

   a. Stock index options are merely options with the underlying asset being the value or price of an index of stocks - for example, the S&P 100.

   b. Interest rate and foreign exchange options are also merely options with the underlying asset being the Treasury bonds or a specific foreign currency.

   c. Options on Treasury bond futures are different from other bond options in that they involve the acquisition of a futures position rather than the delivery of actual bonds. The buyer of an option on a futures contract achieves immunization against any unfavorable price movements, whereas the buyer of a futures contract achieves immunization against any price movements regardless of whether they are favorable or unfavorable.

Self-Tests

TRUE-FALSE

_____ 1. A futures contract requires its holder to buy or sell the asset regardless of what happens to its value during the interim.

_____ 2. An option contract requires its holder to buy or sell the asset regardless of what happens to its value during the interim.

_____ 3. A naked option is illegal in most states.

MULTIPLE CHOICE

1. The term option premium refers to:

    a. The amount the option price exceeds the exercise price.
    b. The amount the exercise price exceeds the option price by.
    c. The price of the option.
    d. None of the above.

2. The intrinsic value of a call option refers to:

    a. The call premium less the amount the stock price exceeds the exercise price by.
    b. The exercise price less the stock price.
    c. The stock price less the exercise price.
    d. None of the above.

21

Corporate Restructuring: Combinations and Divestitures

<u>Orientation</u>: There are two principal ways by which a firm may grow:

(1) internally, through the acquisition of specific assets which are financed by the retention of earnings and/or external financing, or

(2) externally, through the combination with another company. We turn now to a discussion of external growth through mergers with, and acquisition of, other firms.

I. Determining a firm's value

A. The value of a firm depends not only on its earnings capabilities but also on the operating and financial characteristics of the acquiring firm. To determine an acceptable price of a corporation, a number of factors must be carefully evaluated. The final objective of this valuation process is to maximize the stockholders' wealth (stock price) of both firms.

B. Quantitative variables to be evaluated include (1) book value, (2) appraisal value, (3) market price of a firm's common stock, and (4) earnings per share.

1. The book value of a firm's net worth is the depreciated value of the company's assets less its outstanding liabilities. Book value alone is not a significant measure of the worth of a

289

company but should be used as a starting point to be compared with other analyses.

2. Appraisal value, acquired from an independent appraisal firm, may be useful in conjunction with other methods. Advantages include:

    a. The reduction of accounting goodwill by increasing the recognized worth of specific assets.

    b. A test of the reasonableness of results obtained through other evaluation methods.

    c. The discovery of strengths and weaknesses that otherwise might not be recognized.

3. If a stock is listed on a major securities exchange, such as the New York Exchange, and widely traded, an approximate value can be established on the basis of the market value. The justification is based on the fact that the market quotations indicate the investor's different opinions on a firm's earnings potential and the corresponding risk. The market value approach is the one most frequently used in valuing large corporations. However, this value can change abruptly.

4. Earnings per share is important because the value of the prospective acquisition is frequently considered to be a function of the merger's impact on earnings per share.

C. Effect of earnings dilution

1. In examining the effects of a merger on the surviving concern's earnings per share the investigation should include all of the variables affecting future earnings per share, which include (1) the share exchange ratio, (2) the firms' relative sizes and (3) the firms' relative expected future growth rates in earnings.

2. In general, the terms of the merger must be developed in order to provide a mutually satisfactory earnings pattern for the shareholders of both firms.

II. Financing techniques in mergers

    A. Common stock financing. Whenever common stock is used to acquire a new company, the relative price/earnings ratios of the two businesses are important. A corporation that has a high price/earnings ratio has a distinct advantage.

    B. Debt and preferred stock financing. The primary advantages of convertible debt or convertible preferred stock include the following:

        1. Potential earnings dilution may be partially minimized by issuing a convertible security, if this security is designed to sell at a premium over its conversion value.

        2. A convertible issue may allow the acquiring company to comply with the seller's income objectives without changing its own dividend policy.

        3. Convertible preferred stock also represents a possible way of lowering the voting power of the acquired company.

        4. The convertible bond or preferred stock combines senior security protection with a portion of the growth potential of common stock.

    C. Earn-outs, or deferred payment plans

        1. Benefits for the acquiring organization

            a. The earn-out provides a logical method of adjusting the difference between the amount of stock the purchaser is willing to issue and the amount the seller is agreeing to accept for the business.

            b. The merging company will immediately be able to report higher earnings per share because fewer shares of stock will become outstanding at the time of the acquisition.

            c. The acquiring company is provided with down-side protection in the event that the merged business does not fulfill its earnings expectations.

d. The earn-out diminishes the guesswork in establishing an equitable purchase price.

2. Potential problems associated with earn-outs

   a. The acquired corporation must be capable of being operated as an autonomous business entity.

   b. The acquiring firm must be willing to allow the management of the newly acquired business freedom of operation.

   c. The seller must be willing to contribute toward the future growth of the acquiring company.

3. Base period earn-out

   a. An example of an earn-out plan.

   b. An initial payment is made to the acquired company.

   c. Additional payments are made in future years when earnings exceed the base period earnings.

D. A tender offer is a bid by an interested party, usually a corporation, to control another corporation. The prospective purchaser approaches the stockholders of the firm, rather than the management.

   1. The management of the acquiring firm has to provide notice to the target corporation and to the Securities Exchange Commission 30 days prior to the takeover bid.

   2. Managements under attack occasionally rely on state statutes to block or at least delay tender offers.

   3. Disadvantages of the tender offer.

      a. If the target firm's management attempts to block an offer, the costs of executing the offer may increase significantly.

      b. The target firm may strike back in response to a tender offer. Defensive maneuvers may include:

              (1) White knights
              (2) Pac-mans
              (3) Shark repellents.

      c. The purchasing company may fail to acquire a sufficient number of shares to meet the objective of controlling the firm.

  4. Advantages of the tender offer.

      a. If the offer is not strongly contested, it may possibly be less expensive than the normal route for acquiring a company.

      b. The tender offer has proven somewhat less susceptible to judicial inquiries into the fairness of the purchase price.

III. Divestitures

A. Divestitures, or a "reverse merger," have become an important factor in restructuring corporations.

B. A successful divestiture allows the firm's assets to be used more efficiently, and therefore, be assigned a higher value by the market forces.

C. The different types of divestitures may be summarized as follows:

  1. Sell-off. A sell-off is the sale of a subsidiary, division, or product line by one company to another.

  2. Spin-off. A spin-off involves the separation of a subsidiary from its parent, with no change in the equity ownership.

  3. Liquidation. A liquidation in this context is not a decision to shut down or abandon an asset. Rather, the assets are sold to another company, and the proceeds are distributed to the stockholders.

  4. Going private. Going private results when a company, whose stock is traded publicly, is purchased by a small group of investors and the stock is no longer bought and sold on a public exchange.

  5. Leveraged buyout. The leveraged buyout is a special case of going private. The existing

shareholders sell their shares to a small group of investors. The purchasers of the stock use the firm's unused debt capacity to borrow the funds to pay for the stock.

Study Problems

1. The Evans Corporation has negotiated the purchase of E.D.S., Inc. The two firms have agreed that the E.D.S. shareholders are to receive common stock of Evans Corporation in exchange for their shares. The exchange is to be based on the relative earnings per share of the two firms. Evans Corporation currently has 150,000 shares of common stock outstanding with a $128 market value and earnings per share of $8. E.D.S. has issued 50,000 shares, which are selling for $57.20; earnings per share are $5.20. What will be the share exchange ratio for the merger? Will any dilution in earnings occur for either group of shareholders?

SOLUTION

$$\text{exchange ratio} = \frac{\text{EPS of E.D.S., Inc.}}{\text{EPS of Evans Corporation}}$$

$$= \frac{\$5.20}{\$8.00}$$

$$= 0.65:1$$

Company	Original Number of Shares	Earnings per Share	Net Income
Evans	150,000	$8.00	$1,200,000
E.D.S.	50,000	5.20	260,000
	Total post-merger earnings		$1,460,000

Numbers of shares after the merger:
150,000 + (0.65)50,000 =   182,500

Earnings per share for Evans Corporation
stockholders after merger:
$1,460,000 ÷ 182,500 shares =   8.00

Equivalent earnings per share for E.D.S., Inc.

(1) Prior to the merger
Earnings per share after the merger X
share exchange ratio $8.00 x 0.65 =   5.20

            (2)   After the merger
                   Earnings per share before the merger
                   ÷ share exchange ratio $5.20 -.65 = _____ 8.00

        Even though E.D.S. shareholders' earnings per share have
        increased from $5.20 to $8.00, these stockholders only
        have 65% of their original number of shares. Thus, their
        equivalent E.P.S. after the merger is 65% of $8.00, or
        $5.20, and their effective earnings position has not been
        altered by the merger.

2.   Synergistics, Inc. has agreed to purchase the Berne
        Corporation. Synergistics currently has 100,000 shares
        in common stock outstanding; the market value is $122.25,
        and the earnings per share is $8.15. Berne's common
        stock has a market value of $65.25, earnings per share
        are $5.65, and there are 25,000 shares outstanding. The
        two firms have agreed that Berne's stockholders will
        receive Synergistic common stock in exchange for their
        shares at a ratio of 0.5 to 1. What will be the effect
        on the earnings position of each company's stockholders?

        SOLUTION

                      Merger Effect on Earnings
                      (0.5:1 Exchange Ratio)
        _____

                          Original Number   Earnings
        Company   of Shares   per Share   Net Income
        Synergistics   100,000 $8.15 $815,000
        Berne   25,000   5.65   141,250
               Total post-merger earnings $956,250

               Number of shares after the merger:
                   100,000 + (0.5)25,000   112,500

               Earnings per share($956,250 - 112,500)   8.50

        Synergistics, Inc. stockholders:
        Earnings per share before the merger   8.15
        Earnings per share after the merger   8.50
        Accretion in earnings per share $.35

        Berne Corporation stockholders:
        Equivalent earnings per share after the
               merger:
        Earnings per share before the merger -
               share exchange ratio ($5.65 - 0.5)   11.30
        Earnings per share after the merger   8.50
        Dilution in earnings per share $2.80

                               295

3. Simpson Industries has negotiated an acquisition at a price of $50 million. Simpson's common stock is currently selling at $90. A convertible preferred stock could be issued to sell at $135 with a 1.3 conversion ratio. Compare the financing of the acquisition by common stock and by the convertible preferred issue. If Simpson's management wants to minimize the impact of dilution, which financing method should be chosen?

SOLUTION

If common stock financing is used, 555,556 shares would be required ($50 million ÷ $90 per share). If the convertible preferred stock is issued, 370,370 preferred shares would be issued ($50,000,000 ÷ $135). These shares would later be convertible into 481,481 shares of common stock (370,370 shares of preferred stock x 1.3 conversion ratio). The dilution effect would be minimized by issuing the convertible preferred stock since this approach results in 481,481 common shares as opposed to 555,555 under the straight common issue.

4. Widgit Corporation agreed to purchase Gizmo, Inc. under a base-period earn-out plan. Gizmo's base-period profits were $700,000 and its earnings subsequent to the merger are shown below, as are Widgit's common stock market value and earnings. What would be the total number of shares received by Gizmo's stockholders by the end of the fifth year if the initial down payment was 400,000 shares?

Year	Gizmo's Earnings	Widgit's Stock Prices	Widget's EPS
1	$750,000	$68	$4.50
2	775,000	79	6.25
3	815,000	85	8.50
4	800,000	82	8.00
5	830,000	87	8.75

SOLUTION

$$\text{Number of shares each year} = \frac{\text{excess earnings x P/E ratio}}{\text{stock market price}}$$

Year 0 initial down payment   400,000 shares

$$\text{Year 1} \quad \frac{(\$750,000-\$700,000) \times (\$68 \div \$4.50)}{\$68} = 11,111$$

$$\text{Year 2} \quad \frac{(\$775,000-\$700,000) \times (\$79 \div \$6.25)}{\$79} = 12,000$$

$$\text{Year 3} \quad \frac{(\$815{,}000-\$700{,}000) \ \text{x} \ (\$85 \div \$8.50)}{\$85} = 13{,}529$$

$$\text{Year 4} \quad \frac{(\$800{,}000-\$700{,}000) \ \text{x} \ (\$82 \div \$8.00)}{\$82} = 12{,}500$$

$$\text{Year 5} \quad \frac{(\$830{,}000-\$700{,}000) \ \text{x} \ (\$87 \div \$8.75)}{\$87} = 14{,}857$$

Total Shares Received by Gizmo's
Shareholders   <u>463,997</u>

Self-Tests

TRUE-FALSE

_____ 1. Synergism is defined as the state wherein the whole is greater than the sum of the parts.

_____ 2. The higher the P/E ratio of the acquiring company in relation to that of the company being acquired and the larger the earnings of the acquired company in relation to those of the acquiring company, the greater the increase in earnings per share of the acquiring company.

_____ 3. A higher than normal ratio of exchange is not justified, even for a stock that promises high future earnings.

_____ 4. It is wrong to examine the effect on EPS of an acquisition alone as the basis for analyzing the merger, since the effects of synergism may play an important role in determining the attractiveness of the proposed acquisition.

_____ 5. Earnouts provide a means of payment to the acquired company's stockholders for future growth in earnings.

_____ 6. Goodwill is usually expensed during the current accounting period and is not amortized because there is no way to allocate the percentage of goodwill used each period.

_____ 7. If the acquired firm's stockholders prefer dividend income over capital growth, convertible securities may be more satisfactory than issuing common stock.

_____ 8. Conglomerates are the most popular form of corporate merger because of the extremely favorable accounting treatment of mergers.

_____ 9. Use of convertible preferred stock may be preferred to the use of common stock in a merger because it reduces the potential of dilution of earnings per share.

_____10. In response to a tender offer, the management of the target firm may seek a more agreeable partner or white knight.

MULTIPLE CHOICE

1. The appropriate value of a firm:

    a. Depends on the firm's earnings potential.
    b. Depends on the financial characteristics of the acquiring firm.
    c. Is a range of value economically feasible to the prospective buyer within which a final price is negotiated.
    d. All of the above.

2. The two factors considered most important by most business people in estimating a firm's worth is:

      I. The book value of the firm being considered for acquisition.
     II. The appraisal value of the firm being considered for acquisition.
    III. The stock market value of the common shares of the firm being considered for acquisition.
     IV. The after-merger earnings per share of the acquiring company's stockholders.

    a. I, II.
    b. I, III.
    c. II, III.
    d. I, IV.
    e. III, IV.

3. Assume two companies with the following information:

	A	B
Present earnings (millions)	$25	$6
Shares (millions)	5	2
Earnings per share	$5	$3
Price of stock	$80	$30
P/E ratio	13	10

B has offered to exchange its stock at a price of $33 for A's stock. What is the earnings per share after the acquisition?

a. $4.87.
b. $5.25.
c. $5.32.
d. $4.76.

4. Given the information in question 3, but changing the offer of A to purchase B from $33 to $35, what is the effect of EPS?

a. $5.28.
b. $4.95.
c. $4.83.
d. $5.00.

5. The defensive maneuver that involves the target firm to become the attacker, is the:

a. Pac-man.
b. Shark repellent.
c. White Knight.
d. Earn out.

6. Company I has earnings per share of $3.40, and Company J has earnings per share of $2.04. What exchange ratio must Company I give Company J so that no one experiences earnings dilution?

a. .65 to 1.
b. .6 to 1.
c. 1.67 to 1.
d. 1 to 1.

22

Failure and Reorganization

Orientation: Failure can be attributed to both poor internal management and uncontrollable economic conditions. This chapter examines indicators of weakness in a firm and the alternatives open to a firm that actually reaches a point of insolvency. The liquidation procedures under both voluntary and involuntary settlements, as well as possible reorganization plans, are presented.

I.   What failure is

  A.   Economic failure occurs when the company's costs exceed its revenues (internal rates of return on the company's projects are less than its cost of capital).

  B.   Technical insolvency occurs when a firm can no longer honor its financial obligations. This happens when:

    1.   A firm has insufficient liquidity to honor its debts. However, the company's net worth is positive.

    2.   Liabilities actually exceed the fair market value of the company's assets; this is referred to as insolvency in bankruptcy (the company's net worth is negative).

II. Frequent causes of failure

  A.   The following key structural problems within management appear:

1. An imbalance of skills within the top echelon.

2. A chief executive who dominates a firm's operations without regard for the inputs of peers.

3. An inactive board of directors.

4. A deficient finance function within the firm's management.

5. The absence of responsibility of the chief executive officer to the stockholders.

B. The foregoing deficiencies may make the company vulnerable to several mistakes, including the following:

1. Negligence in developing an effective accounting system.

2. Lack of responsiveness to change. The firm may be unable to adjust to a general recession or unfavorable industry developments.

3. An inclination by management to undertake investment projects disproportionately larger relative to the firm's size.

4. Management relying too heavily on debt financing.

C. The primary causes of bankruptcy relate to weakness in the firm's management.

III. Who fails?

A. In a recession the failure rate generally rises then falls during a recovery period.

B. Certain retail or manufacture lines are more vulnerable to failure than others.

C. Typically the young and the small.

1. Fifty percent of the business failures were under five years of age.

2. Eighty percent of the failures were in the first ten years of a company's existence.

D. Failure statistics do not include those firms that would have failed but were either merged with another firm or given government assistance.

IV. Symptoms of bankruptcy

A. Bankruptcy or insolvency cannot be predicted with certainty. However, several financial ratios have proven to be useful indicators of corporate failure.

1. A study by Altman developed a statistical model that found five ratios that are useful in predicting bankruptcy, weighted the ratios, and assembled them into the following equation:

$$\text{Bankruptcy Score} = 1.2X_1 + 1.4X_2 + 3.3X_3 + .6X_4 + .999X_5$$

Where:

X_1 = (net working capital ÷ total assets).

X_2 = (retained earnings ÷ total assets).

X_3 = (earnings before interest and taxes ÷ total assets).

X_4 = (total market value of stock ÷ book value of total debt).

X_5 = (sales ÷ total assets).

2. These ratios seem to indicate that:

a. Potentially failing corporations invest less in current assets (X_1).

b. Younger companies have a greater chance of bankruptcy (X_2).

c. A company approaching failure has suffered a deterioration in general earnings power (X_3). This variable is the best single indicator of impending bankruptcy.

d. Potentially failing corporations often use excessive financial leverage (X_4).

e. A corporation facing possible bankruptcy may be unable to generate sales from the firm's assets (X_5).

302

3. Decision criterion using Altman's model:

   a. If the bankruptcy score is above 2.99, there is little chance for bankruptcy.

   b. If the bankruptcy score is below 1.81, there is a high probability that failure will occur.

   c. If the bankruptcy score is between 1.81 and 2.99, any prediction made using the model involves considerable uncertainty. However, there will be less error if a 2.675 score is used as the cut-off point between the failure and success classifications.

   d. No prediction made using this model is 100% certain.

      (1) Unique factors may affect the eventual fate of the company.

      (2) Management may do some financial "window dressing" of the financial statements that will affect the ratios used in analyzing the firm.

   e. When a firm is facing severe financial problems, the following important question must be answered: "Is the firm worth more dead or alive?" In other words, is the expected value of reorganizing the firm more beneficial than the anticipated liquidation value?

V. Voluntary remedies to insolvency

A. Prerequisites

   The firm must receive unanimous approval of a plan by the creditors, since any one creditor may legally prohibit the arrangement for the remaining creditors. Creditor approval of such a plan is usually based on:

   1. The debtor's proven honesty and integrity.

   2. The firm's potential for recovery.

   3. The economic prospects for the industry.

B. Procedure

   1. The debtor confers with the creditors to
       explain the plan and its benefits. This
       meeting is generally planned under the guidance
       of an adjustment bureau associated with either
       a local credit or trade association.

   2. The creditors appoint a committee to represent
       both large and small claimants.

   3. If a feasible plan can be developed, the
       committee, the firm, and the adjustment bureau
       construct one of the following voluntary
       agreements:

       a. The firm may receive an _extension_ of the
           time allotment for repayment of debts. In
           this case the debts are still payable in
           full. Such an agreement may contain
           stipulations about new purchases or the
           status of new liabilities incurred during
           the period of the contract. It may also
           place restrictions on the payment of
           dividends, require stockholders to place
           their shares in escrow with the creditor's
           committee, or stipulate that a member of
           the creditor's committee countersign
           checks.

       b. A _composition_ actually reduces the balance
           the firm owes its creditors. The credi-
           tors receive a pro rata share of their
           claim. The creditors might opt for this
           method if the only alternative is bank-
           ruptcy with its associated high costs.

       c. A combination of the above remedies.

C. Evaluation of voluntary remedies

   1. The primary advantage of voluntary remedies is
       the minimization of legal, investigative, and
       administrative expenses and the informality of
       the process.

   2. The major disadvantages of voluntary remedies
       are:

       a. A creditor may refuse to participate. In
           order to avoid this problem, a composition
           generally allows small claimants to be
           paid in full.

304

b. The debtor may maintain control of the business.

c. The underlying problems of the firm may not be corrected, allowing the mismanagement of the firm to continue, resulting in further losses.

VI. Reorganization

If a voluntary remedy is not workable, a company can declare or be forced by its creditors into bankruptcy, at which point the company will either be dissolved or reorganized. Chapter 11 of the Bankruptcy Act specifies guidelines for the orderly reorganization of a business.

A. The petition to reorganize

1. Under Chapter 11, bankruptcy may be initiated either:

a. By the firm's management - voluntary.

b. By the firm's creditors - involuntary.

2. To initiate involuntary bankruptcy:

a. The firm's creditors must show the firm is not paying its debts when due.

b. If there are more than 12 creditors to the firm, the petition must be filed by three creditors having a total claim exceeding $50,000.

c. If there are less than 12 creditors, the petition must be filed by either one or more creditors whose total claim is at least $50,000.

3. When filed, a committee of unsecured creditors is appointed to help construct a reorganization plan. A majority of the creditors holding 2/3 of the claim value must approve the plan.

4. The debtor generally continues the business operations unless fraud, incompetence, etc. exist. In this case, a trustee would be given managerial control.

5. Although once an important part of the reorganization process, the role of the SECs has been reduced significantly.

VII. The reorganization decision

    A.   The trustee uses the following procedure in the reorganization process:

        1.   He or she must establish a going concern value for the firm. This may be done by using the following equation:

$$\text{Going Concern Value} = \text{Future Annual Earnings} \times \text{Acceptable P/E Ratio}$$

        2.   If the going concern value exceeds the liquidation value, the trustee must devise a reorganization plan, including a way of reformulating the capital structure, to meet the criteria of fairness and feasibility. The main concerns of the trustee in developing this plan are:

            a.   Changes necessary to place the company in a more profitable posture.

            b.   Developing a capital structure that will enable the firm to cover fixed charges interest, principal repayment, and preferred dividends.

    B.   If the reorganization is determined to be fair and feasible to the respective creditors and stockholders new securities are issued to reflect the revised capital structure.

        1.   The procedure which is generally followed is the <u>rule of absolute priority</u>, which states that the company must completely honor senior claims on assets before settling junior claims.

        2.   Frequently, however, plans are based on a blend of <u>absolute</u> and <u>relative</u> priorities, where a junior claim receives partial payment even though a senior claim has not been paid in full. This is necessary to satisfy small creditors who might otherwise vote against a proposed plan.

VIII. Liquidation

If the liquidation value of the firm exceeds the going concern value, the firm should be dissolved. In other words, if continued operation would only result in further loss, the business should be terminated.

A. Liquidation by assignment

   1. This method of liquidation is done privately
       with a minimum amount of court involvement.
       The debtor transfers title to a third party,
       known as the _assignee_ or _trustee_, who is
       appointed by either the creditors or the court
       and who administers the liquidation process and
       sees to the distribution of the proceeds.
       These proceeds do not automatically discharge
       the debtor of the remaining balance due a
       creditor. The creditor may attempt to obtain
       the remaining balance through the court. This
       problem may be avoided by a prior agreement
       between the debtor and creditor to the effect
       that the liquidation procedure constitutes a
       complete settlement of claims.

   2. The advantages of liquidation by assignment
       over a formal bankruptcy procedure are that:

       a. The assignment is usually quicker and less
           expensive and requires less legal for-
           mality.

       b. The assignee is allowed greater discretion
           and flexibility than a court-appointed
           trustee in bankruptcy because the assignee
           is allowed to maximize the funds received
           from the liquidation.

   3. The disadvantages of the procedure are that:

       a. The debtor is not legally discharged from
           further obligation.

       b. The creditor is not protected from fraud.

B. Liquidation by bankruptcy. A petition for a company
   to be declared bankrupt may be filed in district
   court by either the debtor (voluntary) or by the
   creditors (involuntary) subject to the provisions in
   Chapter 7 of the Bankruptcy Act.

   1. Voluntary declaration of bankruptcy by the
       debtor is usually taken when management con-
       siders a further delay to be detrimental to the
       stockholders' position.

   2. The rules for creditors wishing to initiate
       bankruptcy are the same as those given for
       involuntary reorganization.

3. The liquidation process

    a. After the filing and approval of the bankruptcy petition,

        (1) The court adjudges the debtor bankrupt and names a referee in bankruptcy.

        (2) The referee then may appoint a receiver to serve as the interim caretaker of the company's assets until a trustee can be designated by the creditors.

        (3) The referee acquires a list of assets and liabilities from the debtor, along with other relevant information.

        (4) A meeting of the creditors is called to elect a trustee.

    b. The trustee and creditors' committee initiates plans to liquidate the company's assets.

        (1) An effort is made to collect all money owed to the debtor.

        (2) Appraisers are selected to determine a value to be used as a guideline in liquidating the property. A trustee may not sell an asset for less than 75 percent of its appraised value without court approval.

        (3) The assets are converted to cash through private sale or public auction.

        (4) All expenses incurred in the bankruptcy process are paid.

        (5) The remaining cash is distributed on a pro rata basis to the creditors.

        (6) The trustee provides a final accounting to the creditors and referee; the bankruptcy filing is discharged; and the debtor is relieved of all responsibility for prior debts.

4. Priority of claims. Under the rule of absolute priority, claims are honored in the following order:

    a. Secured creditors, with the proceeds from the sale of specific property going first to these creditors. If any portion of the claim remains unpaid, the balance is treated as an unsecured loan.

    b. Expenses incurred in administering the bankrupt estate.

    c. Expenses incurred after the bankruptcy petition has been filed but prior to a trustee being appointed.

    d. Salaries and commissions not exceeding $2,000 per employee that were earned within the three months preceding the bankruptcy petition.

    e. Federal, state, and local taxes.

    f. Unsecured creditors.

    g. Preferred stock.

    h. Common stock.

Study Problems

1. You are studying three companies and have decided as part of your analysis to use Altman's model to predict the probability of bankruptcy for each. The five ratios needed are given below. What are the bankruptcy scores for these companies and how are they interpreted?

			Ratios		
Company	X_1	X_2	X_3	X_4	X_5
I	0.17	0.19	0.40	3.50	1.80
II	0.21	0.24	0.14	1.20	0.76
III	0.10	0.09	0.11	0.99	9.45

SOLUTION

Bankruptcy
Score $= 1.2(X1) + 1.4(X2) + 3.3(X3) + 0.6(X4) + 0.999(X5)$

Company I

Bankruptcy Score = $1.2(0.17) + 1.4(0.19) + 3.3(0.40)$

$$+ 0.6(3.50) + 0.999(1.80)$$

$$= 5.69$$

Basing your answer on the bankruptcy score, you would predict success. There is very little probability of bankruptcy in the next two years.

Company II

Bankruptcy Score = $1.2(0.21) + 1.4 (0.24) + 3.3(0.14)$

$$+ 0.6(1.20) + 0.999(0.76)$$

$$= 2.53$$

Any prediction based on this bankruptcy score will be questionable. However, a score this low does indicate some strong financial difficulties which may or may not be correctable.

Company III

Bankruptcy Score = $1.2(0.10) + 1.4(0.09) + 3.3(0.11)$

$$+ 0.6(0.99) + 0.999(0.45)$$

$$= 1.653$$

Basing your answer on the bankruptcy scores, you would predict failure. There is a high probability of bankruptcy within the next two years.

2. The Over-Levered Crowbar Company is a recently formed manufacturing firm applying to your firm for credit. Your company follows a very liberal policy in extending credit to young firms. Your company operates under the assumption that as the new business grows, its business with you will increase. However, being aware that the probability of bankruptcy is highest among young firms you do not wish to extend credit to any companies you feel will go bankrupt. Using the following financial statements and data, should you extend credit to this company?

The Over-Levered Crowbar Co.
Statement of Financial Position
December 31, 1986

Assets

Cash	$ 20,000	
Accounts receivable	30,000	
Inventory	30,000	
Total current assets		$100,000
Machines	150,000	
Building	100,000	
Land	50,000	
Total plant and equipment		300,000
Total assets		$400,000

Liabilities and Stockholders' Equity

Accounts payable	20,000	
Notes payable	24,000	
Total current liabilities		44,000
Bonds	56,000	
Pensions	126,000	
Total long-term liabilities		182,000
Capital stock (10,000 shares outstanding)	130,000	
Retained earnings	44,000	
Total stockholders' equity		174,000
Total liabilities and stockholders' equity		$400,000

The Over-Levered Crowbar Co.
Income Statement
December 31, 1986

Sales		$220,000
Cost of goods sold		120,000
Gross Profits		$100,000
Other expenses		
Depreciation	$50,000	
Miscellaneous	10,200	60,200
Earnings before interest and taxes		40,000
Interest		10,000
Taxes		7,900
Net Income		$ 22,100

Market value per share, December 31, 1986 $10.00

SOLUTION

Using the Altman model, you get:

X_1 = net working capital ÷ total assets
  = (current assets - current liabilities) ÷ total assets
  = ($100,000 - 44,000) ÷ $400,000
  = 0.14

X_2 = retained earnings ÷ total assets
  = $44,000 ÷ $400,000
  = 0.11

X_3 = earnings before interest and taxes ÷ total assets
  = $40,000 ÷ $400,000
  = 0.10

X_4 = total market value of stock ÷ book value of total debt
  = (market value per share x number of shares outstanding)
    ÷ (accounts payable + notes payable + bonds)
  = ($10 x 10,000) ÷ ($20,000 + $24,000 + $56,000)
  = 1.0

X_5 = sales ÷ total assets
  = $220,000 ÷ $400,000
  = 0.55

Bankruptcy Score = $1.2(X_1) + 1.4(X_2) + 3.3(X_3) + 0.6(X_4)$
  $+ 0.999(X_5)$

  = 1.2(0.14) + 1.4(0.11) + 3.3(0.10)

  + 0.6(1.0) + 0.999(0.55)

  = 1.80145

This bankruptcy score is in the range in which the probability of failure is very high. Your firm would not want to extend credit to Over-Levered Crowbar Company.

3. Acme, Inc. is currently undergoing a reorganization. The trustee has estimated the firm's going concern value to be $2,480,000. Given the liabilities and equity from the balance sheet, formulate the plan for reorganization under the rule of absolute priority.

```
                         Acme, Inc.
               Statement of Financial Position
                     December 30, 1984
```

Liabilities and Stockholders' Equity

Current liabilities
    Accounts payable $ 350,000
    Notes payable   200,000
    Wages payable   465,000
        Total current liabilities $1,015,000

Long-term liabilities
    Mortgage bonds   1,500,000
    Subordinated debentures*   585,000
        Total long-term liabilities   2,085,000

        Total liabilities   3,100,000

Equity
    Common stock (par $10)   500,000
    Paid in capital   1,840,000
        Total equity   2,340,000
             Total liabilities and equity $5,440,000

---

*Subordinated to mortgage bonds.

SOLUTION

Plan for Reorganization: Acme, Inc. Because the total liabilities exceed the going concern value of the firm, the common stockholders will receive nothing in the reorganization. If it is assumed that no more than $2,000 is owed any single employee, the first priority will be to satisfy the employees in full. After these liabilities have been satisfied there will be $2,015,000 remaining for the creditors ($2,480,000 $465,000). The remaining creditors will therefore receive their proportionate share of the $2,015,000 with the percentage received being equal to 76.47 percent computed as follows:

$$\text{Percentage of Claim} = \frac{\text{Going-Concern Value} - \text{Wages Payable}}{\text{Total Liabilities} - \text{Wages Payable}}$$

$$= \frac{\$2,480,000 - \$465,000}{\$3,100,000 - \$465,000}$$

$$= 76.47\%$$

Liabilities	76.47% of Claim	New Claim After Subordination
Accounts receivable	$ 267,647	$ 267,647
Notes payable	152,941	152,941
Wages payable	465,000*	465,000
Mortgage bonds	1,147,059	1,500,000
Subordinated debentures	447,353	94,412
Going concern value	$2,480,000	$2,480,000

*100% of claim

The amount allocated to the subordinated debentures is available first to satisfy the mortgage bonds, with the remainder going to the holders of the subordinated debentures.

4. The trustee for the reorganization of Miller Corporation has established the going concern value at $10 million. The creditors and the amounts owed are given below. As part of the reorganization plan, the accounts payable are to be settled by renewal of $750,000 of the accounts, with a due date of nine months Any remaining amount to be received by these claimants is to be realized in the form of long-term notes payable. The current notes payable are to be settled by renewing $1 million of the notes payable, with the remaining amount to be settled in preferred stock. The mortgage bondholders will receive one-half of their adjusted claim under the reorganization in the form of newly issued bonds, with the remainder being common stock. The investors who own the subordinated debentures are to receive common stock in settlement of their claim. What will Miller's liabilities and equity be after reorganization?

Miller Corporation

Type of Creditor	Amount of Claim
Accounts Payable	$ 2,500,000
Notes Payable	1,500,000
Mortgage Bonds	4,500,000
Subordinated Debentures*	4,000,000
Total Liabilities	$12,500,000

*Subordinated to the mortgage bonds.

SOLUTION

Eighty percent of the claims are to be honored, repre-
senting the going concern value relative to total liabilities ($10,000,000 + $12,500,000). Therefore, if the
firm were to be liquidated for $10 million instead of
being reorganized, the settlements would be as follows:

	Existing Claims	80% of Claims	Adjustment for Subordination
Accounts Payable	$ 2,500,000	$ 2,000,000	$ 2,000,000
Notes Payable	1,500,000	1,200,000	1,200,000
Mortgage Bonds	4,500,000	3,600,000	4,500,000
Subordinated Debentures	4,000,000	3,200,000	2,300,000*
Total	$12,500,000	$10,000,000	$10,000,000

*Since the debentures are subordinated to the mortgage
bonds, the owners of the bonds are paid prior to the
debenture holders' claims being settled.

Based upon the reorganization plan, the revisions in the
capital structure would be determined as follows:

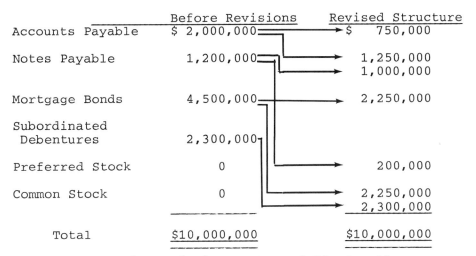

	Before Revisions	Revised Structure
Accounts Payable	$ 2,000,000	$ 750,000
Notes Payable	1,200,000	1,250,000
		1,000,000
Mortgage Bonds	4,500,000	2,250,000
Subordinated Debentures	2,300,000	
Preferred Stock	0	200,000
Common Stock	0	2,250,000
		2,300,000
Total	$10,000,000	$10,000,000

Consequently, the capital structure following the reorganization would appear as follows:

Miller Corporation
Liabilities and Equity (After Reorganization)

Accounts Payable	$ 750,000
Notes Payable	2,250,000
Mortgage Bonds	2,250,000
Preferred Stock	200,000
Common Stock	4,550,000
Total Liabilities and Equity	$10,000,000

5. August Corporation is bankrupt and being liquidated. The liabilities and equity portion of its balance sheet is given below. The book value of the assets was $90 million, but the realized value when liquidated was only $40 million, of which $9 million was from the sale of the firm's office building. Administrative expenses associated with the liquidation were $5 million. Determine the distribution of the proceeds.

August Corporation
Liabilities and Equities

Accounts Payable	$ 5,000,000	
Accrued Wages*	2,000,000	
Notes Payable	15,000,000	
Federal Taxes	2,500,000	
State Taxes	500,000	
Current Debt		$25,000,000
First Mortgage Bonds**	30,000,000	
Subordinated Debentures***	25,000,000	
Long-Term Debt		55,000,000
Preferred Stock	2,500,000	
Common Stock	7,500,000	
Equity		10,000,000
Total		$90,000,000

*No single claim exceeds $2,000.
**Have first lien on office building.
***Subordinated to the first mortgage bonds.

316

Distribution of Proceeds

Liquidation Value of Assets	$40,000,000
Priority of Claims	
1. First Mortgage Receipts from Building Sale	9,000,000
2. Administrative Wages	5,000,000
3. Wages Payable	2,000,000
4. Taxes (State and Federal)	3,000,000
Total Prior Claims	$19,000,000
Amount Available to General Creditors	$21,000,000

Claims of General Creditors

Creditors	Claims	31.82% of Claims*	Claims After Subordination
Accounts Payable	$ 5,000,000	$1,591,000	$ 1,591,000
Notes Payable	15,000,000	4,773,000	4,773,000
Remainder of First Mortgage Bonds	21,000,000	6,682,000	14,636,000
Subordinated Debenture	25,000,000	7,954,000	0
	$66,000,000	$21,000,000	

$$\text{*Percentage of Claims} = \frac{\text{Amount Available}}{\text{to General Creditors}} \div \frac{\text{Amount of}}{\text{Claims}}$$

$$= \$21,000,000 \div \$66,000,000$$

$$= 31.82\%$$

Self-Tests

TRUE-FALSE

_____ 1. A company that has a bankruptcy score below 1.81 will be bankrupt within six months.

_____ 2. An extension usually results in large legal expenses and possible deterioration of assets.

_____ 3. In a composition, creditors receive a pro rata settlement in cash.

_____ 4. Creditors usually prefer a voluntary settlement instead of one brought forth by the court because costs are generally minimized.

_____ 5. During a liquidation procedure the referee has the responsibility of liquidating the assets and distributing the proceeds to the creditors.

_____ 6. Bankruptcy is limited to small firms that have been in existence less than 10 years.

_____ 7. Unsecured creditors must supplement the mortgage bondholders receipts in a reorganization if the bondholders do not receive their full claim.

_____ 8. During informal reorganization, it is sometimes beneficial to partially honor junior claims on assets before all senior claims have been met.

_____ 9. The company is declared a "debtor" in a reorganization as opposed to a "bankrupt" in a liquidation.

_____10. The absolute priority rule is fairest to the common stockholders.

_____11. Under Chapter XI of the Bankruptcy Act, the debtor is no longer allowed any part in the process of satisfying its creditors.

_____12. Under the rule of absolute priority, preferred stockholders have priority over subordinated debenture holders.

_____13. In a liquidation, the debtor is liable for the difference between the liquidation value and the going concern value.

MULTIPLE CHOICE

1. The best single indicator of a forthcoming bankruptcy is:

   a. Net working capital ÷ total assets.
   b. Retained earnings ÷ total assets.
   c. Earnings before interest and taxes ÷ total assets.
   d. Total market value of stock ÷ book value of total debt.
   e. Sales ÷ total assets.

2. Under the rule of absolute priority, which of the following claims would be the first to be honored?

   a. Secured creditors, with the proceeds from the sale of the specific property going first to these creditors.
   b. Common stock.
   c. Unsecured creditors.

d. Federal, state, and local taxes.
e. Preferred stock.

3. A private liquidation is preferred over a public liquidation because it usually results in which of the following?

   a. Lower legal and administrative expenses.
   b. Faster liquidation of the assets.
   c. Less deterioration of the assets' value.
   d. Less disagreement among creditors.

4. Which of the following steps is taken first in a reorganization plan?

   a. Formulation of a new capital structure.
   b. Determination of the total valuation of the reorganized company.
   c. Determination of the total valuation of the old securities.
   d. Determination of a fair exchange of old securities and the new securities.

5. A reorganization and a composition are similar in that:

   a. The company's assets are not liquidated and the company's operations are continued.
   b. Creditors' claims are scaled down.
   c. Both are subject to Chapter 7 of the Bankruptcy Act.

6. The rule of absolute priority states that:

   a. An obligation made prior to another will be the first to be settled.
   b. Obligations that were absolutely essential to the operation of the business will be the first to be settled.
   c. The assignee has the first decision in assigning priority of claims.
   d. The company must completely honor senior claims on assets before settling junior claims.

23

International Business Finance

Orientation: This chapter introduces some of the financial techniques and strategies necessary to the efficient opera- tions of an international business. Problems inherent to these firms include multiple currencies, differing legal and political environments, differing economic and capital markets, and internal control problems. The difficulties arising from multiple currencies are stressed here, including the dimensions of foreign exchange risk and strategies for reducing this risk. We also cover working capital management and direct foreign investment for international firms.

I. The Importance of International Business

    A.   World-trade has grown faster over the last few decades than has world GNP.

    B.   In less-developed countries, long-run overseas investments of the United States companies have yielded high returns.

    C.   Many American multi-national corporations (MNC) have significant assets, sales, and profits attributable to foreign investments.

    D.   Many foreign MNCs have significant operations in the United States.

    E.   Many firms, investment companies, and individuals invest in the capital markets of foreign companies to receive:

1. Higher returns than those available in domestic capital markets.

2. Reduced portfolio risk through international diversification.

F. Companies are increasingly turning to the Eurodollar market to raise funds. In 1985 U.S. companies raised almost $40 billion in foreign financial markets.

II. Exchange Rates

A. Recent history of exchange rates

1. Exchange rates between the major currencies were fixed from 1949 and 1970.

2. Countries were required to set a parity rate with the U.S. dollar, around which the daily exchange rate could narrowly fluctuate.

3. In order to effect a major adjustment, a currency either had to undergo a devaluation (reducing the cost relative to the dollar) or an upvaluation/revaluation (increasing the cost relative to the U.S. dollar).

4. Since 1973, a floating rate international currency system has operated, wherein the currencies are allowed to fluctuate freely.

5. Two major types of transactions now occur in the foreign exchange markets: spot and forward transactions.

B. Spot Exchange Rates

1. The rate at which one currency can be immediately exchanged for another currency.

2. Direct quote expresses the exchange rate in the units of home currency required to buy one unit of foreign currency. For example, 1.4845 U.S. dollars per pound.

3. Indirect Quotes indicate the number of foreign currency units needed to purchase one unit of home currency. For example, .6691 pounds per U.S. dollar.

EXAMPLE

Using the rates listed above, how many dollars would a U.S. manufacturer pay for a part costing 250 pounds?

250 (pounds) x 1.4845 ($/pound) = $371.13

4. The direct and indirect quotes should have a reciprocal relationship. In formula:

$$\text{Direct Quote} = \frac{1}{\text{Indirect Quote}}$$

or

$$\text{Indirect Quote} = \frac{1}{\text{Direct Quote}}$$

5. When these quotes are not equal, <u>arbitrage</u> will occur, where a trader (or arbitrager) makes a riskless profit, by exchanging currency in two markets.

6. The <u>asked rate</u> is the rate which the bank or foreign exchange trader "asks" the buyer to pay for the foreign currency.

7. The <u>bid rate</u> is the rate which the bank or foreign exchange trader buys the foreign currency from the customer.

8. The <u>spread</u> is the difference in the bid and the asked rates.

9. The narrower the spread, the greater is the efficiency in the spot exchange market.

10. A <u>cross rate</u> is the result of an indirect computation of one currency's exchange rate from the exchange rate of two other currencies. For example, the calculation of marks per pound from U.S. dollars per pound and marks per U.S. dollars.

11. Triangular arbitrage will occur when the cross rates calculated are not equal to the exchange rates offered.

C. Forward Exchange Rates

1. A <u>forward exchange rate</u> specifies <u>today</u> the rate at which currencies will be exchanged at in the future, usually 30, 90, or 180 days from today.

2. Rates are quoted in both the direct and indirect form.

3. Forward rates are often quoted at a <u>premium</u> or a <u>discount</u> to the existing spot rate. This is also referred to as the forward-spot differential.

4. These differentials may either be stated in absolute terms or as an annualized percent premium or discount.

5. The use of forward contracts allows for risk reduction in that future cash outlays are known with certainty.

D. The Interest Parity Theorem

1. Theorem states that the forward premium or discount should be equal and opposite in sign to the difference in the national interest rates for securities of the same maturity. (Except for the effects of small transaction costs). Notationally, this is expressed as:

$$P(\text{or } D) = -\left(\frac{I^f - I^d}{1 + I^f} \right) = \left(\frac{I^d - I^f}{1 + I^f} \right)$$

where

$P(\text{or } D)$ = the percent-per-annum premium or discount on the forward rate.

I^f = the annual interest rate on a foreign instrument having the same maturity as the forward contract.

I^d = the annualized interest rate on a domestic instrument having the same maturity as the forward contract.

EXAMPLE

The premium (P) on 30-day forward mark contracts is 4.368 percent. If the 30-day T-Bill is yielding 10 percent, what must the 30-day German instrument yield.

$$P = \frac{I^f - I^d}{1 + I^f}$$

323

$$.04368 = \frac{I^f - .10}{1 + I^f}$$

$$I^f = .1502 \text{ or } 15.02\%$$

2. If the forward differentials are not those predicted by the interest parity theorem, then <u>covered interest arbitrage</u> can occur and be profitable at no risk.

E. Purchasing Power Parity

1. According to purchasing power parity, exchange rates will adjust over time so that the currencies of different countries will have the same purchasing power. The exchange rates will adjust to cover the inflation rate differential between the two countries.

2. Purchasing power parity can be demonstrated by the equation:

$$S_{t+1} = S_t (1 + P_d)/(1 + P_f)^n$$

$$= S_t (1 + P_d - P_f)^n$$

where:

S_t = units of domestic currency per unit of the foreign currency at time t.

P_f = the foreign inflation rate.

P_d = the domestic inflation rate.

n = the number of time periods.

EXAMPLE

The inflation rate in Great Britain is 6% and in the U.S. it is 10%. The current spot rate of the pound is $2.00. According to purchasing power parity, what will be the expected value of the pound at the end of the year?

$$S = \$2.00 (1 + .10 + - .06)^1$$

$$= \$2.00 (1.04)^1$$

$$= \$2.08$$

F. International Fisher Effect

1. According to the Fisher effect, interest rates reflect not only the real rate of return but the expected inflation rate.

2. The Fisher effect can be expressed as:

$$I = P + I_r + PI_r$$

where:

I = the nominal interest rate.

I_r = the real rate of return.

P = the expected inflation rate.

3. The international Fisher effect suggests that the exchange rate adjusts to cover the interest rate differential between two countries.

4. This theory suggests that in efficient markets, with rational expectations, the forward rate is an unbiased forecast of the future spot rate.

III. Exchange Rate Risk

A. Risk arises from not knowing the value of the future spot rate today.

B. Types of exchange risk

1. Risk in international trade contracts - when an agreement exists to purchase some good at a future date in foreign currency, uncertainty exists as to the future cash outlay.

2. Risk in foreign portfolios - because of exchange rate fluctuations in foreign securities the returns are more variable and thus more risky than investment in domestic securities.

3. Risk in direct foreign investment (DFI) - the balance sheet and income statement are dominated in foreign currency. Thus, for the parent company, risk arises from both the fluctuations in the asset's value and the profit streams.

C. Exposure to exchange rate risk

1. Transaction exposure refers to the net total foreign currency transactions whose monetary

325

value was fixed at a time different from when the transactions are actually completed. Examples of transactions exposed to this kind of risk are receivables, payables, and fixed price sales or purchase contracts. Fluctuations in exchange rates can affect the value of these assets and liabilities.

2. Translation exposure is actually a paper gain or loss. Translation exposure refers to gains or losses caused by the translation of foreign currency assets and liabilities into the currency of the parent company for accounting purposes.

3. Economic exposure refers to the extent to which the economic value of a company can decline due to exchange rate changes. It is the overall impact of exchange rate changes on the value of the firm. A decline in value can be attributed to an exchange rate induced decline in the level of expected cash flows and/or by an increase in the riskiness of these cash flows.

D. Hedging Strategies

1. The standard procedure to hedge is to match the amount and the duration of the asset (liability) position.

2. The money market hedge offsets the exposed position in a foreign currency by borrowing or lending in the foreign and domestic money markets. This may be costly for small or infrequent users.

3. The forward market hedge matches the asset (liability) position with an offsetting forward contract of equal value and maturity. Generally, this is less costly than the money market hedge.

4. Foreign currency futures contracts and foreign currency options are two relatively new instruments used for hedging. Futures contracts are similar to forward contracts in that they provide a fixed price for the required delivery. Options, on the other hand, permit a fixed price anytime before their expiration date. Options and futures both differ from forward contracts in that they are traded in standardized amounts with standardized maturity dates

and are traded through organized exchanges and individual dealers. The difference between the futures contract and the currency option is that the option requires delivery only if it is exercised. The option can be exercised any time before its maturity date, this can provide additional flexibility for a company.

IV. Multinational Working Capital Management

A. The MNC must be careful to make decisions concerning working capital management that are optimal for the corporation as a whole and not just the best for the individual entities.

B. Leading and lagging are important risk reduction techniques for a MNC's working capital management.

   1. When holding an asset in a:

      a. Strong (appreciating) currency, we should lag (delay) conversion to the domestic currency.

      b. Weak (depreciating) currency, we should lead (expedite) conversion to the domestic currency.

   2. When holding a liability in a:

      a. Strong currency, we should lead (expedite) payment of the liability.

      b. Weak currency, we should lag (delay) payment of the liability.

C. Cash management

   1. A MNC may wish to position funds in a specific subsidiary in another country such that the foreign exchange exposure and the tax liability of the MNC are minimized as a whole. This strategy may not, however, be the optimal strategy for the specific subsidiary.

   2. The transfer of funds is effected by royalties, fees, and transfer-pricing. The transfer price is the price charged for goods or services transferred from a subsidiary or parent company to another subsidiary.

D. Managing receivables

1. The strategies of lead and lag should be followed for managing accounts receivable.

2. Sales made in weak (depreciating) currency should be collected sooner - leading.

3. Sales made in a strong (appreciating) currency should be collected later - lagging.

4. The terms of the sales should encourage payment according to the MNC's desired lead-lag strategy.

V. International Financing Decisions

A. A multinational corporation (MNC) may have a lower cost of capital than a domestic firm due to its ability to tap a larger number of financial markets.

1. A multinational company has access to financing sources in the countries in which it operates.

2. Host countries often provide access to low-cost subsidized financing to attract foreign investment.

3. A MNC may enjoy preferential credit treatment due to its size and investor preference for its home currency.

4. A MNC may be able to access third country capital markets.

5. A MNC has access to external currency markets variously known as Eurodollar, Eurocurrency, or Asiandollar markets. These markets are unregulated and because of their lower spread, can offer attractive rates for financing and investment.

B. To increase their visibility in foreign capital markets, MNCs are increasingly listing their stocks in the foreign capital markets.

C. A MNC's capital structure should reflect its wider access to financial markets, the ability to diversify economic and political risks, and several of its other advantages over domestic firms.

328

VI. Direct Foreign Investment

   A. Risk in international capital budgeting

      1. Political risk arises from operating a business in a different and possibly less stable business climate than the United States.

      2. Exchange risk incorporates changes in the future earnings stream because of currency fluctuations, possibly in both foreign and domestic currencies.

      3. Business risk is affected by the response of business and the MNC to economic conditions within the foreign country.

      4. Financial risk arises from the financial structure of the firm and its effect on the profit stream.

   B. Cash flows must be estimated considering the potential effects of exchange rate changes, governmental policy, and other items that determine product demand and sales.

   C. A foreign investment can be evaluated from either a parent or a local firm perspective. If a firm uses a local perspective the initial investment and all of its cash flows should be discounted at a rate that reflects the local inflation rate and the riskiness of the project. When using the parent company perspective, the discount rate should reflect the expected inflation rate in the parent currency and foreign currency cash flows should be converted to the parent currency cash flows using projected exchange rates.

   D. The net present value (NPV) must be calculated using the above factors.

      1. If NPV is greater than zero, generally accept direct foreign investments.

      2. If NPV is less than zero, the MNC may decide to:

         a. Reject direct foreign investment.

         b. Establish a sales office in the foreign country.

       c.   License a local company to manufacture the product, where the MNC receives royalty payments.

Study Problems

1.   An American manufacturer owes 5000 marks to a German supplier. How much does he owe in U.S. dollars, using the textbook's exchange rates for February 28, 1984?

SOLUTION

Exchange rate = .3846 U.S. dollar per mark

5000 (marks) x .3846 (U.S. dollar/mark) = 1923 U.S. dollars

2.   A fashion designer in France owes $65,000, due in 30 days, to a counterpart in the U.S. How much is the foreign liability today using the February 28, 1984 exchange rates for 30-day forward contracts?

SOLUTION

30-day forward exchange rate - 8.0451 francs per U.S. dollar

65,000 ($) x 8.0451 (francs per U.S. dollar) = 522,931.5 francs

3.   You own $20,000. The dollar rate in London is .6501. The pound rate is given in the textbook. Are arbitrage profits possible? Set up an arbitrage scheme with your capital. What is the gain (loss) in dollars?

SOLUTION

The London rate is .6501 pounds/U.S. dollar. The indirect New York rate is .6691 pounds/U.S. dollar.

Assuming no transaction costs, the rates between London and New York are out of line. Arbitrage profits are possible.

Pounds are cheaper in New York. Buy pounds in New York with the $20,000.

20,000 ($) x .6691 (pounds/dollars) = 13,382 pounds.

Sell pounds in London.
13,382 (pounds) ÷ .6501 (pounds/U.S. dollars) = $20,584.52.

Your net gain is $20,584.52 - $20,000 = $584.52.

4. Interest rates on the 30-day instruments in the United States and Germany are 12 and 10 percent (annualized), respectively. What is the correct price of the 30-day forward mark? Use spot rates from textbook.

SOLUTION

The spot rate is .3846 U.S. dollar per mark. The annual premium via equation (23-3) is

$$= \frac{.12 - .10}{1 + .10} = \frac{.02}{1.10} = .0182$$

P = 1.82%

Using this premium in equation (23-2), compute the "correct" forward price.

$$\frac{F - .3846}{.3846} \times \frac{12}{1} \times 100 = .0182 \qquad \underline{F = .3852}$$

Self-Tests

TRUE-FALSE

_____ 1. One of the most difficult aspects of operating a business in a foreign country is the problem of multiple currencies.

_____ 2. International business affairs affect very few firms, and therefore is of little concern to most businesses.

_____ 3. Exchange rates are fixed according to the U.S. dollar and must be maintained within the narrow margins unless a major adjustment is enacted.

_____ 4. The forward contract states the exchange rate to be used in the spot market on a specific date in the near future.

_____ 5. A narrow spread between the bid and asked rates indicates an efficient spot market.

_____ 6. The interest parity theorem states that (except for effect of transaction costs) the forward premium or discount should be equal and opposite in sign to the difference in the respective country's interest rates for securities of the same maturities.

_____ 7. Extensive profit opportunities exist for arbitrageurs in the foreign exchange markets.

_____ 8. Exchange rate risk constitutes only a small portion of the risk associated with international business.

_____ 9. An investor with foreign currency liabilities may want to hedge against exchange rate changes in the money markets.

_____10. Leading and lagging are strategies for optimal working capital management.

_____11. Covered interest arbitrage can be taken advantage of when the premiums in the forward rate are not equal to the interest rate differentials.

_____12. Purchasing power parity suggests that exchange rates in countries with high inflation rates tend to decline.

_____13. Translation exposure results in exchange rate related losses or gains that have little or no impact on taxable income.

_____14. Futures contracts are customized with regard to the amount and maturity date of the contract.

_____15. Receivables and payables are subject to transaction exposure.

_____16. The objective of a hedging strategy is to have a positive net asset position in the foreign currency.

MULTIPLE CHOICE

1. A direct 30-day forward quote of 1.4957 U.S dollars per pound is equivalent to what 30-day indirect quote?

   a. .6686 U.S dollars per pound.
   b. .6671 marks per U.S. dollar.
   c. 1.4957 U.S. dollars per pound.
   d. .6686 pounds per U.S. dollar.
   e. .6671 pounds per U.S. dollar.

2. An example of a cross rate, when the exchange rates are given in U.S. dollars, would be:

   a. marks per U.S. dollar.
   b. pounds per yen.
   c. yen per mark.
   d. U.S. dollars per yen.
   e. both b and c.

3. Forward rate contracts are used in international transactions to:

   a. reduce the risk for the buyer.
   b. reduce the risk for the seller.
   c. both a and b.
   d. neither a or b.

4. If an investor noticed a discrepancy in the exchange rates of two countries and acted upon it, he would be engaging in:

   a. money market hedging.
   b. forward hedging.
   c. arbitrage.
   d. sabotage.
   e. leading strategies.

5. If your firm held liabilities in a strong currency, it would be wise to _____.

   a. lead.
   b. lag.
   c. engage in money market hedging.
   d. engage in forward hedging.
   e. all of the above.

6. Direct foreign investment involves:

   a. political risk.
   b. business risk.
   c. financial risk.
   d. exchange rate risk.
   e. all of the above.

7. If the net present value of a direct foreign investment project for a MNC is less than zero, they should:

   a. reject it.
   b. open a sales office.
   c. license a foreign company.
   d. accept it.
   e. a, b, and c are all possibilities.

8. If the U.S. experiences a 7% inflation rate while France is experiencing a 4% inflation rate, then according to purchasing power parity:

   a. The value of the U.S. dollar should increase by approximately 3% against the French Franc.
   b. The U.S. dollar should decline against the French Franc by 3%.

c.   The French Franc would decline by 3% against the U.S. dollar.

d.   There would be no change in either currency.

9.   A paper loss/gain best describes which type of risk:

a.   economic.
b.   transaction.
c.   interest rate.
d.   translation.

10. Which of the following do not provide a hedge against some risk:

a.   forward contract.
b.   money market hedge.
c.   currency options.
d.   futures contracts.
e.   all are forms of hedging.

24

Small Business Finance

Orientation: This chapter explores the basic concepts of financial management for the small business enterprise, along with the means available for financing the small firm.

I.   The Small Business

    A.   The Small Business Administration (SBA) defines a small business as one that is independently owned and operated and meets certain employee and sales restrictions dependent on the specific industry. Also the firm should not be the dominant constituent in its field of operations.

    B.   Observed differences in large and small firms

        1.   Dividend policy - small firms that are experiencing growth pay little or no dividends to their investors as compared to their larger counterparts.

        2.   Liquidity - small firms have "tighter" cash flows as seen in lower current ratios and frequent shortages of working capital.

        3.   Business risk - small firms have more variability of earnings before interest and taxes.

        4.   Financial risk - the capital structure for the small enterprise is much more debt oriented, with a strong tendency to use short-term credit.

II. Importance of Cash Management in the Small Firm

    A. The following conditions, typical of the small firm, require careful cash management:

        1. Firms encountering change.

        2. Firms that are undercapitalized.

        3. Firms facing expansion and growth.

        4. Firms approaching potential sources of financing, especially the banker.

    B. Small businesses typically do not spend time planning and forecasting cash flow budgets, despite its importance.

III. Financing the Small Company

    A. Stages of financing.

        1. Initial investment sources might include:

            a. Owner's personal capital.
            b. Commercial banks.
            c. Savings and loan associations.
            d. Small Business Administration.
            e. Friends and relatives.
            f. Leasing companies.
            g. Commercial finance companies.

        2. The gap - the time for private placements either placed directly or through an investment banker, consisting of debt and/or equity sources including:

            a. Financial institutions.
            b. Private investor groups.
            c. Venture capital.
            d. Small business investment company.
            e. Large corporations.

        3. The public offerings.

            a. Over-the-counter.
            b. Regional exchanges.
            c. American or New York Exchanges.

    B. Venture capital and the small firm.

        1. Investment interests of the venture capitalist.

336

<ol type="a">
<li>Providing capital for high risk operation.</li>
<li>Providing start-up or "seed" capital.</li>
<li>Investing in firms unable to raise conventional capital.</li>
<li>Investing in high risk publicly traded corporations.</li>
</ol>

2. General attributes of venture capitalists.

<ol type="a">
<li>Monies are generally committed for specific period of time wherein the opportunity to make quick gains or losses is not available.</li>
<li>The venture capitalist often represents the first "independent" source of equity financing to the small firm.</li>
<li>Venture capital groups have divergent interests.</li>
</ol>

3. Concerns of the venture capital investor.

<ol type="a">
<li>Protective covenants similar to loan restrictions.</li>
<li>Trade-off between interest rate and conversion privileges.</li>
</ol>

C. Debt as a source of financing.

1. Commercial banks.

<ol type="a">
<li>Banks are the leading source of borrowed funds for the small company.</li>
<li>Two types of loans; short term notes and mortgage bonds are available.</li>
<li>Long term credit is often provided by the continued renewal of short-term credit.</li>
<li>A personal and professional relationship with a banker can be very beneficial to the small business person.</li>
<li>Selection of bank should depend on the expertise of the bank's loan officers as well as their capabilities in terms of loan size.</li>
</ol>

2. Insurance companies.

<ol type="a">
<li>Loans are generally in the form of mortgage loans.</li>
<li>The size of the loan is generally large.</li>
</ol>

3. Small business investment companies - historically loans have been long-term and in excess of

$75,000 to companies with a good record in a high technology field.

4. Governmental agencies.

    a. Mostly offered at the federal level from the Small Business Administration and several other agencies sponsoring firms in specific industries and/or for specific purposes.

    b. The Small Business Administration.

        (a) Mainly <u>facilitates</u> the acquisition of small business loans.

        (b) To be eligible for an SBA loan, must meet certain size and operational criteria.

        (c) Application for an SBA loan should be subsequent to the denial of a commercial bank loan.

        (d) Loan size is limited to a maximum of $150,000, but typically ranges between $5,000 and $25,000.

    c. State and local agencies - many and varied.

D. Common Stock as a source of financing.

1. Problems of common stock for the small firm.

    a. Lack of marketability of stock leads to higher cost of common capital.

    b. Prohibitive flotation costs exist for a small issue.

    c. Issuing new common results in a potential dilution of control.

2. Forms of common stock.

    a. Class A stock has a higher claim on dividend income and assets but less extensive voting power.

    b. Class B has greater voting power but lower claim on assets and dividend income.

c. "Founders' shares" are similar to Class B stock but maintain sole voting rights and forfeit dividend income for a specified number of years.

3. Sources of common equity for the small firm.

   a. Relatives and friends.

   b. Venture capitalists.

      (a) Small business investment corporations (SBICs).

      (b) Publicly owned venture capital investment companies.

      (c) Private venture capital investors.

      (d) Wealthy individuals.

      (e) Large corporations.

      (f) Other sources.

E. Retention of earnings as a source of financing.

   1. Retained earnings are a major source of equity financing for any size organization.

   2. An inverse relationship exists between the company's size and percentage profits retained for reinvestment.

   3. Retention of earnings precludes the payment of dividends. Informational content and income preference seem to be of lesser importance in a small firm.

IV. Going public

A. Disadvantages to going public.

   1. Registration process is both timely and expensive.

   2. Principal owner-manager is no longer able to run the operations in a personal manner.

   3. Disclosure of inside transactions are timely and expensive.

4. Decision-making process of the company must now incorporate the views of the stockholders.

5. Personal liability for directors and officers is significantly increased.

6. Public market is an unreliable source of funds.

B. Reasons for going public.

1. It establishes a market for future financing.

2. Stock options can be used as encouragement for key personnel.

3. Broad distribution may result in favorable public relations.

4. Owner can diversify his holdings constrained by his desire to maintain control.

5. Public securities are easier to use as collateral for personal credit.

C. Prerequisites for going public.

1. Size of the issue constraint.

2. Marketability of securities.

3. Established earnings record.

4. Quality and philosophies of management.

5. Growth potential.

6. Favorable reputation and image of the firm's products and services.

Self-Test

TRUE-FALSE

_____ 1. A small firm might be a company with annual sales of $10 million in the wholesaling business or a retailer with annual sales of only $250,000 as defined by the SBA.

_____ 2. Insurance firms provide a viable source of equity financing to the small business community.

_____ 3.   The Small Business Administration more frequently acts as a guarantor to a loan rather than to loan the actual funds to the small business.

_____ 4.   Since the management/owner of a small business enterprise is so familiar with the operations of the business, cash management and planning provides very few benefits for the costs and time entailed.

_____ 5.   Small businesses generally retain a larger percentage of their earnings than do their larger counterparts.

_____ 6.   The "gap" is the period of time in which the small business has outgrown the owner's capability to finance all investments, but is not yet large enough to justify a public offering.

_____ 7.   Small businesses borrow frequently a large amount of short-term credit that is renewed continuously to become a means of long-term financing.

_____ 8.   Most small business investment corporations (SBICs) were established as non-profit corporations regulated by the SBA, to provide a source of financing to the small business community.

_____ 9.   Issuing public securities requires a lot of time and expense but has historically been viewed as a positive move by the firm's management.

_____ 10. The image of the products or services of the small business may be an important consideration to the owner/manager deciding to make a public offering.

MULTIPLE CHOICE

1. If a particular group of venture capitalists has been approached for equity capital and the request denied, the management of the small firm should proceed by:

    a.   requesting more bank loans.
    b.   seeking out another venture capital group.
    c.   making a public offering.
    d.   none of the above.
    e.   both a and b.

2. The means available to finance a small business include:

    a.   financial institutions.
    b.   venture capitalists.
    c.   wealthy investors.

341

d.   commercial banks.
e.   all of the above.

3.   Venture capitalists

a.   provide capital for any high risk financial venture.
b.   provide "seed capital" for a start-up situation.
c.   invest in a firm that is unable to raise capital from conventional sources.
d.   invest in large publicly traded corporations where the risk is significant.
e.   all of the above.
f.   only a, b, and c.

4.   The SBA makes loans to

a.   small businesses.
b.   non-profit businesses.
c.   magazine and newspaper publishers.
d.   monopolies.
e.   all of the above.
f.   only a and b.

5.   The following is not a problem of common stock for the small business.

a.   lack of marketability of stock.
b.   higher flotation costs.
c.   establishes market for future financing.
d.   higher cost of equity capital.
e.   potential dilution of control for existing owners.

6.   The size of a public offering is important to the investment banker because of

a.   the potential for developing an active market.
b.   the flotation costs of a small issue.
c.   the growth potential of future offerings.
d.   both a and b.
e.   both a and c.

ANSWERS TO SELF-TESTS

Chapter 1 TRUE-FALSE	Chapter 2 TRUE-FALSE	Chapter 3 TRUE-FALSE	Chapter 4 TRUE-FALSE
1. F	1. F	1. F	1. T
2. T	2. T	2. T	2. T
3. F	3. T	3. F	3. F
4. T	4. F	4. T	4. T
5. T	5. F	5. T	5. F
6. F	6. F	6. F	6. T
7. F	7. F	7. T	7. F
8. T	8. T	8. F	8. F
9. T	9. F	9. T	9. T
10. F	10. T	10. T	10. F
11. T			

Chapter 1 MULTIPLE CHOICE	Chapter 2 MULTIPLE CHOICE	Chapter 3 MULTIPLE CHOICE	Chapter 4 MULTIPLE CHOICE
1. d	1. e	1. b	1. c
2. e	2. e	2. e	2. d
3. e	3. a	3. a	3. e
4. e	4. b	4. d	4. c
5. d	5. c	5. b	5. e
6. d	6. b	6. b	6. c
7. c	7. e	7. d	
8. d	8. c	8. d	
		9. c	
		10. b	

Chapter 5 TRUE-FALSE	Chapter 6 TRUE-FALSE	Chapter 7 TRUE-FALSE	Chapter 8 TRUE-FALSE
1. F	1. F	1. F	1. F
2. F	2. F	2. T	2. F
3. T	3. T	3. T	3. T
4. F	4. F	4. T	4. F
5. T	5. T	5. F	5. F
6. T	6. F	6. T	6. T
7. F	7. T	7. T	7. F
8. T	8. F	8. F	8. F
9. F	9. F	9. T	9. T
10. T	10. F	10. F	10. T
	11. F		
	12. F		
	13. F		
	14. F		
	15. F		
	16. F		
	17. T		
	18. T		
	19. F		
	20. F		
	21. T		
	22. T		
	23. F		
	24. F		
	25. T		
	26. T		
	27. T		
	28. F		
	29. T		
	30. F		
	31. T		

Chapter 5	Chapter 6	Chapter 7	Chapter 8
MULTIPLE CHOICE	MULTIPLE CHOICE	MULTIPLE CHOICE	MULTIPLE CHOICE
1. d	1. a	1. c	1. c
2. f	2. d	2. c	2. b
3. c	3. c	3. e	3. a
4. a	4. a	4. d	4. c
5. c	5. d	5. d	5. b
6. e	6. c	6. b	6. b
	7. d	7. a	
	8. e	8. d	
	9. c		
	10. d		
	11. e		
	12. d		
	13. c		
	14. b		

Chapter 9	Chapter 10	Chapter 11	Chapter 12
TRUE-FALSE	TRUE-FALSE	TRUE-FALSE	TRUE-FALSE
1. T	1. T	1. F	1. T
2. T	2. T	2. T	2. T
3. F	3. T	3. F	3. T
4. T	4. T	4. T	4. F
5. T	5. T	5. F	5. F
6. T	6. F	6. F	6. F
7. T	7. F	7. T	7. T
8. F	8. F	8. T	8. T
9. T	9. T	9. F	9. T
10. F	10. T	10. T	10. T
	11. T	11. F	11. T
	12. F	12. T	12. F
	13. F	13. T	13. F
		14. F	14. T
		15. F	15. F

Chapter 9	Chapter 10	Chapter 11	Chapter 12
MULTIPLE CHOICE	MULTIPLE CHOICE	MULTIPLE CHOICE	MULTIPLE CHOICE
1. a	1. c	1. b	1. a
2. c	2. e	2. c	2. a
3. d	3. a	3. c	3. b
4. b	4. c	4. b	4. e
5. c	5. e	5. d	5. a
6. c	6. c	6. d	6. d
7. a	7. d		7. c
	8. b		8. b

Chapter 13 TRUE-FALSE	Appendix 13A TRUE-FALSE	Chapter 14 TRUE-FALSE	Chapter 15 TRUE-FALSE
1. F	1. T	1. F	1. F
2. F	2. F	2. F	2. T
3. T	3. F	3. T	3. F
4. F	4. T	4. T	4. F
5. F	5. F	5. F	5. T
6. T		6. T	6. F
7. F		7. F	7. F
8. F		8. T	8. F
9. T		9. F	9. F
10. F		10. F	10. T
11. T		11. F	11. T
12. T		12. F	12. F
13. T		13. F	13. F
		14. F	14. F
		15. T	15. T
		16. T	16. T
		17. T	17. T
		18. T	18. T
		19. T	19. F
		20. T	20. F
		21. F	

Chapter 13 MULTIPLE CHOICE	Appendix 13A MULTIPLE CHOICE	Chapter 14 MULTIPLE CHOICE	Chapter 15 MULTIPLE CHOICE
1. f	1. b	1. c	1. c
2. d	2. c	2. c	2. e
3. b	3. b	3. c	3. b
4. d	4. b	4. c	4. d
5. b		5. b	5. b
		6. b	6. b
		7. b	7. a
		8. b	8. d
		9. b	9. b
		10. d	10. d
		11. b	11. a
		12. c	12. c
		13. a	13. e
		14. b	
		15. c	
		16. d	
		17. b	

Chapter 16 TRUE-FALSE	Chapter 17 TRUE-FALSE	Chapter 18 TRUE-FALSE	Chapter 19 TRUE-FALSE
1. T	1. F	1. F	1. F
2. F	2. T	2. T	2. F
3. F	3. F	3. T	3. F
4. F	4. F	4. T	4. F
5. T	5. F	5. F	5. F
6. F	6. F	6. T	6. T
7. T	7. T	7. F	7. T
8. T	8. T	8. F	8. F
9. F	9. F	9. T	9. F
10. T	10. T	10. T	10. F
11. T	11. T		11. T
12. F	12. F		12. F
13. F	13. T		13. F
14. F	14. F		
15. F	15. F		
	16. T		
	17. T		
	18. F		
	19. F		
	20. T		
	21. F		

Chapter 16 MULTIPLE CHOICE	Chapter 17 MULTIPLE CHOICE	Chapter 18 MULTIPLE CHOICE	Chapter 19 MULTIPLE CHOICE
1. b	1. c	1. e	1. d
2. d	2. d	2. a	2. d
3. d	3. e	3. a	3. d
4. c	4. b	4. e	4. c
5. d	5. b	5. d	5. b
6. d	6. a		6. d
7. d	7. c		7. a
8. d	8. d		8. d
9. e	9. c		9. c
10. f	10. c		
11. b	11. d		
12. b	12. b		
13. d	13. b		
	14. c		
	15. c		
	16. d		

Chapter 20 TRUE-FALSE	Chapter 21 TRUE-FALSE	Chapter 22 TRUE-FALSE	Chapter 23 TRUE-FALSE
1. T	1. T	1. F	1. T
2. F	2. T	2. F	2. F
3. F	3. F	3. F	3. F
4. F	4. T	4. T	4. F
5. T	5. T	5. F	5. T
6. F	6. F	6. F	6. T
7. T	7. T	7. F	7. F
8. F	8. F	8. T	8. F
9. T	9. T	9. T	9. T
10. T	10. T	10. F	10. T
11. F		11. F	11. T
12. T		12. F	12. T
13. F		13. T	13. T
			14. F
			15. T
			16. F

Appendix 20A
TRUE-FALSE

1. T
2. F
3. F

Chapter 20 MULTIPLE CHOICE	Chapter 21 MULTIPLE CHOICE	Chapter 22 MULTIPLE CHOICE	Chapter 23 MULTIPLE CHOICE
1. c	1. d	1. c	1. d
2. a	2. e	2. a	2. e
3. b	3. c	3. a	3. c
4. b	4. a	4. b	4. c
5. c	5. a	5. b	5. a
6. c	6. b	6. d	6. e
7. b			7. e
			8. b
			9. d
			10. e

Appendix 20A
MULTIPLE
CHOICE

1. c
2. c

Chapter 24
TRUE-FALSE

1. T
2. F
3. T
4. F
5. T
6. T
7. T
8. F
9. F
10. T

Chapter 24
MULTIPLE
CHOICE

1. b
2. e
3. e
4. a
5. c
6. d

COMPOUND SUM AND PRESENT-VALUE TABLES

Appendix A COMPOUND SUM OF $1

n	1%	2%	3%	4%	5%	6%	7%	8%	9%	10%
1	1.010	1.020	1.030	1.040	1.050	1.060	1.070	1.080	1.090	1.100
2	1.020	1.040	1.061	1.082	1.102	1.124	1.145	1.166	1.188	1.210
3	1.030	1.061	1.093	1.125	1.158	1.191	1.225	1.260	1.295	1.331
4	1.041	1.082	1.126	1.170	1.216	1.262	1.311	1.360	1.412	1.464
5	1.051	1.104	1.159	1.217	1.276	1.338	1.403	1.469	1.539	1.611
6	1.062	1.126	1.194	1.265	1.340	1.419	1.501	1.587	1.677	1.772
7	1.072	1.149	1.230	1.316	1.407	1.504	1.606	1.714	1.828	1.949
8	1.083	1.172	1.267	1.369	1.477	1.594	1.718	1.851	1.993	2.144
9	1.094	1.195	1.305	1.423	1.551	1.689	1.838	1.999	2.172	2.358
10	1.105	1.219	1.344	1.480	1.629	1.791	1.967	2.159	2.367	2.594
11	1.116	1.243	1.384	1.539	1.710	1.898	2.105	2.332	2.580	2.853
12	1.127	1.268	1.426	1.601	1.796	2.012	2.252	2.518	2.813	3.138
13	1.138	1.294	1.469	1.665	1.886	2.133	2.410	2.720	3.066	3.452
14	1.149	1.319	1.513	1.732	1.980	2.261	2.579	2.937	3.342	3.797
15	1.161	1.346	1.558	1.801	2.079	2.397	2.759	3.172	3.642	4.177
16	1.173	1.373	1.605	1.873	2.183	2.540	2.952	3.426	3.970	4.595
17	1.184	1.400	1.653	1.948	2.292	2.693	3.159	3.700	4.328	5.054
18	1.196	1.428	1.702	2.026	2.407	2.854	3.380	3.996	4.717	5.560
19	1.208	1.457	1.753	2.107	2.527	3.026	3.616	4.316	5.142	6.116
20	1.220	1.486	1.806	2.191	2.653	3.207	3.870	4.661	5.604	6.727
21	1.232	1.516	1.860	2.279	2.786	3.399	4.140	5.034	6.109	7.400
22	1.245	1.546	1.916	2.370	2.925	3.603	4.430	5.436	6.658	8.140
23	1.257	1.577	1.974	2.465	3.071	3.820	4.740	5.871	7.258	8.954
24	1.270	1.608	2.033	2.563	3.225	4.049	5.072	6.341	7.911	9.850
25	1.282	1.641	2.094	2.666	3.386	4.292	5.427	6.848	8.623	10.834
30	1.348	1.811	2.427	3.243	4.322	5.743	7.612	10.062	13.267	17.449
40	1.489	2.208	3.262	4.801	7.040	10.285	14.974	21.724	31.408	45.258
50	1.645	2.691	4.384	7.106	11.467	18.419	29.456	46.900	74.354	117.386

Appendix A COMPOUND SUM OF $1 (cont.)

n	11%	12%	13%	14%	15%	16%	17%	18%	19%	20%
1	1.110	1.120	1.130	1.140	1.150	1.160	1.170	1.180	1.190	1.200
2	1.232	1.254	1.277	1.300	1.322	1.346	1.369	1.392	1.416	1.440
3	1.368	1.405	1.443	1.482	1.521	1.561	1.602	1.643	1.685	1.728
4	1.518	1.574	1.630	1.689	1.749	1.811	1.874	1.939	2.005	2.074
5	1.685	1.762	1.842	1.925	2.011	2.100	2.192	2.288	2.386	2.488
6	1.870	1.974	2.082	2.195	2.313	2.436	2.565	2.700	2.840	2.986
7	2.076	2.211	2.353	2.502	2.660	2.826	3.001	3.185	3.379	3.583
8	2.305	2.476	2.658	2.853	3.059	3.278	3.511	3.759	4.021	4.300
9	2.558	2.773	3.004	3.252	3.518	3.803	4.108	4.435	4.785	5.160
10	2.839	3.106	3.395	3.707	4.046	4.411	4.807	5.234	5.695	6.192
11	3.152	3.479	3.836	4.226	4.652	5.117	5.624	6.176	6.777	7.430
12	3.498	3.896	4.334	4.818	5.350	5.936	6.580	7.288	8.064	8.916
13	3.883	4.363	4.898	5.492	6.153	6.886	7.699	8.599	9.596	10.699
14	4.310	4.887	5.535	6.261	7.076	7.987	9.007	10.147	11.420	12.839
15	4.785	5.474	6.254	7.138	8.137	9.265	10.539	11.974	13.589	15.407
16	5.311	6.130	7.067	8.137	9.358	10.748	12.330	14.129	16.171	18.488
17	5.895	6.866	7.986	9.276	10.761	12.468	14.426	16.672	19.244	22.186
18	6.543	7.690	9.024	10.575	12.375	14.462	16.879	19.673	22.900	26.623
19	7.263	8.613	10.197	12.055	14.232	16.776	19.748	23.214	27.251	31.948
20	8.062	9.646	11.523	13.743	16.366	19.461	23.105	27.393	32.429	38.337
21	8.949	10.804	13.021	15.667	18.821	22.574	27.033	32.323	38.591	46.005
22	9.933	12.100	14.713	17.861	21.644	26.186	31.629	38.141	45.923	55.205
23	11.026	13.552	16.626	20.361	24.891	30.376	37.005	45.007	54.648	66.247
24	12.239	15.178	18.788	23.212	28.625	35.236	43.296	53.108	65.031	79.496
25	13.585	17.000	21.230	26.461	32.918	40.874	50.656	62.667	77.387	95.395
30	22.892	29.960	39.115	50.949	66.210	85.849	111.061	143.367	184.672	237.373
40	64.999	93.049	132.776	188.876	267.856	378.715	533.846	750.353	1051.642	1469.740
50	184.559	288.996	450.711	700.197	1083.619	1670.669	2566.080	3927.189	5988.730	9100.191

Appendix A COMPOUND SUM OF $1 (cont.)

n	21%	22%	23%	24%	25%	26%	27%	28%	29%	30%
1	1.210	1.220	1.230	1.240	1.250	1.260	1.270	1.280	1.290	1.300
2	1.464	1.488	1.513	1.538	1.562	1.588	1.613	1.638	1.664	1.690
3	1.772	1.816	1.861	1.907	1.953	2.000	2.048	2.097	2.147	2.197
4	2.144	2.215	2.289	2.364	2.441	2.520	2.601	2.684	2.769	2.856
5	2.594	2.703	2.815	2.932	3.052	3.176	3.304	3.436	3.572	3.713
6	3.138	3.297	3.463	3.635	3.815	4.001	4.196	4.398	4.608	4.827
7	3.797	4.023	4.259	4.508	4.768	5.042	5.329	5.629	5.945	6.275
8	4.595	4.908	5.239	5.589	5.960	6.353	6.767	7.206	7.669	8.157
9	5.560	5.987	6.444	6.931	7.451	8.004	8.595	9.223	9.893	10.604
10	6.727	7.305	7.926	8.594	9.313	10.086	10.915	11.806	12.761	13.786
11	8.140	8.912	9.749	10.657	11.642	12.708	13.862	15.112	16.462	17.921
12	9.850	10.872	11.991	13.215	14.552	16.012	17.605	19.343	21.236	23.298
13	11.918	13.264	14.749	16.386	18.190	20.175	22.359	24.759	27.395	30.287
14	14.421	16.182	18.141	20.319	22.737	25.420	28.395	31.691	35.339	39.373
15	17.449	19.742	22.314	25.195	28.422	32.030	36.062	40.565	45.587	51.185
16	21.113	24.085	27.446	31.242	35.527	40.357	45.799	51.923	58.808	66.541
17	25.547	29.384	33.758	38.740	44.409	50.850	58.165	66.461	75.862	86.503
18	30.912	35.848	41.523	48.038	55.511	64.071	73.869	85.070	97.862	112.454
19	37.404	43.735	51.073	59.567	69.389	80.730	93.813	108.890	126.242	146.190
20	45.258	53.357	62.820	73.863	86.736	101.720	119.143	139.379	162.852	190.047
21	54.762	65.095	77.268	91.591	108.420	128.167	151.312	178.405	210.079	247.061
22	66.262	79.416	95.040	113.572	135.525	161.490	192.165	228.358	271.002	321.178
23	80.178	96.887	116.899	140.829	169.407	203.477	244.050	292.298	349.592	417.531
24	97.015	118.203	143.786	174.628	211.758	256.381	309.943	374.141	450.974	542.791
25	117.388	144.207	176.857	216.539	264.698	323.040	393.628	478.901	581.756	705.627
30	304.471	389.748	497.904	634.810	807.793	1025.904	1300.477	1645.488	2078.208	2619.936
40	2048.309	2846.941	3946.340	5455.797	7523.156	10346.879	14195.051	19426.418	26520.723	36117.754
50	13779.844	20795.680	31278.301	46889.207	70064.812	104354.562	154942.687	229345.875	338440.000	497910.125

Appendix A COMPOUND SUM OF $1 (cont.)

n	31%	32%	33%	34%	35%	36%	37%	38%	39%	40%
1	1.310	1.320	1.330	1.340	1.350	1.360	1.370	1.380	1.390	1.400
2	1.716	1.742	1.769	1.796	1.822	1.850	1.877	1.904	1.932	1.960
3	2.248	2.300	2.353	2.406	2.460	2.515	2.571	2.628	2.686	2.744
4	2.945	3.036	3.129	3.224	3.321	3.421	3.523	3.627	3.733	3.842
5	3.858	4.007	4.162	4.320	4.484	4.653	4.826	5.005	5.189	5.378
6	5.054	5.290	5.535	5.789	6.053	6.328	6.612	6.907	7.213	7.530
7	6.621	6.983	7.361	7.758	8.172	8.605	9.058	9.531	10.025	10.541
8	8.673	9.217	9.791	10.395	11.032	11.703	12.410	13.153	13.935	14.758
9	11.362	12.166	13.022	13.930	14.894	15.917	17.001	18.151	19.370	20.661
10	14.884	16.060	17.319	18.666	20.106	21.646	23.292	25.049	26.924	28.925
11	19.498	21.199	23.034	25.012	27.144	29.439	31.910	34.567	37.425	40.495
12	25.542	27.982	30.635	33.516	36.644	40.037	43.716	47.703	52.020	56.694
13	33.460	36.937	40.745	44.912	49.469	54.451	59.892	65.830	72.308	79.371
14	43.832	48.756	54.190	60.181	66.784	74.053	82.051	90.845	100.509	111.119
15	57.420	64.358	72.073	80.643	90.158	100.712	112.410	125.366	139.707	155.567
16	75.220	84.953	95.857	108.061	121.713	136.968	154.002	173.005	194.192	217.793
17	98.539	112.138	127.490	144.802	164.312	186.277	210.983	238.747	269.927	304.911
18	129.086	148.022	169.561	194.035	221.822	253.337	289.046	329.471	375.198	426.875
19	169.102	195.389	225.517	260.006	299.459	344.537	395.993	454.669	521.525	597.625
20	221.523	257.913	299.937	348.408	404.270	468.571	542.511	627.443	724.919	836.674
21	290.196	340.446	398.916	466.867	545.764	637.256	743.240	865.871	1007.637	1171.343
22	380.156	449.388	530.558	625.601	736.781	866.668	1018.238	1194.900	1400.615	1639.878
23	498.004	593.192	705.642	838.305	994.653	1178.668	1394.986	1648.961	1946.854	2295.829
24	652.385	783.013	938.504	1123.328	1342.781	1602.988	1911.129	2275.564	2706.125	3214.158
25	854.623	1033.577	1248.210	1505.258	1812.754	2180.063	2618.245	3140.275	3761.511	4499.816
30	3297.081	4142.008	5194.516	6503.285	8128.426	10142.914	12636.086	15716.703	19517.969	24201.043
40	49072.621	66519.313	89962.188	121388.437	163433.875	219558.625	294317.937	393684.687	525508.312	700022.688

Appendix B PRESENT VALUE OF $1

n	1%	2%	3%	4%	5%	6%	7%	8%	9%	10%
1	.990	.980	.971	.962	.952	.943	.935	.926	.917	.909
2	.980	.961	.943	.925	.907	.890	.873	.857	.842	.826
3	.971	.942	.915	.889	.864	.840	.816	.794	.772	.751
4	.961	.924	.888	.855	.823	.792	.763	.735	.708	.683
5	.951	.906	.863	.822	.784	.747	.713	.681	.650	.621
6	.942	.888	.837	.790	.746	.705	.666	.630	.596	.564
7	.933	.871	.813	.760	.711	.665	.623	.583	.547	.513
8	.923	.853	.789	.731	.677	.627	.582	.540	.502	.467
9	.914	.837	.766	.703	.645	.592	.544	.500	.460	.424
10	.905	.820	.744	.676	.614	.558	.508	.463	.422	.386
11	.896	.804	.722	.650	.585	.527	.475	.429	.388	.350
12	.887	.789	.701	.625	.557	.497	.444	.397	.356	.319
13	.879	.773	.681	.601	.530	.469	.415	.368	.326	.290
14	.870	.758	.661	.577	.505	.442	.388	.340	.299	.263
15	.861	.743	.642	.555	.481	.417	.362	.315	.275	.239
16	.853	.728	.623	.534	.458	.394	.339	.292	.252	.218
17	.844	.714	.605	.513	.436	.371	.317	.270	.231	.198
18	.836	.700	.587	.494	.416	.350	.296	.250	.212	.180
19	.828	.686	.570	.475	.396	.331	.277	.232	.194	.164
20	.820	.673	.554	.456	.377	.312	.258	.215	.178	.149
21	.811	.660	.538	.439	.359	.294	.242	.199	.164	.135
22	.803	.647	.522	.422	.342	.278	.226	.184	.150	.123
23	.795	.634	.507	.406	.326	.262	.211	.170	.138	.112
24	.788	.622	.492	.390	.310	.247	.197	.158	.126	.102
25	.780	.610	.478	.375	.295	.233	.184	.146	.116	.092
30	.742	.552	.412	.308	.231	.174	.131	.099	.075	.057
40	.672	.453	.307	.208	.142	.097	.067	.046	.032	.022
50	.608	.372	.228	.141	.087	.054	.034	.021	.013	.009

Appendix B PRESENT VALUE OF $1 (cont.)

n	11%	12%	13%	14%	15%	16%	17%	18%	19%	20%
1	.901	.893	.885	.877	.870	.862	.855	.847	.840	.833
2	.812	.797	.783	.769	.756	.743	.731	.718	.706	.694
3	.731	.712	.693	.675	.658	.641	.624	.609	.593	.579
4	.659	.636	.613	.592	.572	.552	.534	.516	.499	.482
5	.593	.567	.543	.519	.497	.476	.456	.437	.419	.402
6	.535	.507	.480	.456	.432	.410	.390	.370	.352	.335
7	.482	.452	.425	.400	.376	.354	.333	.314	.296	.279
8	.434	.404	.376	.351	.327	.305	.285	.266	.249	.233
9	.391	.361	.333	.308	.284	.263	.243	.225	.209	.194
10	.352	.322	.295	.270	.247	.227	.208	.191	.176	.162
11	.317	.287	.261	.237	.215	.195	.178	.162	.148	.135
12	.286	.257	.231	.208	.187	.168	.152	.137	.124	.112
13	.258	.229	.204	.182	.163	.145	.130	.116	.104	.093
14	.232	.205	.181	.160	.141	.125	.111	.099	.088	.078
15	.209	.183	.160	.140	.123	.108	.095	.084	.074	.065
16	.188	.163	.141	.123	.107	.093	.081	.071	.062	.054
17	.170	.146	.125	.108	.093	.080	.069	.060	.052	.045
18	.153	.130	.111	.095	.081	.069	.059	.051	.044	.038
19	.138	.116	.098	.083	.070	.060	.051	.043	.037	.031
20	.124	.104	.087	.073	.061	.051	.043	.037	.031	.026
21	.112	.093	.077	.064	.053	.044	.037	.031	.026	.022
22	.101	.083	.068	.056	.046	.038	.032	.026	.022	.018
23	.091	.074	.060	.049	.040	.033	.027	.022	.018	.015
24	.082	.066	.053	.043	.035	.028	.023	.019	.015	.013
25	.074	.059	.047	.038	.030	.024	.020	.016	.013	.010
30	.044	.033	.026	.020	.015	.012	.009	.007	.005	.004
40	.015	.011	.008	.005	.004	.003	.002	.001	.001	.001
50	.005	.003	.002	.001	.001	.001	.000	.000	.000	.000

Appendix B PRESENT VALUE OF $1 (cont.)

n	21%	22%	23%	24%	25%	26%	27%	28%	29%	30%
1	.826	.820	.813	.806	.800	.794	.787	.781	.775	.769
2	.683	.672	.661	.650	.640	.630	.620	.610	.601	.592
3	.564	.551	.537	.524	.512	.500	.488	.477	.466	.455
4	.467	.451	.437	.423	.410	.397	.384	.373	.361	.350
5	.386	.370	.355	.341	.328	.315	.303	.291	.280	.269
6	.319	.303	.289	.275	.262	.250	.238	.227	.217	.207
7	.263	.249	.235	.222	.210	.198	.188	.178	.168	.159
8	.218	.204	.191	.179	.168	.157	.148	.139	.130	.123
9	.180	.167	.155	.144	.134	.125	.116	.108	.101	.094
10	.149	.137	.126	.116	.107	.099	.092	.085	.078	.073
11	.123	.112	.103	.094	.086	.079	.072	.066	.061	.056
12	.102	.092	.083	.076	.069	.062	.057	.052	.047	.043
13	.084	.075	.068	.061	.055	.050	.045	.040	.037	.033
14	.069	.062	.055	.049	.044	.039	.035	.032	.028	.025
15	.057	.051	.045	.040	.035	.031	.028	.025	.022	.020
16	.047	.042	.036	.032	.028	.025	.022	.019	.017	.015
17	.039	.034	.030	.026	.023	.020	.017	.015	.013	.012
18	.032	.028	.024	.021	.018	.016	.014	.012	.010	.009
19	.027	.023	.020	.017	.014	.012	.011	.009	.008	.007
20	.022	.019	.016	.014	.012	.010	.008	.009	.006	.005
21	.018	.015	.013	.011	.009	.008	.007	.006	.005	.004
22	.015	.013	.011	.009	.007	.006	.005	.004	.004	.003
23	.012	.010	.009	.007	.006	.005	.004	.003	.003	.003
24	.010	.008	.007	.006	.005	.004	.003	.003	.002	.002
25	.009	.007	.006	.005	.004	.003	.003	.002	.002	.001
30	.003	.003	.002	.002	.001	.001	.001	.001	.000	.000
40	.000	.000	.000	.000	.000	.000	.000	.000	.000	.000
50	.000	.000	.000	.000	.000	.000	.000	.000	.000	.000

Appendix B PRESENT VALUE OF $1 (cont.)

n	31%	32%	33%	34%	35%	36%	37%	38%	39%	40%
1	.763	.758	.752	.746	.741	.735	.730	.725	.719	.714
2	.583	.574	.565	.557	.549	.541	.533	.525	.518	.510
3	.445	.435	.425	.416	.406	.398	.389	.381	.372	.364
4	.340	.329	.320	.310	.301	.292	.284	.276	.268	.260
5	.259	.250	.240	.231	.223	.215	.207	.200	.193	.186
6	.198	.189	.181	.173	.165	.158	.151	.145	.139	.133
7	.151	.143	.136	.129	.122	.116	.110	.105	.100	.095
8	.115	.108	.102	.096	.091	.085	.081	.076	.072	.068
9	.088	.082	.077	.072	.067	.063	.059	.055	.052	.048
10	.067	.062	.058	.054	.050	.046	.043	.040	.037	.035
11	.051	.047	.043	.040	.037	.034	.031	.029	.027	.025
12	.039	.036	.033	.030	.027	.025	.023	.021	.019	.018
13	.030	.027	.025	.022	.020	.018	.017	.015	.014	.013
14	.023	.021	.018	.017	.015	.014	.012	.011	.010	.009
15	.017	.016	.014	.012	.011	.010	.009	.008	.007	.006
16	.013	.012	.010	.009	.008	.007	.006	.006	.005	.005
17	.010	.009	.008	.007	.006	.005	.005	.004	.004	.003
18	.008	.007	.006	.005	.005	.004	.003	.003	.003	.002
19	.006	.005	.004	.004	.003	.003	.003	.002	.002	.002
20	.005	.004	.003	.003	.002	.002	.002	.002	.001	.001
21	.003	.003	.003	.002	.002	.002	.001	.001	.001	.001
22	.003	.002	.002	.002	.001	.001	.001	.001	.001	.001
23	.002	.002	.001	.001	.001	.001	.001	.001	.001	.000
24	.002	.001	.001	.001	.001	.001	.001	.000	.000	.000
25	.001	.001	.001	.000	.001	.000	.000	.000	.000	.000
30	.000	.000	.000	.000	.000	.000	.000	.000	.000	.000
40	.000	.000	.000	.000	.000	.000	.000	.000	.000	.000

Appendix C SUM OF AN ANNUITY OF $1 FOR _n_ PERIODS

n	1%	2%	3%	4%	5%	6%	7%	8%	9%	10%
1	1.000	1.000	1.000	1.000	1.000	1.000	1.000	1.000	1.000	1.000
2	2.010	2.020	2.030	2.040	2.050	2.060	2.070	2.080	2.090	2.100
3	3.030	3.060	3.091	3.122	3.152	3.184	3.215	3.246	3.278	3.310
4	4.060	4.122	4.184	4.246	4.310	4.375	4.440	4.506	4.573	4.641
5	5.101	5.204	5.309	5.416	5.526	5.637	5.751	5.867	5.985	6.105
6	6.152	6.308	6.468	6.633	6.802	6.975	7.153	7.336	7.523	7.716
7	7.214	7.434	7.662	7.898	8.142	8.394	8.654	8.923	9.200	9.487
8	8.286	8.583	8.892	9.214	9.549	9.897	10.260	10.637	11.028	11.436
9	9.368	9.755	10.159	10.583	11.027	11.491	11.978	12.488	13.021	13.579
10	10.462	10.950	11.464	12.006	12.578	13.181	13.816	14.487	15.193	15.937
11	11.567	12.169	12.808	13.486	14.207	14.972	15.784	16.645	17.560	18.531
12	12.682	13.412	14.192	15.026	15.917	16.870	17.888	18.977	20.141	21.384
13	13.809	14.680	15.618	16.627	17.713	18.882	20.141	21.495	22.953	24.523
14	14.947	15.974	17.086	18.292	19.598	21.015	22.550	24.215	26.019	27.975
15	16.097	17.293	18.599	20.023	21.578	23.276	25.129	27.152	29.361	31.772
16	17.258	18.639	20.157	21.824	23.657	25.672	27.888	30.324	33.003	35.949
17	18.430	20.012	21.761	23.697	25.840	28.213	30.840	33.750	36.973	40.544
18	19.614	21.412	23.414	25.645	28.132	30.905	33.999	37.450	41.301	45.599
19	20.811	22.840	25.117	27.671	30.539	33.760	37.379	41.446	46.018	51.158
20	22.019	24.297	26.870	29.778	33.066	36.785	40.995	45.762	51.159	57.274
21	23.239	25.783	28.676	31.969	35.719	39.992	44.865	50.422	56.764	64.002
22	24.471	27.299	30.536	34.248	38.505	43.392	49.005	55.456	62.872	71.402
23	25.716	28.845	32.452	36.618	41.430	46.995	53.435	60.893	69.531	79.542
24	26.973	30.421	34.426	39.082	44.501	50.815	58.176	66.764	76.789	88.496
25	28.243	32.030	36.459	41.645	47.726	54.864	63.248	73.105	84.699	98.346
30	34.784	40.567	47.575	56.084	66.438	79.057	94.459	113.282	136.305	164.491
40	48.885	60.401	75.400	95.024	120.797	154.758	199.630	259.052	337.872	442.580
50	64.461	84.577	112.794	152.664	209.341	290.325	406.516	573.756	815.051	1163.865

Appendix C SUM OF AN ANNUITY OF $1 FOR n PERIODS (cont.)

n	11%	12%	13%	14%	15%	16%	17%	18%	19%	20%
1	1.000	1.000	1.000	1.000	1.000	1.000	1.000	1.000	1.000	1.000
2	2.110	2.120	2.130	2.140	2.150	2.160	2.170	2.180	2.190	2.200
3	3.342	3.374	3.407	3.440	3.472	3.506	3.539	3.572	3.606	3.640
4	4.710	4.779	4.850	4.921	4.993	5.066	5.141	5.215	5.291	5.368
5	6.228	6.353	6.480	6.610	6.742	6.877	7.014	7.154	7.297	7.442
6	7.913	8.115	8.323	8.535	8.754	8.977	9.207	9.442	9.683	9.930
7	9.783	10.089	10.405	10.730	11.067	11.414	11.772	12.141	12.523	12.916
8	11.859	12.300	12.757	13.233	13.727	14.240	14.773	15.327	15.902	16.499
9	14.164	14.776	15.416	16.085	16.786	17.518	18.285	19.086	19.923	20.799
10	16.722	17.549	18.420	19.337	20.304	21.321	22.393	23.521	24.709	25.959
11	19.561	20.655	21.814	23.044	24.349	25.733	27.200	28.755	30.403	32.150
12	22.713	24.133	25.650	27.271	29.001	30.850	32.824	34.931	37.180	39.580
13	26.211	28.029	29.984	32.088	34.352	36.786	39.404	42.218	45.244	48.496
14	30.095	32.392	34.882	37.581	40.504	43.672	47.102	50.818	54.841	59.196
15	34.405	37.280	40.417	43.842	47.580	51.659	56.109	60.965	66.260	72.035
16	39.190	42.753	46.671	50.980	55.717	60.925	66.648	72.938	79.850	87.442
17	44.500	48.883	53.738	59.117	65.075	71.673	78.978	87.067	96.021	105.930
18	50.396	55.749	61.724	68.393	75.836	84.140	93.404	103.739	115.265	128.116
19	56.939	63.439	70.748	78.968	88.211	98.603	110.283	123.412	138.165	154.739
20	64.202	72.052	80.946	91.024	102.443	115.379	130.031	146.626	165.417	186.687
21	72.264	81.698	92.468	104.767	118.809	134.840	153.136	174.019	197.846	225.024
22	81.213	92.502	105.489	120.434	137.630	157.414	180.169	206.342	236.436	271.028
23	91.147	104.602	120.203	138.295	159.274	183.600	211.798	244.483	282.359	326.234
24	102.173	118.154	136.829	158.656	184.166	213.976	248.803	289.490	337.007	392.480
25	114.412	133.333	155.616	181.867	212.790	249.212	292.099	342.598	402.038	471.976
30	199.018	241.330	293.192	356.778	434.738	530.306	647.423	790.932	966.698	1181.865
40	581.812	767.080	1013.667	1341.979	1779.048	2360.724	3134.412	4163.094	5529.711	7343.715
50	1668.723	2399.975	3459.344	4994.301	7217.488	10435.449	15088.805	21812.273	31514.492	45496.094

Appendix C SUM OF AN ANNUITY OF $1 FOR n PERIODS (cont.)

n	21%	22%	23%	24%	25%	26%	27%	28%	29%	30%
1	1.000	1.000	1.000	1.000	1.000	1.000	1.000	1.000	1.000	1.000
2	2.210	2.220	2.230	2.240	2.250	2.260	2.270	2.280	2.290	2.300
3	3.674	3.708	3.743	3.778	3.813	3.848	3.883	3.918	3.954	3.990
4	5.446	5.524	5.604	5.684	5.766	5.848	5.931	6.016	6.101	6.187
5	7.589	7.740	7.893	8.048	8.207	8.368	8.533	8.700	8.870	9.043
6	10.183	10.442	10.708	10.980	11.259	11.544	11.837	12.136	12.442	12.756
7	13.321	13.740	14.171	14.615	15.073	15.546	16.032	16.534	17.051	17.583
8	17.119	17.762	18.430	19.123	19.842	20.588	21.361	22.163	22.995	23.858
9	21.714	22.670	23.669	24.712	25.802	26.940	28.129	29.369	30.664	32.015
10	27.274	28.657	30.113	31.643	33.253	34.945	36.723	38.592	40.556	42.619
11	34.001	35.962	38.039	40.238	42.566	45.030	47.639	50.398	53.318	56.405
12	42.141	44.873	47.787	50.895	54.208	57.738	61.501	65.510	69.780	74.326
13	51.991	55.745	59.778	64.109	68.760	73.750	79.106	84.853	91.016	97.624
14	63.909	69.009	74.528	80.496	86.949	93.925	101.465	109.611	118.411	127.912
15	78.330	85.191	92.669	100.815	109.687	119.346	129.860	141.302	153.750	167.285
16	95.779	104.933	114.983	126.010	138.109	151.375	165.922	181.867	199.337	218.470
17	116.892	129.019	142.428	157.252	173.636	191.733	211.721	233.790	258.145	285.011
18	142.439	158.403	176.187	195.993	218.045	242.583	269.885	300.250	334.006	371.514
19	173.351	194.251	217.710	244.031	273.556	306.654	343.754	385.321	431.868	483.968
20	210.755	237.986	268.783	303.598	342.945	387.384	437.568	494.210	558.110	630.157
21	256.013	291.343	331.603	377.461	429.681	489.104	556.710	633.589	720.962	820.204
22	310.775	356.438	408.871	469.052	538.101	617.270	708.022	811.993	931.040	1067.265
23	377.038	435.854	503.911	582.624	673.626	778.760	900.187	1040.351	1202.042	1388.443
24	457.215	532.741	620.810	723.453	843.032	982.237	1144.237	1332.649	1551.634	1805.975
25	554.230	650.944	764.596	898.082	1054.791	1238.617	1454.180	1706.790	2002.608	2348.765
30	1445.111	1767.044	2160.459	2640.881	3227.172	3941.953	4812.891	5873.172	7162.785	8729.805
40	9749.141	12936.141	17153.691	22728.367	30088.621	39791.957	52570.707	69376.562	91447.375	120389.375

Appendix C SUM OF AN ANNUITY OF $1 FOR *n* PERIODS (cont.)

n	31%	32%	33%	34%	35%	36%	37%	38%	39%	40%
1	1.000	1.000	1.000	1.000	1.000	1.000	1.000	1.000	1.000	1.000
2	2.310	2.320	2.330	2.340	2.350	2.360	2.370	2.380	2.390	2.400
3	4.026	4.062	4.099	4.136	4.172	4.210	4.247	4.284	4.322	4.360
4	6.274	6.362	6.452	6.542	6.633	6.725	6.818	6.912	7.008	7.104
5	9.219	9.398	9.581	9.766	9.954	10.146	10.341	10.539	10.741	10.946
6	13.077	13.406	13.742	14.086	14.438	14.799	15.167	15.544	15.930	16.324
7	18.131	18.696	19.277	19.876	20.492	21.126	21.779	22.451	23.142	23.853
8	24.752	25.678	26.638	27.633	28.664	29.732	30.837	31.982	33.167	34.395
9	33.425	34.895	36.429	38.028	39.696	41.435	43.247	45.135	47.103	49.152
10	44.786	47.062	49.451	51.958	54.590	57.351	60.248	63.287	66.473	69.813
11	59.670	63.121	66.769	70.624	74.696	78.998	83.540	88.335	93.397	98.739
12	79.167	84.320	89.803	95.636	101.840	108.437	115.450	122.903	130.822	139.234
13	104.709	112.302	120.438	129.152	138.484	148.474	159.166	170.606	182.842	195.928
14	138.169	149.239	161.183	174.063	187.953	202.925	219.058	236.435	255.151	275.299
15	182.001	197.996	215.373	234.245	254.737	276.978	301.109	327.281	355.659	386.418
16	239.421	262.354	287.446	314.888	344.895	377.690	413.520	452.647	495.366	541.985
17	314.642	347.307	383.303	422.949	466.608	514.658	567.521	625.652	689.558	759.778
18	413.180	459.445	510.792	567.751	630.920	700.935	778.504	864.399	959.485	1064.689
19	542.266	607.467	680.354	761.786	852.741	954.271	1067.551	1193.870	1334.683	1491.563
20	711.368	802.856	905.870	1021.792	1152.200	1298.809	1463.544	1648.539	1856.208	2089.188
21	932.891	1060.769	1205.807	1370.201	1556.470	1767.380	2006.055	2275.982	2581.128	2925.862
22	1223.087	1401.215	1604.724	1837.068	2102.234	2404.636	2749.294	3141.852	3588.765	4097.203
23	1603.243	1850.603	2135.282	2462.669	2839.014	3271.304	3767.532	4336.750	4989.379	5737.078
24	2101.247	2443.795	2840.924	3300.974	3833.667	4449.969	5162.516	5985.711	6936.230	8032.906
25	2753.631	3226.808	3779.428	4424.301	5176.445	6052.957	7073.645	8261.273	9642.352	11247.062
30	10632.543	12940.672	15737.945	19124.434	23221.258	28172.016	34148.906	41357.227	50043.625	60500.207

Appendix D PRESENT VALUE OF AN ANNUITY OF $1 FOR n PERIODS

n	1%	2%	3%	4%	5%	6%	7%	8%	9%	10%
1	.990	.980	.971	.962	.952	.943	.935	.926	.917	.909
2	1.970	1.942	1.913	1.886	1.859	1.833	1.808	1.783	1.759	1.736
3	2.941	2.884	2.829	2.775	2.723	2.673	2.624	2.577	2.531	2.487
4	3.902	3.808	3.717	3.630	3.546	3.465	3.387	3.312	3.240	3.170
5	4.853	4.713	4.580	4.452	4.329	4.212	4.100	3.993	3.890	3.791
6	5.795	5.601	5.417	5.242	5.076	4.917	4.767	4.623	4.486	4.355
7	6.728	6.472	6.230	6.002	5.786	5.582	5.389	5.206	5.033	4.868
8	7.652	7.326	7.020	6.733	6.463	6.210	5.971	5.747	5.535	5.335
9	8.566	8.162	7.786	7.435	7.108	6.802	6.515	6.247	5.995	5.759
10	9.471	8.983	8.530	8.111	7.722	7.360	7.024	6.710	6.418	6.145
11	10.368	9.787	9.253	8.760	8.306	7.887	7.499	7.139	6.805	6.495
12	11.255	10.575	9.954	9.385	8.863	8.384	7.943	7.536	7.161	6.814
13	12.134	11.348	10.635	9.986	9.394	8.853	8.358	7.904	7.487	7.103
14	13.004	12.106	11.296	10.563	9.899	9.295	8.746	8.244	7.786	7.367
15	13.865	12.849	11.938	11.118	10.380	9.712	9.108	8.560	8.061	7.606
16	14.718	13.578	12.561	11.652	10.838	10.106	9.447	8.851	8.313	7.824
17	15.562	14.292	13.166	12.166	11.274	10.477	9.763	9.122	8.544	8.022
18	16.398	14.992	13.754	12.659	11.690	10.828	10.059	9.372	8.756	8.201
19	17.226	15.679	14.324	13.134	12.085	11.158	10.336	9.604	8.950	8.365
20	18.046	16.352	14.878	13.590	12.462	11.470	10.594	9.818	9.129	8.514
21	18.857	17.011	15.415	14.029	12.821	11.764	10.836	10.017	9.292	8.649
22	19.661	17.658	15.937	14.451	13.163	12.042	11.061	10.201	9.442	8.772
23	20.456	18.292	16.444	14.857	13.489	12.303	11.272	10.371	9.580	8.883
24	21.244	18.914	16.936	15.247	13.799	12.550	11.469	10.529	9.707	8.985
25	22.023	19.524	17.413	15.622	14.094	12.783	11.654	10.675	9.823	9.077
30	25.808	22.397	19.601	17.292	15.373	13.765	12.409	11.258	10.274	9.427
40	32.835	27.356	23.115	19.793	17.159	15.046	13.332	11.925	10.757	9.779
50	39.197	31.424	25.730	21.482	18.256	15.762	13.801	12.234	10.962	9.915

Appendix D PRESENT VALUE OF ANNUITY OF $1 FOR *n* PERIODS (cont.)

n	11%	12%	13%	14%	15%	16%	17%	18%	19%	20%
1	.901	.893	.885	.877	.870	.862	.855	.847	.840	.833
2	1.713	1.690	1.668	1.647	1.626	1.605	1.585	1.566	1.547	1.528
3	2.444	2.402	2.361	2.322	2.283	2.246	2.210	2.174	2.140	2.106
4	3.102	3.037	2.974	2.914	2.855	2.798	2.743	2.690	2.639	2.589
5	3.696	3.605	3.517	3.433	3.352	3.274	3.199	3.127	3.058	2.991
6	4.231	4.111	3.998	3.889	3.784	3.685	3.589	3.498	3.410	3.326
7	4.712	4.564	4.423	4.288	4.160	4.039	3.922	3.812	3.706	3.605
8	5.146	4.968	4.799	4.639	4.487	4.344	4.207	4.078	3.954	3.837
9	5.537	5.328	5.132	4.946	4.772	4.607	4.451	4.303	4.163	4.031
10	5.889	5.650	5.426	5.216	5.019	4.833	4.659	4.494	4.339	4.192
11	6.207	5.938	5.687	5.453	5.234	5.029	4.836	4.656	4.487	4.327
12	6.492	6.194	5.918	5.660	5.421	5.197	4.988	4.793	4.611	4.439
13	6.750	6.424	6.122	5.842	5.583	5.342	5.118	4.910	4.715	4.533
14	6.982	6.628	6.303	6.002	5.724	5.468	5.229	5.008	4.802	4.611
15	7.191	6.811	6.462	6.142	5.847	5.575	5.324	5.092	4.876	4.675
16	7.379	6.974	6.604	6.265	5.954	5.669	5.405	5.162	4.938	4.730
17	7.549	7.120	6.729	6.373	6.047	5.749	5.475	5.222	4.990	4.775
18	7.702	7.250	6.840	6.467	6.128	5.818	5.534	5.273	5.033	4.812
19	7.839	7.366	6.938	6.550	6.198	5.877	5.585	5.316	5.070	4.843
20	7.963	7.469	7.025	6.623	6.259	5.929	5.628	5.353	5.101	4.870
21	8.075	7.562	7.102	6.687	6.312	5.973	5.665	5.384	5.127	4.891
22	8.176	7.645	7.170	6.743	6.359	6.011	5.696	5.410	5.149	4.909
23	8.266	7.718	7.230	6.792	6.399	6.044	5.723	5.432	5.167	4.925
24	8.348	7.784	7.283	6.835	6.434	6.073	5.747	5.451	5.182	4.937
25	8.442	7.843	7.330	6.873	6.464	6.097	5.766	5.467	5.195	4.948
30	8.694	8.055	7.496	7.003	6.566	6.177	5.829	5.517	5.235	4.979
40	8.951	8.244	7.634	7.105	6.642	6.233	5.871	5.548	5.258	4.997
50	9.042	8.305	7.675	7.133	6.661	6.246	5.880	5.554	5.262	4.999

Appendix D PRESENT VALUE OF AN ANNUITY OF $1 FOR n PERIODS (cont.)

n	21%	22%	23%	24%	25%	26%	27%	28%	29%	30%
1	.826	.820	.813	.806	.800	.794	.787	.781	.775	.769
2	1.509	1.492	1.474	1.457	1.440	1.424	1.407	1.392	1.376	1.361
3	2.074	2.042	2.011	1.981	1.952	1.923	1.896	1.868	1.842	1.816
4	2.540	2.494	2.448	2.404	2.362	2.320	2.280	2.241	2.203	2.166
5	2.926	2.864	2.803	2.745	2.689	2.635	2.583	2.532	2.483	2.436
6	3.245	3.167	3.092	3.020	2.951	2.885	2.821	2.759	2.700	2.643
7	3.508	3.416	3.327	3.242	3.161	3.083	3.009	2.937	2.868	2.802
8	3.726	3.619	3.518	3.421	3.329	3.241	3.156	3.076	2.999	2.925
9	3.905	3.786	3.673	3.566	3.463	3.366	3.273	3.184	3.100	3.019
10	4.054	3.923	3.799	3.682	3.570	3.465	3.364	3.269	3.178	3.092
11	4.177	4.035	3.902	3.776	3.656	3.544	3.437	3.335	3.239	3.147
12	4.278	4.127	3.985	3.851	3.725	3.606	3.493	3.387	3.286	3.190
13	4.362	4.203	4.053	3.912	3.780	3.656	3.538	3.427	3.322	3.223
14	4.432	4.265	4.108	3.962	3.824	3.695	3.573	3.459	3.351	3.249
15	4.489	4.315	4.153	4.001	3.859	3.726	3.601	3.483	3.373	3.268
16	4.536	4.357	4.189	4.033	3.887	3.751	3.623	3.503	3.390	3.283
17	4.576	4.391	4.219	4.059	3.910	3.771	3.640	3.518	3.403	3.295
18	4.608	4.419	4.243	4.080	3.928	3.786	3.654	3.529	3.413	3.304
19	4.635	4.442	4.263	4.097	3.942	3.799	3.664	3.539	3.421	3.311
20	4.657	4.460	4.279	4.110	3.954	3.808	3.673	3.546	3.427	3.316
21	4.675	4.476	4.292	4.121	3.963	3.816	3.679	3.551	3.432	3.320
22	4.690	4.488	4.302	4.130	3.970	3.822	3.684	3.556	3.436	3.323
23	4.703	4.499	4.311	4.137	3.976	3.827	3.689	3.559	3.438	3.325
24	4.713	4.507	4.318	4.143	3.981	3.831	3.692	3.562	3.441	3.327
25	4.721	4.514	4.323	4.147	3.985	3.834	3.694	3.564	3.442	3.329
30	4.746	4.534	4.339	4.160	3.995	3.842	3.701	3.569	3.447	3.332
40	4.760	4.544	4.347	4.166	3.999	3.846	3.703	3.571	3.448	3.333
50	4.762	4.545	4.348	4.167	4.000	3.846	3.704	3.571	3.448	3.333

Appendix D PRESENT VALUE OF AN ANNUITY OF $1 FOR n PERIODS (cont.)

n	31%	32%	33%	34%	35%	36%	37%	38%	39%	40%
1	.763	.758	.752	.746	.741	.735	.730	.725	.719	.714
2	1.346	1.331	1.317	1.303	1.289	1.276	1.263	1.250	1.237	1.224
3	1.791	1.766	1.742	1.719	1.696	1.673	1.652	1.630	1.609	1.589
4	2.130	2.096	2.062	2.029	1.997	1.966	1.935	1.906	1.877	1.849
5	2.390	2.345	2.302	2.260	2.220	2.181	2.143	2.106	2.070	2.035
6	2.588	2.534	2.483	2.433	2.385	2.339	2.294	2.251	2.209	2.168
7	2.739	2.677	2.619	2.562	2.508	2.455	2.404	2.355	2.308	2.263
8	2.854	2.786	2.721	2.658	2.598	2.540	2.485	2.432	2.380	2.331
9	2.942	2.868	2.798	2.730	2.665	2.603	2.544	2.487	2.432	2.379
10	3.009	2.930	2.855	2.784	2.715	2.649	2.587	2.527	2.469	2.414
11	3.060	2.978	2.899	2.824	2.752	2.683	2.618	2.555	2.496	2.438
12	3.100	3.013	2.931	2.853	2.779	2.708	2.641	2.576	2.515	2.456
13	3.129	3.040	2.956	2.876	2.799	2.727	2.658	2.592	2.529	2.469
14	3.152	3.061	2.974	2.892	2.814	2.740	2.670	2.603	2.539	2.477
15	3.170	3.076	2.988	2.905	2.825	2.750	2.679	2.611	2.546	2.484
16	3.183	3.088	2.999	2.914	2.834	2.757	2.685	2.616	2.551	2.489
17	3.193	3.097	3.007	2.921	2.840	2.763	2.690	2.621	2.555	2.492
18	3.201	3.104	3.012	2.926	2.844	2.767	2.693	2.624	2.557	2.494
19	3.207	3.109	3.017	2.930	2.848	2.770	2.696	2.626	2.559	2.496
20	3.211	3.113	3.020	2.933	2.850	2.772	2.698	2.627	2.561	2.497
21	3.215	3.116	3.023	2.935	2.852	2.773	2.699	2.629	2.562	2.498
22	3.217	3.118	3.025	2.936	2.853	2.775	2.700	2.629	2.562	2.498
23	3.219	3.120	3.026	2.938	2.854	2.775	2.701	2.630	2.563	2.499
24	3.221	3.121	3.027	2.939	2.855	2.776	2.701	2.630	2.563	2.499
25	3.222	3.122	3.028	2.939	2.856	2.776	2.702	2.631	2.563	2.499
30	3.225	3.124	3.030	2.941	2.857	2.777	2.702	2.631	2.564	2.500
40	3.226	3.125	3.030	2.941	2.857	2.778	2.703	2.632	2.564	2.500
50	3.226	3.125	3.030	2.941	2.857	2.778	2.703	2.632	2.564	2.500